BURUNDI

I spent whole afternoons gazing at the slopes of our mountains, the splendid plateaux, the springs, the tumultuous torrents, the trees that seemed to spring up in the twinkling of an eye, cow-dung, the banana trees which sprouted almost without being tended, the fallow gardens, the rudimentary hoes that my sisters used for turning the soil....

Michel Kayoya, *My Father's Footsteps*

Peace

What's peace? Now first of all it's really
Not a simple issue of no-war.
It's no-injustice, no-intolerance, no-hatred
It's thinking good, not bad of everyone.

It recognises one humanity
In which all lives are precious
And worthy to be loved and given help
Towards fulfilment.

(Extract from a poem by Adam Curle, the first Professor of Peace Studies at the University of Bradford, published in Barbara Mitchels, *Love in Danger*, John Carpenter, 2006 reproduced by permission of the publisher.)

NIGEL WATT

Burundi
Biography of a Small African Country

HURST & COMPANY, LONDON

First published in the United Kingdom in 2008 by
C. Hurst & Co (Publishers) Ltd,
41 Great Russell Street, London, WC1B 3PL
© Nigel Watt, 2016
This revised and updated edition 2016
All rights reserved.
Printed in India

Distributed in the United States, Canada and Latin America by
Oxford University Press, 198 Madison Avenue, New York, NY 10016,
United States of America.

A catalogue data record for this volume is available
from the British Library.

ISBN 978-1-84904-509-4 *paperback*

www.hurstpublishers.com

CONTENTS

v

THE PRESENT AND THE FUTURE

ANNEXES

ACKNOWLEDGMENTS

I am most grateful to all those who helped me during my visit to Burundi in May 2007: especially to Bindende Kamwanga and his family for hospitality and logistical support of all kinds.

I would like to thank all those who agreed to be interviewed or gave me the benefit of their wisdom and knowledge: Christophe Hakizimana, Eugene Nindorera, Emmanuel Hakizimana, Dismas Hicintuka, Phocas Ndimubandi, Claudette Manariyo, Jérémie Sindayirwanya, Archbishop Bernard Ntahoturi, Samson Munahi, Floribert Kubwayezu, Perpétue Kankindi, Alexis Sinduhije, Fidèle Kanyugu, Jean-Marie Nibizi, Emmanuel Nsanganiye, Jean-Louis Nahimana, Robert Abel, Jean-Sebastien Munie, Didace Kanyugu, Chantal Mutamuriza, Adrien Tuyaga, Mohamed Nibaruta, David Niyonzima, Tracy Dexter, Eddy Ndakunze, Alexis Ndayizeye, Osias Habingabwa, Joseph Ntiruhungwa, Sue Hogwood, Melchior Nsigamasabo, Pie Ntakarutimana, Libérate Nicayenzi, Delfin Sebitwa, Emmanuel Nengo, Alexis Kwizera, Maggie Barankitse, Innocent Mawikizi, Aloys Ningabira, Levy Ndikumana, Athanase Bagorikunda, Samson Gahungu, Matthias Ndimurwanko, Jérôme Nkurubanka, Apollinaire Nsengiyumva, Juvenal Ntakarashira, Louis-Marie Nindorera, André Nsengiyumva, Liz McClintock, Peter Uvin, Denise Holland, Nepomucène Hasabintwari, Jenny Theron, Christophe Nkurunziza, Thierry Rwagatore, Janine Nayigombeye, Matthias Manirakiza, Jean-Marie Badionona, Etoile Kazeruke, Adrien Sindayigaya, ex-President Jean-Baptiste Bagaza, Fr Claudio Marino, Joseph Nindorera, Jean-Marie Vianney Kavumbagu, ex-President Domitien Ndayizeye, Isabelle Brouillard, Fr Emmanuel Ntakarutimana, Samuel Braimah, Sylvestre Barancira, Charles

Ndayiziga, Christophe Sebudandi, Paul Natulya, Kassie McIlvaine, Nona Zicherlan, Serge Ntabikiyoboka, Vital Bambanze, Pascal Benimana, Violette Mukarashema, Rory Beaumont, Vital Ndikumana, Terence Mbonabuca, Pacifique Ntawuyamara, David and Gloria Rothrock, Dismas Nzeyimana, Margaret Sweeney.

I am also most grateful to friends who have checked and advised on the text: Fidèle Kanyugu, Alexis Sinduhije, Jean-Marie Nibizi, Kris Berwouts, Tracy Dexter, Tony Jackson and my dear wife, Edyth.

PREFACE TO THE 2008 EDITION
IN THE SHADOW OF RWANDA

On the night of 6 April 1994 an aircraft was shot down close to Kigali, the capital of Rwanda. The plane was carrying two presidents. The death of President Habyarimana of Rwanda, a Hutu, led directly to the well-documented genocide, mainly of Tutsis. President Ntaryamira of Burundi, also a Hutu, was aboard also. He had been chosen to be president as a result of events in Burundi in 1993 which were a direct cause of what happened in Rwanda. The fateful date in Burundi was 21 October 1993 when a coup led by elements of the mainly Tutsi army resulted in the death of Melchior Ndadaye, the country's first democratically elected president. This led to a double genocide in Burundi, first of Tutsis all over the country, then of Hutus as the army took its revenge. Seeing what had happened in Burundi, extreme Hutus in Rwanda wanted to make sure that no Tutsis would survive to take their revenge.

Burundi is Rwanda's twin. Both were kingdoms which retained their pre-colonial boundaries, sharing the same culture, almost the same language and the same division of the population into Hutus, Tutsis and Batwa (singular Twa). They were governed as one Mandated and later Trust Territory by Belgium, known as Ruanda-Urundi. There are significant differences between the two countries but events in one always infect the other. Yet, because of Rwanda's notoriety, Burundi is often forgotten. This is especially true in the UK, the USA and Anglophone Africa. Go to a specialist bookshop in Paris or Brussels and you will find two shelves of books about Burundi. In London you will find nothing. Look on a map and you may not notice this very small, very poor country squeezed between

Tanzania and the Democratic Republic of Congo, both of which are hundreds of times larger.

It was this low level of awareness about Burundi which prompted me to sit down and write this book. I wish it had been written by a Burundian, but I hope the voices of people I have interviewed provide at least some authenticity. From 1998 to 2003 I spent about four years in the country working for Christian Aid and later briefly for Care International. This was enough time to make many friends, to learn to love the place and to see that Burundi should not be forgotten because it is small and not rich in strategic minerals. This is not intended to be an academic treatise but a general introduction to what the country is like and how it has suffered, especially during what everyone calls 'the crisis' (*la crise*), the period of war which began in 1993. I have tried to describe how a process of peace building and healing has been helped by many distinguished outsiders including former Presidents Julius Nyerere and Nelson Mandela—but especially by some very wonderful Burundians. I hope this book will lead to a fuller recognition of their efforts, and I hope that it may encourage more people to get to know this beautiful and friendly country, to speak up in its favour, to lobby for aid and good governance, and not to be afraid of going there to see for themselves.

Apart from my own experiences and perceptions, this book is based on a number of interviews conducted in Burundi in May and June 2006 and on published material as indicated in the bibliography, footnotes and acknowledgments. The names of those interviewed are shown in italics, as are Kirundi and French words. Big acronyms such as FRODEBU and UPRONA (a very Belgian tradition), I have put into upper and lower case to stop them leaping out of the page, as they occur frequently in the text.

There are usually two versions of history in Burundi—a Tutsi one and a Hutu one—and it is hard to keep a balance and be impartial. I have tried, and I hope to be forgiven if I have failed. Bringing the story up to date is also impossible, as events keep on unfolding even as I write. Many people have helped me with their time and their wisdom. They are listed in the acknowledgments. Any errors of fact or interpretation are my own.

London, October 2007   N.W.

LIST OF ILLUSTRATIONS

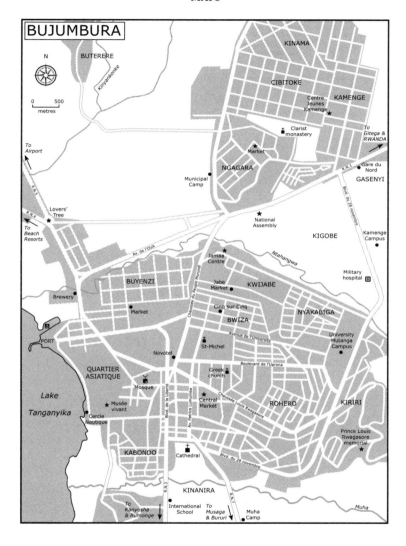

1

A QUICK TOUR OF THE COUNTRY

Arriving

When I first set off for Burundi in 1998, the country faced an international boycott and in theory there were no international flights. Arriving at Kigali airport in Rwanda I was put on a plane which, according to the announcement, was going to Kalemie, a town way south in the Democratic Republic of Congo (DRC). It was, in fact, going to Bujumbura—a 12-seater belonging to an embargo-breaking company. As I looked down from the little plane as it descended over Burundi, everything was hazy green. The forest smothered the mountains on the border with Rwanda. I began to see small brown roads winding into the hills, and scattered homesteads[1]. Soon we were over a flat plain with a large meandering river on the right. As we got lower, we could see irrigated fields and, finally, the airport at Bujumbura, Burundi's capital city. This north western corner of Burundi consists mainly of the flat flood plain of the Rusizi River, irrigated in some places, which produces rice, cotton and tomatoes. To the east lies the Kibira Forest, at the time a safe haven for rebel fighters. The homesteads are typical: there are no villages in Burundi, only *collines* (hills) with families living in scattered settlements, each

---

1   Burundi's traditional homesteads (*rugo*, pl. *ingo*) are family enclosures containing several thatched huts with provision for cattle.

one consisting of a couple of houses and huts, fenced in with their livestock. The plain is part of the Imbo, the lowland region that stretches south along the shore of Lake Tanganyika.

It was reassuring that my plane did land at Bujumbura, but less reassuring that the pretty white airport terminal was totally deserted. I sat and read my book. Finally a security man offered me his mobile phone, the big, heavy sort which was the latest thing in 1998. Although it was a Saturday, Andy Nicholson, the Project Officer at Christian Aid who was to be my future colleague, chanced to be in the office listening to the BBC, and he came to fetch me. The road we had seen from the air, running dead straight through the plain on its way from Cibitoke Province, Rwanda and Bukavu (in the DRC), led into town past billboards advertising YES cigarettes (*Say 'Yes'*) and Primus beer (*'Kirinyota mugenzi'*). Apart from occasional cars from the airport, the main traffic was bicycles wobbling on and off the tarmac, the rider obscured by huge bundles of grass and leaves, food for the city's population of cattle, displaced by the war. With steep escarpments left and right, this was the Great Rift Valley—in the west the *Haut Plateau* of South Kivu in the Congo,[2] in the east the *ruguru*, the undulating central plateau of Burundi. South of Bujumbura, Lake Tanganyika fills the floor of the rift valley for a further 600 kilometres, the world's longest freshwater lake and its second deepest.

The capital

Approaching town, towering over the first roundabout is a colossal, magnificent and ancient tree, known as the lovers' tree, where newly-weds pose for photographs. The road then passes through an area of warehouses and moribund light industries. The smell intensifies outside the brewery, one of the country's only growth industries. The *Quartier Asiatique* is on the right. Bujumbura grew up as a trading post and port at the north end of Lake Tanganyika and this was

---

2   The Democratic Republic of Congo (DRC), known during President Mobutu's time as Zaire. There is another Congo, usually known as Congo-Brazzaville. References to the Congo in this book mean the DRC unless indicated otherwise.

its oldest neighbourhood, originally inhabited by Arabs and Indians. For most of the colonial period Kiswahili speakers from Congo and from what is now Tanzania outnumbered Burundians in Usumbura, which was the city's Kiswahili name, used until Independence. Similarly the country was known as Urundi. The little town developed into the capital of the Belgian trust territory of Ruanda-Urundi. Many of its streets preserve buildings of a typically Belgian art-deco style of the mid-twentieth century. In the ex-Belgian Congo (DRC) such buildings have crumbled and decayed, but Bujumbura remains for the moment a fascinating place for historians of architecture.

There are other hangovers from colonial times. There is a large horse riding club surrounded by a golf course where former President Buyoya sometimes used to turn up unexpectedly to do a little jogging. (On such occasions it was wise to move off quickly and discreetly.) Bujumbura still has some good restaurants serving exotic things like *coquilles St. Jacques* and locally produced *cuisses de grenouilles* (frogs' legs), as well as very good lake fish such as *sangala* and *capitaine*. The stunning white and blue Greek Orthodox Church is witness to what has been a much larger Greek community,[3] but the Greeks are still present at Dimitri's supermarket, the *Boucherie Nouvelle* and the *Gymnase Club*. Belgians, too, are still in evidence. If you seek colonial nostalgia, Bujumbura should be on your itinerary—and it is something of a shock to find that Burundians seem to still regard Belgium as a Great Power!

Things have changed, however. Bujumbura is now an African city, small for a capital but growing rapidly in size and in congestion. The central market[4], a modern structure (reputedly chosen as an aid project in preference to a new stadium), swarms with shoppers, traders, small boys selling plastic bags and men carrying bleeding animal carcasses or huge bunches of bananas. Turn into the Avenue de l'Amitié and, especially if you are a *muzungu* (a white), you will be pursued by hopeful money changers. Park your car and it will quickly

---

3   The first Greeks came from the Ottoman Empire. They arrived with the Germans via the lake.

4   Sadly destroyed by fire in 2013.

be surrounded by street kids telling you they are called Jean-Marie and asking to protect your car.

In the days of colonial segregation, the Belgians built the model suburb of Ngagara for their junior civil servants, almost all Tutsis, and some of these neat little houses survive. Also on the north side of town is the suburb of Cibitoke, a Tutsi stronghold during the 'crisis', the period of civil war from 1993 to 1997. Next door are the Hutu dominated suburbs of Kinama, Kamenge and Buterere. In fact, all these neighbourhoods contained a mixture of Hutus and Tutsis before 'the crisis'. Pre-crisis Kamenge was a lively place full of night clubs and bars. It had been completely destroyed but it is finally coming back to life and, as elsewhere, Hutus and Tutsis are again living side by side.

South of the city are the suburbs of Musaga, traditionally mainly Tutsi, and Kanyosha, mainly Hutu. In the centre and south along the lake shore are the smarter residential areas of Rohero, Kinindo, Kinanira and the newly developed Kibenga. Up the hill is the smartest of all, Kiriri, with magnificent views over the lake. Continue up this winding road and you reach the memorial to the assassinated Prime Minister Prince Louis Rwagasore, and, higher still, a heavy, white landmark, the former Jesuit college most of which is now the Kiriri Campus of the University of Burundi, where I used to go for a swim in the big open-air pool. Also along the hillside are Mutanga Sud and Mutanga Nord, the latter the most tolerant of suburbs, inhabited by intellectuals, politicians and bishops, where Tutsi and Hutu neighbours used to warn each other of approaching trouble.

For me the most interesting *quartiers* (neighbourhoods) are Bwiza (and the adjoining Jabe market) and Buyenzi. These, along with the *Quartier Asiatique*, are the most cosmopolitan parts of Bujumbura. Pre-crisis Bwiza was home to a large West African community, so many that the Malian government sent a plane to evacuate its nationals. A few remain, running tailoring shops and serving *michopo*[5] and beer in the open air 'cafés' on Second Avenue, where you can sit in the street to the sound of Congolese music and watch the moon

---

5   Plates of rather greasy meat with cold cassava *ugali*, but it goes down well with a beer.

behind the minaret. Buyenzi, even more than Bwiza, is home to many Muslims and it was here that both Hutus and Tutsis were welcomed during the worst of the crisis. Buyenzi at first sight is a dirty slum with muddy puddles in the roads and plenty of rusty corrugated iron, but inside its cramped courtyards there is a lot of wealth. These are traders, mechanics, handymen of all kinds and other business people—but also many poor people struggling to survive. I learned about Buyenzi in my first week in the country. The petrol cap was stolen from our vehicle. Benoit, the driver, went down to Buyenzi market and bought it back within minutes! The segregation during colonial times shows up in the Kiswahili words used at that time: *azunguni* (place of the whites = the city centre), *warabuni* (Arabs = the *Quartier Asiatique*) and just *mjini* (town = Buyenzi).

There are many Congolese in Bujumbura and they liven the place up. *Soukous* and rumba music can be heard all over Bwiza, especially at the Cinq sur Cinq night club, while on Sunday afternoons in Buyenzi ladies in dazzling costumes enjoyed the *taarab* (Zanzibar style) music of the Orchestre Jasmine, climbing on stage to stick 100 franc notes on the forehead of any singer they appreciate. Although many were chased out in the 1980s, the Congolese are still active in Burundian life, in spheres such as business, education and sport. Some of them joined together with local and expatriate staff from international aid agencies in a football team called Kibinda n'koye (leopards). This mixed team created quite a stir, showing how sport was a good way of overcoming differences. Andy once made a memorable save and when kids in town spotted him at the wheel of his little Renault 5 they would shout out the name of the team—'*Kibinda n'koye!*'

Bujumbura exists because of its port, yet the town has mostly turned its back on the lake and faces up to the hills. Next to the port is Bujumbura's small 'people's beach' where brides and grooms come on Saturdays to have their photos taken.

Up country

Apart from the flat Imbo plain north of Bujumbura, most of the interior of the country is high plateau, sloping gradually down towards the eastern border with Tanzania. This is the real Burundi where

5

people eat beans, not fish. The King of Burundi would never leave the highlands. It was said that if he ever saw the lake he would die. Mwezi Gisabo, who reigned from 1850 to 1908, was the first king to see the lake when he visited the Germans at Usumbura. He did indeed die, of malaria, on his way home.

Driving up country usually means taking the Route National 1 (RN1) which winds steeply up the escarpment, through dense banana plantations hanging onto the sides of the hills, with occasional views of the plain far below. During the time I lived in Burundi this was rebel territory. Soldiers lounged about by the road, looking rather nervous and very bored. The road would close for the night at 4.30pm, the soldiers would disappear and the rebels would hold sway. It is a busy road, the main link to Rwanda, Tanzania and the outside world, as well to Gitega and the centre of the country. On this road it is normal to be stuck behind a lorry which is impossible to overtake owing to the many sharp curves. Hanging on behind the lorries are cyclists who pay 100 francs for the privilege of being pulled up the hill. These are the cyclists who have passed us in the down direction with two huge sacks of charcoal tied on the back, or an equal weight of bananas, propelled by gravity at breakneck speed down to Bujumbura—or death. My colleague Jean-Marie always described them as 'helicopters'.

As you reach Bugarama the temperature has dropped by a few degrees. This is really just a road junction and military post with clusters of stalls selling onions, carrots, cabbages, cauliflowers, leeks, peas, strawberries, maize cobs, big wild mushrooms, flowers, even rhubarb and, lower down the hill, fancy baskets, wooden beds and chairs and, of course, bananas.[6] Turning north, this road used to pass through a beautiful glade of large, grey-barked trees: now no more. Security during the crisis demanded a clearing on both sides of the road. A few kilometres north is an even better roadside market where the ingenious sellers split bamboo canes in half to create a channel for cool spring water to moisten the fruit and vegetables, making them glisten

---

6   Paul Mirerekano, who founded the Uprona party together with Prince Louis
     Rwagasore, was an agronomist and was responsible for the development of
     this fruit and vegetable production around Bugarama.

in the sunlight. Getting towards Kayanza, the first proper town after leaving Bujumbura, first you see small boys standing by the roadside holding live rabbits by their ears for sale, then you are in the brickworks zone, with huge piles of red bricks on both sides, a booming trade with so much building going on throughout the country. North from Kayanza the main road drops steeply, crossing the Kanyaru river into Rwanda. Once I was in a bus here and we came upon two dead cyclists who had hit a car as they raced downhill and round a bend, leaving their heavy loads and their blood on the road.

Here and all over the north and centre of the country you cannot miss the small fields of coffee bushes, tended by the peasant farmers. Turning right at Kayanza is the road to Ngozi, Burundi's third city. (Don't be fooled, it's tiny!) Politically sidelined in the past, Ngozi is proud to be the province of President Nkurunziza.[7] It is also the home of Burundi's first independent university, set up by some of Ngozi's prominent sons. Further north east is Kirundo, in the ancient kingdom of Bugesera, a land of lakes but also of open grassland with scattered acacia trees. Formerly a main food producing area, unreliable rainfall now makes this region the worst affected by drought and famine.

The RN2 which branches off at Bugarama leads through Muramvya to Gitega. Muramvya province is one of the most densely populated. This was the royal province, the base of the *mwami,* the King of Burundi. There is still an old sign by the road pointing to the historical site of the royal drums (and if you go there and ask, drummers will come out and drum). After Muramvya town, a scrawny, straggling place, the next stop is Rutegama, famous for a market which used to spill all over the main road, but a new market place has recently been built up the side of the hill. Climbing up from the valley of the Mubarazi, the buildings of Kibimba mission and school can be seen on the horizon but, before getting there, on the left is the memorial to commemorate the Tutsi schoolchildren killed in the massacre of 1993.[8]

---

7   Not to mention three former prime ministers.

8   The monument was inaugurated by President Buyoya on 22 October 1998 on the site of the petrol station where the massacre occurred. Sadly the

Finally, past another brewery, a motel and the rather dusty and inadequate national museum, the road gets to Gitega. This was briefly the capital during the German period and the prison is the old German *boma* (government building). Its hilly situation makes Gitega a difficult place to expand, but this has not stopped it doing so. We used to stay at the Songa Hotel, by the central square. To get a good night's sleep you had to choose the room carefully. If you were at the back you would be woken up by a collection of crowing cocks at 4am. If you were at the front you were opposite a new mosque with an extremely noisy muezzin, on the edge of the Swahili Quarter, Gitega's answer to Buyenzi. South of the town, across a valley, is Mushasha, Gitega's Vatican City, the seat of the Catholic Archbishop, with its imposing cathedral, schools and convents. Today the nuns sell home-cooked biscuits. In 1993 they tried to protect those fleeing for their lives.

Northeast from Gitega, a bad road leads to the small, sleepy and uninteresting provincial headquarters of Karuzi, not far from which is the rather charming Anglican 'village church' at Buhiga. Further northeast is Muyinga, on the Tanzanian border and more easily accessible on the tarmac road from Ngozi and Kirundo. To the south east is Ruyigi, as nondescript a tiny town as the others, but now, thanks to Maison Shalom,[9] home of Burundi's most modern cinema and other attractions. Furthest east is the least known and most thinly populated province of the country, Cankuzo.

The other main route into the interior is RN7, one of the big development projects of the era of President Bagaza (1976-87), with another panoramic view over Bujumbura and Lake Tanganyika. This route passes Buhonga, one of the first Catholic mission churches. Leaving the province of Bujumbura Rural at Ijenda, the road passes through parts of the provinces of Mwaro and Bururi. This is the region called Bututsi, the only area with a Tutsi majority, generally infertile but good cattle country. Some of the most photogenic tea gardens are up on this plateau. The commune of Rutovu contains

---

opportunity was not taken to remember the many Hutus also killed in 1993, which would have made this a healing memorial; see chapter 6.

9   See chapter 16.

the most southerly source of the Nile, Burundians would say the real source. A small pyramid was built there in the 1930s and it counts as one of Burundi's tourist attractions. This commune is also famous for producing Burundi's three military presidents, Micombero (1966-76), Bagaza (1976-87) and Buyoya (1987-93 and 1996-2003).

At the southern tip of the country are the provinces of Rutana and Makamba. The low-lying valley of Kumoso in Rutana province contains the large sugar cane plantations and refinery of Sosumo[10] and also the nickel deposits in Musongati commune, a mirage of future development. Makamba province, a stronghold of the CNDD-FDD[11] rebels, was the scene of much fighting during the crisis.

Due south from Bujumbura is the RN3 along the shore of Lake Tanganyika. Just south of the city is a large rock marking the spot where Dr. Livingstone met Stanley, though it was not their famous first encounter.[12] The road hugs the lakeside south to Rumonge. This little town is of great historical significance for Burundi. It is where the Burundian king, Mwezi Gisabo, defeated the Swahili slave traders who had advanced from the coast. As a result, unlike most of eastern Africa, no slaves were ever traded in Burundi. Later, other Swahili-speaking traders did settle there and it became the country's most Muslim town as well as being the centre of palm oil production. Just to the north of Rumonge is the recently restored lakeside resort of Saga Resha, the site of Castela, or *Château Maus*. This 'stately home' was built before independence by Albert Maus, an eccentric and extremist leader of the white community.[13] The coast road con-

---

10 Société Sucrière du Moso.

11 The main rebel movement after 1994 (see chapter 10), and now the governing party.

12 The first meeting of Stanley and Livingstone ('Dr. Livingstone, I presume?') was at Ujiji in present day Tanzania on 10 November 1871. The two men stayed together for about four months, during which time they visited the northern end of Lake Tanganyika to try and check whether it flowed into the Nile or not. They were together at the site of this rock on 25 November 1871.

13 He was a former priest who had, it is said, turned to worshipping the Egyptian sun god. He was the leader of the small community of hardline white settlers in Ruanda-Urundi and played a part in creating pro-colonial political parties in both countries—see chapter 3. He hated the nationalists

tinues to Nyanza Lac and links up with Makamba. In this region there are Swahili-style villages strung along the roads.

Westwards from Bujumbura, the RN4 runs for 20 kilometres along the north shore of the lake to the Congo border at Gatumba, passing on the way a burgeoning number of beach resorts, with thatched sunshades and waiters staggering across the sand with trays of beer, where wealthier Burundians and expatriates drink and play at weekends. Crossing the Rusizi river there is a small and somewhat rundown game reserve, good for watching hippos, birds and crocodiles.

It was at one of these beach resorts, now the very smart Hotel Club Lac Tanganyka, that Andy's French neighbour, Patrice, happened to end up in Burundi. He left France on a bicycle and cycled through Africa, arriving in Bujumbura in the 1980s. To earn some money to travel on southwards, he got a job helping to build the hotel. He never left, and he became an expert on reptiles. His home swarmed with chameleons, snakes of all different sizes and kinds, purple crested lowries, African grey parrots and anything else that local people might bring along. This even included a cerval, a spotted cat about the size of a Labrador dog. With such a household next door, Andy found he had few burglars or security threats.

Watching the sunset across the lake or climbing into the hills, it is hard to imagine that this little country has been tearing itself apart for over forty years. To know the country, its sad history has to be told.

---

so much that he swore to kill himself if the pro-independence party, Uprona, won the pre-Independence election. He duly committed suicide.

2

TRANSPORT, LANGUAGE, CULTURE, RELIGION

Le Murundi en général est essentiellement routinier, vit de la tradition, se contente d'un bon champ de haricots et d'une bananeraie. S'il a la bonne fortune de posséder une ou plusieurs vaches, il est comblé de bonheur. 'The Burundian is a creature of habit. His life is based on tradition and he is content with a good field of beans and a banana grove. If he is lucky enough to possess one or several cows his happiness is complete.'—a missionary writing during colonial times.

Anyone who has travelled much in Africa will be struck by the quietness and order in Burundi. Compare this with the noise and chaos at airports and bus stations in Kinshasa or Lagos. This reflects the self-control of Burundians, who tend to keep their thoughts to themselves, to face tragedy stoically and to be publicly very polite. This natural discipline and obedience has been inculcated through the centuries of a highly structured society with a monarch at its head. These excellent qualities have their down side: false rumours circulate fast, creating fear, hatred and, on occasion, cold-blooded killing.

Burundians are not great travellers. From colonial times some went as migrant workers to Uganda and the Congo but otherwise, until some of them felt the need to become refugees and apart from a handful who went abroad to study, there were few who wanted to go outside the country. Even in 1999, when I sailed down Lake Tanganyika on the *Liemba*, there was only one Burundian among the fifty

11

or so passengers. This ancient ship used to serve Bujumbura before the crisis and again in 1999. It is a scruffy looking ship which does not betray its amazing old age. It was built by the Germans before 1914, sunk by the British in the First World War, brought to the surface and restored, and has been running ever since. It no longer comes to Bujumbura but sails weekly from Kigoma in Tanzania to Mpulungu in Zambia, serving various villages on the lake shore. Until recently to get to Kigoma meant finding a freight ship, not always a pleasant experience. A friend travelling to Zambia in 1999 found himself with forty others in a small open boat with no toilet. Worse, it was held up overnight for security reasons. A minibus service has now started from Bujumbura to Kigoma.

Getting to Rwanda is easier. Minibuses leave Bujumbura every day around 9am and reach Kigali in the afternoon. From there it is possible to connect to Kampala and eventually to Nairobi. The doomed 'Titanic Express' stopped running after a massacre in 2000.[1] Some buses run through to Kampala. There is also a daily bus from Bujumbura to Bukavu in the DRC, which is only 113 kilometres but involves two leisurely border crossings in and out of Rwanda.

Bujumbura is not very well connected by air. Kenya Airways now has two flights most days to Nairobi. Ethiopian Airlines flies to Addis Ababa, Rwandair to Kigali and Entebbe and the only direct intercontinental flight is by SN Brussels Airlines.

Inside Burundi, social necessity makes some people travel—to funerals, weddings and other family occasions. Quite understandably people feared to travel far during the crisis and there are very many residents of Bujumbura, especially Tutsis, who have never visited the interior. The departure point for most parts of the country is the '*Gare du Nord*' in Kamenge where—not at all like Paris—lines of minibuses are surrounded by swarms of hopeful passengers and people selling food for the journey. To get to some of the more remote places you can get off the minibus and find a *taxi vélo* (bicycle taxi) or, if you are lucky, a *taxi moto* (motorbike).

In Bujumbura there are minibuses which follow regular routes but, in contrast to places like Addis Ababa or Kampala, there is no

---

1   See chapter 8.

limit enforced on the number of sardines in the tin. Nearly all the vehicles have been bought second-hand from East Africa or Japan, so they have the passenger door on the left. The result is that passengers pour out into the middle of the road with little regard for oncoming traffic. The brightly painted city taxis and many private cars also have right hand drive. Rwanda is very strict and insists that all vehicles on its roads are designed for driving on the right. So Burundi is full of third hand vehicles bought from Rwanda.

The *taxi vélo*, which was well known in rural areas, in smaller towns such as Gitega and in some of the outer suburbs of Bujumbura, is now sometimes found, unofficially, on the roads of the city centre. The taxi men are often newly arrived villagers or demobilised soldiers who are hazy about the rules of the road. They scrape a living. Competition is tough and they do not (and cannot afford to) pay tax or insurance. They provide a new hazard for everyone else on the road, to add to the mass of pedestrians, an increased number of cars and minibuses, and the more than occasional pothole.

One very positive development has been the upgrading of many side roads in the capital with stone sets and deep drainage ditches. Originally the brainchild of Belgian Cooperation, this idea has been taken up by the World Bank as a job creation programme. These stone roads are now even to be found in Bwiza and Buyenzi as well as in some of the more prosperous suburbs and in parts of the town centre. This is a project which could well be replicated all over Africa.

Saturdays in Burundi are busy days for many of the more prosperous families as there will be a betrothal ceremony (*la dot*), a wedding or a *levée de deuil*, the end of a mourning period. (President Bagaza tried to discourage these 'unproductive' social occasions in the 1980s.) The hosts have to provide quantities of '*fanta*'[2] and beer and usually serve a spread of grilled bananas, rice, chicken, salad and *brochettes*[3] of beef or goat. A bar is known as a *kabare* (cabaret) and you usually sit at a table outdoors and eat *brochettes* or fish, served in a very Belgian way with chips and mayonnaise. You call for the

---

2 *Ifanta* (Fanta) has become the generic term for any fizzy drink, so you can be asked: 'Which Fanta do you want, Orange, Coca or Sprite?'

3 Shish kebabs.

'vétérinaire' ('the vet') who comes out of kitchen to take your order.[4] All beer is brewed by Brarudi and is a choice between Primus and Amstel. Primus was the first to establish itself and sells the most, especially to villagers. The French word *bière* became *ibiyeri* in Kirundi, but since this looked like a plural it had to have a singular, so Primus became known as *ikiyeri*. Amstel never got a Kirundi name. Many Burundians do not like beer to be cold, especially in the cool interior of the country, so the next question is, 'Hot or cold?'. In rural areas where there is no refrigeration the only choice is 'hot'![5] Production of beer was one thing that no amount of strife in the country could stop. The two breweries, always protected by the military, produce up to 30 million bottles each month and are the biggest contributor to the state budget. Home produced beer is also popular—*impeke*, made from sorghum, *insongo*, *urwarwa* and *mugomozi*, made from bananas.

Kirundi is one of the large family of Bantu languages which are spoken all the way from Kenya and the Congo south to the Cape. It is basically the same as Kinyarwanda and this makes it one of the most widely spoken languages in the family, spreading into border areas of Tanzania, Uganda and the Congo. It is not as easy for a foreigner as some of the other Bantu languages, such as Kiswahili, having a rather complicated system of past tenses and some weird spelling rules. Like all African languages it is very rich in words dealing with rural life: crops, trees and especially cattle and their ceremonial use. There are verbs for 'to return a cow to someone from whom one has received a cow' and 'to put the skin of a dead calf in front of a cow to make her give milk' and many more. Even within Burundi there are regional variations such as the almost aspirated pronunciation of the letter 't' in the south of the country (*ifanta* sounds like ifan'a). Naturally Kirundi has needed to borrow words for anything modern or urban. Two of the earliest borrowings were from German—*ishure* (school, from *Schule)* and *amahera* (money, from *Heller* which was the equivalent of a cent used in the German colonies). Newer words

---

4   The custom is to rinse your glass with a little beer and pour this on the ground. This is not done with soft drinks nor, understandably, with whisky!

5   As a change from bad news, a new small bottle of Primus was launched in July 2015 nicknamed *akabajou*, a sweet little baby.

from French, English or Kiswahili include *umuduga* (motor car), *indege* (airplane, originally Swahili for bird), *amashu* (cabbages, from *choux*), and of course *kabare, ikiyeri* and *ifanta.*

Being lucky enough to have one national language, Burundians, even highly educated ones, use French much less than do educated Congolese—and less than Ugandans or Zambians use English. Yet the standard of spoken French is good, even if the intonation sometimes has a Kirundi lilt. Kiswahili is used a lot in Buyenzi and Bwiza, in the markets in Bujumbura, Ngozi and Gitega, but even in these places almost everyone knows Kirundi as well. It is of course the 'French' version of Kiswahili that is spoken, where French words are frequently scattered through the conversation—my favourite, quoted by John Abuya of ActionAid, is *patron iko réunion*[6]—far from the pure Kiswahili of the East African coast.

The length of Burundians' names is often remarked upon. Apart from Muslims nearly everybody has two names, a traditional one which is given to the individual at birth and a Christian name.[7] Sometimes they are given an extra nickname or praise name. A few families such as the Nindorera began the modern practice of taking the father's name but this is unusual, so each person has his or her own name and keeps it for life. Women do not change their name when they get married. There is a wide variety of Christian names, often obscure saints (Népomucène, Herménégilde, Jean-Berchmans), or names from the Bible such as Joseph or Moïse. Traditional names are more complex. Philippe Ntahombaye has written a fascinating book explaining the way traditional names are chosen and even this does not include all of them.[8] The kings of Burundi used only four dynastic names: the first king was *Ntare* (lion), the next *Mwezi* (moon), then *Mutaga* (midday) and finally *Mwambutsa* (crossing over). There were other special names for different officials in the royal court. In general names were used as a way of protecting a child, either by minimizing its importance with names such as *Mu-*

---

6   'The boss is in a meeting.'

7   Before colonial times Burundians only had the one name.

8   Philippe Ntahombaye, *Des noms et des hommes, Aspects psychologiques et sociologiques du nom au Burundi* (Paris: Karthala, 1983).

gayo (contempt or shame) or *Ntazina* (no name), or by entrusting it to God. Sometimes a name might be changed when the danger seemed to be past. The former President writes that his parents named him *Buyoya*, meaning 'baby', fearing that they would lose him as they had lost other children, but that they planned to change his name later. He remains 'baby' up to now. Sometimes a nickname is used a lot and becomes a person's name, e.g. *Mpozagara* (a baby that burps after breast feeding), *Ntabona* (does not see well), *Rukundo* (love). An event during pregnancy or birth can suggest a name, e.g. *Nyangoma* (of the drum, meaning that a king was enthroned) or *Kibiriti* (matches), a name given in the First World War when huts were being burned down. The most common type of names these days are those where God (*Imana*) is to be thanked, or begged for help and protection: *Nshimirimana* (I thank God), *Havyarimana* (God gives children), *Manirakiza* or *Hakizimana* (God heals), *Bizimana* (God knows), *Ndayizeye* or *Nzeyimana* (my hope is in God).

Traditional culture in Burundi is not very different from that in many parts of Africa. History, legends, and stories were passed down by old people to their children and grandchildren. Fables, poems and praises of the king were set to music, with rhythmic clapping and chanting. Musical instruments included the thumb piano (*ikembe*), flute (*umwironge*), a kind of sitar (*inanga*), a rattle (*inyagara*), a zither (*amazina)*, a trumpet (*inzamba)*, a type of violin (*indonongo*), a one-stringed bow (*umuduri*), bells (*amayugi)* and, of course, drums.

Drums (*ingoma*) were the symbol of the kings of Burundi. They are also on the national flag. Legend tells us that a king came to Burundi from a foreign land with his ox. He killed the ox and spread the skin over a hole to dry. He lay down to sleep but he was woken up suddenly by the sound of a snake which slid out of the hole and stopped with its head next to the ox hide. The king then told his underlings to make a drum out of a hollowed out tree where the skin was stretched out. This became the holy drum, *inkiranya*, symbolising the legitimacy of the royal family and the welfare of the kingdom. The royal drums were kept in sacred sanctuaries, guarded mainly by Hutu families. They were used for many royal events and rituals including the huge annual sorghum festival (*umuganuro*) at the start of the sowing season, when drummers from all over the country would come to the royal capital. The drumming ritual is still always the same. The drummers enter and leave carrying the drums (which weigh from 25 to 50 kgs) on their heads. Each member of the team comes forward in turn to dance around and beat the big, holy drum, with the national flag painted on it, while the others drum frantically in the background on the smaller *amashako* drums, which provide a continuous beat, and the *ibishikizo* drums, which pick up the rhythm of the big drum. The Drummers of Burundi are among the most famous in Africa, a continent of drummers. They have performed all over the world, including the WOMAD festival in Britain, and have recorded several albums.

There are also various traditional dances (*uruvyino*), the best known being the *intore* war dance from the north of Burundi (and Rwanda). Among traditional handicrafts, Burundian basketwork is special. It is very tightly woven and is used most often to make baskets with tall, conical lids such as are carried on the heads of the relatives and guests who bring gifts to a married couple the day after their wedding, the *gutwikurura* ceremony. Pottery, always the work of the Twa, ranges from large, undecorated water carriers to decorated pots of all shapes and sizes, made by hand without a potter's wheel.

Burundi's 'modern' cultural output has been small. Up to 2014 the only Burundian feature film was *Gito l'ingrat* (Gito the ungrateful), the amusing story of a Burundian returning from France, made in 1992 by Léonce Ngabo, who is better known as a musician. Léonce launched an annual film festival in 2007 and this has encouraged the production of several feature films. Among the handful of musical stars, Khadja Nin is the best known. She left Burundi for Zaire (as the Congo was then called) and Europe when she was very young but had an incredibly lucky break when the French television channel, TF1, selected her album *Sambolera* as its summer promotion in 1996. She sings in French, Kiswahili and Kirundi and some of her songs make poignant commentaries on African affairs, as for example her 1998 song about the Burundi embargo. Another well known singer is the late Jean-Christophe Matata who started singing in the 1980s in Burundi, moved to Rwanda where he became a star, and finally to Belgium. He used his talent to promote peace, with songs like, *Hutus, Tutsis, nous sommes tous des frères* (Hutus, Tutsis, we are

17

all brothers), *Ntuntumeyo* ('Don't send me there', i.e. where the Hutus and Tutsis hate each other) and *V-Ibuzima uje Ibuntu* ('Return to reason' or you will be lost!). When he returned to perform in Burundi, the Mayor of Bujumbura presented him with the national and unity flags in recognition of his role as a 'combatant for peace'. Other musicians of note are Kadumu, whose popular blues-like songs also carry a strong peace message; Bahaga, who lives in Germany; Lion Story, a reggae group very critical of Nkurunziza and exiled for that; Sogo, now in the U.S. and Mudibu who is based in London.[9] There are several theatrical groups, some with a message on peace, human rights or AIDS.

Burundi has a rich tradition of storytelling and poetry. Herding cattle all day can be boring. To break the monotony tales of monsters, kings and animals were composed and exchanged. The doings of King Ntare Rushatsi were told and retold. Arrogant animals, especially the leopard, ended up being tricked and biting the dust. Such tales were also exchanged over a pot of *urwagwa* (banana beer) in the evening, along with songs, riddles, proverbs and poems. Recitation of poetry is still popular: traditionally much of this was in praise of that cultural icon, the cow—its milk, its beauty, its value as a payment at a marriage ceremony.[10]

With modern education the oral tradition has, of course, had to give way to literature. Burundi has not yet produced any world-famous authors, but many books have been written about Burundi's society and history, including memoirs of tragic events. The best loved writer was Michel Kayoya who trained as a priest and published two books about traditional life, *My Father's Footsteps*[11] and *Entre*

---

9   Mudibu was in fact one of the Tutsi students who escaped from Kibimba just in time to save his life. See chapter 6.

10 I am grateful to Kris Berwouts for parts of this chapter. If you can read Dutch, his book provides excellent basic information and analysis: Kris Berwouts, *Burundi* (Landenreeks, Koninklijk Instituut voor de Tropen, Amsterdam, 2007).

11 *Sur les traces de mon père* (the English version was published by the East African Publishing House in 1973). Kayoya was killed along with most other Hutu intellectuals in 1972. His body was thrown into a ditch with those of other priests. An association was founded in 1992 to honour Kayoya's heritage and to give him a proper burial.

deux mondes ('Between two worlds'). Many of the other works by Burundian authors can be found in the bibliography. I have particularly appreciated Augustin Mariro's *Burundi 1965: la première crise éthnique* ('Burundi 1965: the first ethnic crisis'), Antoine Kaburahe's *Mémoires blessées* ('Wounded memories'), Perpétue Nshimirimana's *Lettre à Isidore* and the two volumes of memoirs by ex-president Sylvestre Ntibantunganya.

Burundian traditional religion had one God, *Imana,* and a kind of high priest or intermediary between man and God, called *Kiranga.* This ceremonial cult was called *ukubandwa.* The spirits of ancestors, the 'living dead', were also greatly revered. There was also the equivalent of the Devil in the form of *Urupfu* (death). Christian missionaries sensibly presented their religion not as something totally new which involved the destruction of the old. Thus the name of the Christian God is now *Imana* (or *Mungu* in Kiswahili), even if *Kiranga* has been replaced by bishops, priests and pastors.

Somebody once described Lake Tanganyika as a very long lake completely surrounded by White Fathers. These Roman Catholic missionaries[12] got this label because of the colour of their robes, not of their faces. They had a struggle to establish themselves at the Burundian end of the lake. The first two who arrived in 1879 were killed. The king, Mwezi Gisabo, did not want them, neither did local people, nor the Arab traders. The White Fathers finally established missions during the period of German colonisation. Mostly French speakers, they became much more influential after the arrival of the Belgians, who helped to fund their schools and hospitals. They never converted King Mwambutsa but succeeded in suppressing most of the traditional religious rituals connected with the monarchy and in converting most of the other princes. The first Protestants, German Lutherans who had started work in 1911, had to leave with the German officials five years later. Seventh Day Adventists and Danish Baptists arrived in the 1920s, followed by Anglicans, Swedish Pentecostals, American Quakers and Free Methodists in the 1930s. Conversions and baptisms increased after 1940 and Burundi became

---

12 The name of their order is the Missionaires de Notre Dame d'Afrique and it was founded by Cardinal Lavigerie in 1868.

one of the most Christianised countries in Africa, with the Catholics estimated to account for about 60 per cent of the population, the many forms of Protestants and Evangelicals 25 per cent. The Muslims have increased to an estimated 13 per cent. There is at present a movement away from the Catholics and the older Protestant churches towards the Evangelicals and the Muslims.

The unity of the Catholic Church and its backing by the colonial regime gave it strength, but the proliferation of the Protestant churches continued nonetheless, including United Methodists and Kimbanguists.[13] The Protestants met to parcel out the country between the different missions. Most of these older churches are now members of the National Council of Churches of Burundi (CNEB) while the more evangelical ones form a separate alliance. More recently, as elsewhere in Africa, large numbers of independent evangelical 'mushroom' churches have been established. In some cases these ('a church in a suitcase') are more of a fund-raising scheme by the pastor than a beacon of spirituality, but many are genuine. They provide non-stop free entertainment for hours on Sundays, and not just on Sundays. They are a big growth industry all over Africa and clearly satisfy people's spiritual needs. In the process the mainstream churches have had to accept the loss of some of their followers. The Pentecostal churches have expanded fastest of all. One reason for this is their method of converting not individuals but whole communities at a time, and of refusing to help non-members. They have built large new churches and they pay their pastors well. Owing to their strength in the south of the country and their presence on both sides of the border, many of the Hutu refugees in Tanzania belonged to this church.[14]

In a poor country there are material advantages in trying to become a church leader. Bishops are relatively wealthy and respected. A former British Anglican missionary recalled how a young man had

---

13　Simon Kimbangu was a Congolese prophet who began preaching and healing in 1921. The Belgians almost immediately put him in prison where he remained till his death in 1951. His church grew fast and followed some of the ways of the Salvation Army—brass bands, no alcohol, strict discipline.

14　See Marc Sommers, *Fear in Bongoland* pp. 158-62. Their main funding comes from Sweden.

come up to him asking how he could become a bishop. He was told that this involved long service in a humbler role. He changed his allegiance and managed to get a scholarship to study in America with another church—and he ended up a bishop!

Muslim (Sunni) influence came into Burundi with the Arab traders at the end of the 19th century. They established centres of Swahili culture around the markets along the lake shore at Rumonge and Bujumbura, and also up country at Gitega and Ngozi. At first few Burundians converted. It seemed to be a faith for the traders using the Kiswahili language. During the crisis after 1993 Muslims, who did not categorise themselves as Hutus or Tutsis, welcomed displaced families from both sides, especially into Buyenzi, the mainly Muslim *quartier* in Bujumbura. They were neutral and had no part in the killings. Their exemplary role has been recognised by all Burundians, which may be part of the reason for a big increase in the number of Muslims. Another reason is that the Koran has been translated and Kirundi is used at prayers, although there is a shortage of Imams fluent in the language. New mosques are being built,[15] one even in the very Catholic and Tutsi suburb of Ngagara. The festival of Eid has been declared a national holiday. A Muslim, *Sheikh Mohamed Nibaruta,* took the lead in helping to set up the inter-faith Council of Religious Organisations (COR). COR provides a useful channel for dialogue and discussion between Christian and Muslim organisations and a coordination of joint action. For example, COR was one of the bodies chosen to help prepare and monitor the 2005 election.

---

15 No less than four mosques have been built in the burgeoning suburb of Kanyosha.

HISTORY AND PAINFUL MEMORIES

3

KINGS, GERMANS, BELGIANS, HUTUS, TUTSIS, TWA

Burundi was colonised three times—first by Germany, then by Belgium and fi-nally by Bururi—Burundian joke.

Burundi is very small. Its 27,834 sq km make it larger than Wales and smaller than Belgium. More than half its area is over 1,500m above sea level, rising to 2,685m at the highest peak. Most of the country is fertile with two rainy seasons. This has permitted an aver-age population density of almost 290 per square kilometre which is, after Rwanda, the highest in Africa. The total population is already 8 million.[1] When the population was smaller, land was not a prob-lem. The increasing pressure on the land was one of the causes of Burundi's crisis and the reason that there are no longer many wild animals. The undulating plateau in the centre of the country was the heart of the pre-colonial kingdom of Burundi, an area with a moder-ate climate, good rain and, in those days, free from malaria.

Burundi was one of a number of centralised kingdoms in the Great Lakes region and, though its boundaries changed as a result of local wars, its shape on the map stabilised after 1850 and this was the kingdom that was incorporated, along with Rwanda, into

---

1   Annual births per 1,000 are approximately 42, deaths 13.5. Average life expectancy has dropped from 50 to 39 in the last 15 years owing to violence and AIDS.

German East Africa from 1890. The king (*mwami)* was revered as an embodiment of God (*Imana)* and presided over a relatively stable and cohesive social structure, where the elements composing society were classified as Tutsi, Hutu and Twa (in the Kirundi language, singular *mututsi,* plural *batutsi* and so on*).*[2] The oversimplified explanation of the origins of these groups is that the Twa (pygmies)[3] were the first inhabitants, living from hunting in the forests; that the Hutu, Bantu-speaking agriculturalists, were next to arrive; and that the Tutsi were a Hamitic cattle-owning people who moved in later, perhaps from the Horn of Africa. The origin of the Twa (Batwa) is accepted. There is no archaeological, biological or linguistic evidence for the rest of the story—but there is not a lot of evidence for any alternative interpretation. In addition, the extended royal family in Burundi is considered (at least by themselves) to be a separate group, the Ganwa.[4] There has been no recent census but it is normally accepted that the Hutus number around 85 per cent, the Tutsis around 14 per cent and the Twa less than 1 per cent. There are a few areas, such as most of the province of Mwaro, where the Tutsis are the majority and other areas, such as Cibitoke and Bubanza provinces, where native Tutsis are very few indeed.

These groups are always described by Burundians as *ethnies* (ethnic groups)—or *ubwoko* in Kirundi[5]—but they are not 'tribes' such as are found elsewhere in Africa and other parts of the world. Perhaps 'categories' is the best word, but I will, like the Burundians, continue to refer to them in this book as ethnic groups. The Tutsis and Hutus lived for centuries on the same *collines,* spoke the same language, had the same culture, worshipped the

---

2   For clarity I have normally referred to them Tutsis, Hutus, Twa, Ganwa rather than *Batutsi, Bahutu, Batwa and Baganwa.*

3   There are various pygmy populations throughout central Africa. The Twa are the eastern grouping, found in Burundi, Rwanda, eastern Congo and southwestern Uganda. See Jerome Lewis, *The Batwa Pygmies of the Great Lakes Region* (London: Minority Rights Group International 2000).

4   Most people consider them to be Tutsis and they are not recognised in the Constitution as a separate group.

5   *Ubwoko* really means, sort, kind or species.

same God and honoured the same king. This was a stable, almost feudal, system—which is not to say it was idyllic or specially harmonious. Just as peasants were exploited in Europe in the Middle Ages, there was certainly a degree of repression, especially in areas like Cibitoke and Kayanza provinces where the population was overwhelmingly Hutu. Revolts by Hutu peasants were not unknown and the king's army was composed mainly of Tutsis and Ganwas. *Ubugererwa,* where a Tutsi leased a plot of land to a Hutu, and *ubugabire,* where a cow was loaned, in both cases in return for loyal service, are not unlike medieval practices in Europe, and the tribute which the king received in kind resembles the tithe. Radical Hutus such as Rémy Gahutu, the founder of the Hutu political movement, Palipehutu, liked to emphasise these deep historical roots of conflict.[6] In contrast, social cohesion was helped by the tradition of nominating *bashingantahe* (wise men, counsellors, elders) chosen from both main groups.[7] Outstanding citizens were formally invested with moral authority by becoming *bashingantahe.* They were the guardians of tradition and of good behaviour. They were able to resolve inter-personal conflicts and dispense justice on their *colline.* This institution (the abstract noun is *ubushingantahe*) was weakened when it was politicised in the 1980s. There have been attempts to revive it, so that the *bashingantahe* can have a role as agents of development and can aid the post-war reconciliation process, but some see this as 'cultural nostalgia' inappropriate for today's world.

The 'ethnic' division is not a matter of social class either: traditionally Tutsi men looked after cattle and Tutsi women tilled the land, whereas Hutus either worked for Tutsis or tilled the land. These days there are numerous cattle-owning Hutus and bean-growing Tutsi men. Then there is the simplistic idea that Tutsis (and Ganwa) are tall, lighter coloured and have long noses

---

6   See chapter 10.

7   The name derives from the words *intahe* (a staff of wisdom) and *gushinga* (to plant or establish). In 1993 some outstanding citizens helped calm the situation; many but not all of these were *bashingantahe.* See chapter 6.

whereas Hutus are short and stocky with flat noses.[8] Because of centuries of intermarriage, these are very rough guidelines indeed. One scholar has suggested that up to 70 per cent of Burundians are of mixed ethnicity. Thus plenty of people do not fit the stereotype: the Tutsi Michel Micombero, President of Burundi from 1966 to 1976, for example, had all the supposedly Hutu features.[9] In this patrilineal society, if your father is a Hutu then you are labelled Hutu even if you resemble your Tutsi mother—and vice versa. During the recent 'crisis', some were killed in error because of their appearance. The Twa are a bit different and I have written a whole chapter on them. They are classified as pygmies and most of them are indeed quite short. I am told they speak Kirundi with a distinctive accent, and, interestingly, they refer to the other groups as 'Burundians'.

René Lemarchand in his outstanding book, *Burundi, Ethnic Conflict and Genocide*[10] remarks that when considering the precolonial history of Burundi, the problem is to know what is reality and what is invention. 'Oral traditions are a tangled web. Some tell stories that others deny; many are manipulated to suit the interests of particular individuals or communities...' There are different interpretations of Burundi's origins just as there are of its post-independence experience. However, everyone agrees that the kingdom was founded by Mwami Ntare Rushatsi[11] around the year 1680. Mwami Ntare Rugamba greatly enlarged the kingdom in the early 19th century, partitioning the old kingdom of Bugesera with Rwanda, thus giving Burundi the area around Kirundo. There were local conflicts, usually between different Ganwa princes, especially during the long reign of Mwami Mwezi

---

8   Rwandan Interahamwe, it was reported, would insert a thumb into a person's nostril; if it fitted, you were a Hutu and your life was spared. The historical origins of the 'ethnic' question throughout the Great lakes region are examined in Jean-Pierre Chrétien, *The Great Lakes of Africa* (New York: Zone Books, 2003), pp. 74-83.

9   The four tallest members of the government in 1994-95 were all Hutus.

10   René Lemarchand, *Burundi: Ethnic Conflict and Genocide* (Cambridge University Press, 1995).

11   His name means 'Hairy Lion'.

Gisabo (1850-1908). The princes needed to have support from local Hutus and Tutsis to bolster their power base and to extend their power into new areas. Thus the monarchy never became as authoritarian as in Rwanda. These conflicts were not based on Hutu-Tutsi rivalry, except in the case of Kilima, an 'anti-king' who cashed in on the popular discontent of Hutu peasants. There are also the folk stories about Samandari, a semi-legendary folk leader, which are passed down orally. A hero especially to Hutus, Samandari makes fun of Tutsis, saying that they are as useless as their cows. There are several stories where he traps the king, such as the one where he leaves the king to boil some spinach. When he returns he accuses the king of stealing some of the spinach, which has reduced in the pot. This, and other similar tales, proved the need for witnesses and led to the tradition that people were innocent until proved guilty. Another story recounts that when Samandari was being sent into exile, he climbed a tree and urinated on the king.

The king and princes were Ganwas but Tutsis and some Hutus had high-up positions, the difference being that the Hutu roles were generally by favour rather than by right. For example, some Hutus were responsible for looking after the royal drums and tombs and Twa had a role as court dancers and musicians. Ethnicity was not totally rigid: a Hutu with lots of cattle might, in some cases, be 'promoted'. There is even a word for it: *kwihutura*, 'to de-Hutuise'[12].

There are other important divisions in Burundian society. The clan (*umuryango*) is often considered more important than the ethnic group, particularly among Tutsis. Social stratification was normally based on clan. Tutsis from Muramvya (Banyaruguru) saw themselves as superior to those from Bururi (Bahima), a source of political bitterness later. It may be that the Bahima arrived later than the other Tutsis and thus got the poorest land. Within the Banyaruguru there was a bitter rift between the Bezi and Batare sub-clans (which was behind the murder of the Prime Minister

---

12 This did not happen much in Burundi before colonial times. Ganwa could also be demoted to Tutsi status.

Prince Louis Rwagasore in 1961). Some clans are exclusively Tutsi or Hutu; others can include both, even Twa in some cases. Among the Hutus the division between Banyaruguru Hutus and Ababo from the Imbo plain was equally deep, not least as far as diet was concerned, those from Imbo living on fish and cassava and those from the interior on beans and maize.[13] In spite of the small size of the country, the cleavage between north and south was a reality which was not just a matter of clans. This difference has, as with the ethnic division, been deepened by post-independence politics, but it existed under the monarchy.

When the colonialists arrived they found what appeared to be a stratified society which fitted nicely into their prejudiced world view. King Mwazi Gisabo resisted any kind of outside interference whether it came from missionaries, Germans or even cotton clothing. He did not submit to a German protectorate until 1904, after which the Germans ruled indirectly through the king and the Ganwa princes. The aristocratic colonial officials looked favourably on the Tutsis and the Ganwa. There was economic hardship during the German period: a rinderpest epidemic destroyed cattle and sleeping sickness halved the population of the Rusizi plain. Otherwise the short period of German rule had little impact. The Belgians took over the country in 1916, and their control was confirmed in 1922 as a League of Nations mandate, which implied a responsibility to lead the country towards independence. They continued the German policy of indirect rule, though their version of it was less indirect and involved much more interference in local affairs. They exploited the ethnic divisions and the prejudices that went with them. This fitted in well with the racist theories that were current in Europe at the time. The Tutsis were seen as a superior race, intelligent and good looking; the Hutus as simple peasants. (There was a rough parallel with Belgium where at that time the French speaking Walloons were politically and socially dominant over the Flemings.) It seemed logical to educate the Tutsis as a collaborating class, a typical 'divide and

---

13 See Marc Sommers, *Fear in Bongoland* (Oxford: Bergbahn Books 2001) who describes differences among exiled Hutus in Tanzania.

rule' way of running a colony.[14] The Belgians introduced identity cards indicating ethnic origin and this only deepened the divisions. The commission set up in 1989 by President Pierre Buyoya to study the 'ethnic' question blamed the Belgians for promoting the 'Hamitic myth', the idea that the Tutsis were related to the Ethiopians. Later, at the height of the crisis, people sometimes shouted to Tutsis to go back to Ethiopia.[15] Understandably, Tutsis are generally opposed to the myth, suggesting as it does, last in, first out.

The Belgians took little account of the League of Nations and ruled Burundi as a colony, though the *mwami's* administration was responsible for certain things such as customary law and land allocation. Pierre Ryckmans, the Belgian Resident,[16] described this style of government neatly: 'The native kings…are the familiar décor that permits us to act behind the scenes without alarming the people.'[17] Some were alarmed, however, and there was a revolt in the centre of the country in 1922. Economic development began slowly through peasant coffee production and the development of the port at Bujumbura. Forced labour and taxation brought villagers into the cash economy: 'The money came to demystify the cow'.[18] Many went to Uganda or the Congo as temporary labourers. The first motor road into Rwanda was opened in 1932. Education was strictly limited, even for Tutsis.

In 1946 the newly-established United Nations established a trusteeship to replace the mandate and started putting pressure on Belgium to democratise and to push both Burundi and Rwanda to

---

14 The Belgians progressively reduced the number of Hutu and Tutsi chiefs and sub-chiefs in favour of Ganwa.

15 Very few Tutsis resemble Ethiopians.

16 The Resident was in fact the deputy governor responsible for Urundi. His autobiography is entitled *Dominer pour servir* (To serve through domination). He believed that the Tutsis' 'mere demeanour lends them considerable prestige over the inferior races that surround them'.

17 This is quoted by J.-P. Chrétien, op. cit. (note 127, p. 399) from Ministère des Colonies, *Rapport sur l'administration belge.*

18 Léonce Ndarubagiye, *The Origins of the Tutsi-Hutu Conflict* (self-published, available in School of Oriental and African Studies library, London).

independence. Belgian politics had also evolved by this time and tended to favour the Hutu majority in both countries, believing that the Hutus preferred Belgian tutelage to continue. The Belgian governor, Jean-Paul Harroy, supported vocally by the leader of the *colons*, Albert Maus, gave every support to the Hutu-led revolution in 1959 in Rwanda and the overthrow of the monarchy there. This was the moment when the relationship between the two countries, like non-identical Siamese twins, began to poison the history of both. In Rwanda ethnic polarisation went much deeper and the monarchy was not such a unifying factor as it was in Burundi. In Burundi the Belgians wanted another prince, Baranyanka, to replace Mwami Mwambutsa, whose son, Prince Louis Rwagasore, led the Union pour le Progrès National (Uprona), a genuine nationalist independence movement which was on good terms with Nyerere, Lumumba and Nkrumah. The Belgians saw Uprona as dangerously pro-communist and anti-Belgian. The governor put all his weight behind the pro-Belgian Christian Democrat Party (PDC) supported by the rival royal Batare clan, but Uprona easily won the pre-independence election in September 1961 and Prince Louis Rwagasore became Prime Minister.[19]

He had little time to make his mark. Three weeks after the election, Prince Louis was assassinated by Karageorgis, a Greek settler in the pay of the PDC and the rival royals. If the Belgians were not directly implicated, they were certainly not sorry.[20] Rwagasore had the prestige of royalty but was as much a popular nationalist as Nyerere, Kaunda or Kenyatta. He opposed continued union or federation with Rwanda for he despised its ethnic extremism. Maintaining the twin countries as one had been the aim of both

---

19 Eight parties contested the 1961 election. Alongside the PDC was the collaborationist People's Party (PP) created by the same Albert Maus. An excellent detailed description of this confused pre- and post-independence period is provided by Augustin Mariro's book, *Burundi 1965: la première crise ethnique*. Uprona's victory led Albert Maus to commit suicide.

20 Patrice Lumumba, the Congolese leader, was killed earlier in 1961 and the Belgian role in this has been confirmed by the recent inquiry. There has been no such inquiry in the case of Prince Louis. Belgium threatened to deny aid to Burundi if certain people implicated in the killing were not exonerated.

the UN and the Belgians. He did, however, propose that Burundi should federate with Tanganyika after independence. Rwagasore was an intellectual, an idealist and a businessman. He had a vision of a united Burundi, economically and socially developed, and he had enough charisma to make it a reality.[21] His assassination was independent Burundi's first great tragedy and an event which led to all the later tragedies.

As it was, Burundi staggered to independence with a weak king and a divided political class. In Rwanda the 1959 revolution had led to many killings and the flight of thousands of Tutsis, many of whom came to Burundi filled with hatred for Hutus, fuelling the fears of Burundi's Tutsi minority. Hutus and Tutsis, known as the 'Casablanca' and 'Monrovia' groups, jostled for power inside Uprona and there were constant changes of government. Early in 1965, one week after taking office for the second time, the Prime Minister, Pierre Ngendandumwe, was killed by a Tutsi refugee. He was the most competent politician of this chaotic period, a Hutu with a Tutsi wife and, like Rwagasore, a unifying influence. This was Burundi's second great tragedy.

Another general election provided a big Hutu majority[22] but perversely the King nominated a prince as prime minister. Hutu opinion became inflamed. Meanwhile, King Mwambutsa, who had been on the throne for the entire period of Belgian rule, began to feel increasingly powerless and politically isolated. He went on a long visit to Europe from which he was never to return. In October 1965 Hutus in the police and the army started a revolt. It was brutally crushed: many villagers in Muramvya province were slaughtered, along with Hutu army officers and politicians. Among these was the charismatic Paul Mirerekano, who had been co-founder of Uprona with Rwagasore but had moved to an increasingly hardline Hutu position. The Tutsis saw this revolt as an attempt at ethnocide. They reacted by excluding Hutus from

---

21 Even Governor Harroy recognised his charisma, his natural authority and the moderation of his remarks after the election: J.-P. Harroy, *Burundi 1955-62* (Brussels: Editions Hayez, 1987).

22 Uprona had 20 deputies, 11 of whom were Hutu. The People's Party, the old pro-Belgian party aiming at Rwandan-style Hutu domination, had 10.

the army and from political power. From this moment, history started to look different depending on your ethnic standpoint.

The end of the monarchy came in 1966. King Mwambutsa was deposed by his son, Ntare V, who was himself almost immediately removed by Captain Michel Micombero, a young army officer from Bururi whom the new king had appointed as Prime Minister. Micombero was the first, and worst, of the three Tutsi military presidents, all of the Hima clan, from Rutovu commune. An interlude of only four years divided Belgian rule from Bururi rule.

4

MICOMBERO AND THE
TRAGEDY OF 1972

What is it to be Hutu or Tutsi? ... It is to remember who killed one of your close relations fifteen years ago or to wonder who will kill your child in ten years. —Jean-Pierre Chrétien

Having effectively excluded the Hutus (most of whom were kept out of the army by a rule that recruits had to be of a certain height and girth.) Micombero set about creating a dictatorship, abolishing parliament and running the country through a National Revolutionary Council. Micombero accused Belgium of supporting a minor revolt by Hutus in 1969. Belgium withdrew military aid and France eagerly stepped in. A plot in 1971 by Tutsis from Muramvya who felt excluded from power was followed by a serious Hutu revolt on 29 April 1972. Symbols of authority were attacked in Rumonge in the south, in Gitega and in the capital. The then US Ambassador, Thomas Patrick Melady,[1] witnessed events in Bujumbura. Up to 3,000 Tutsis lost their lives. At the same time the deposed King, Ntare V, who had been invited to Uganda by Idi Amin, was handed over to the Burundi government. The Hutu rebels expected to get support from the many Tutsis who were angry at the King's arrest but the

---

1   Thomas Patrick Melady, *Burundi, the Tragic Years* (New York: Orbis Books, 1974).

government acted quickly. The King was killed on 30 April and his body was thrown in a ditch at Gitega.[2]

The failure of the coup was attributed, according to one story, to the fact that Micombero had been sleeping with the Tutsi wife of one of the few Hutu army officers and she told the President that something was afoot. He had therefore dismissed his entire cabinet and distributed arms on 28 April. Another story is that the plotters had agreed on a time to strike but some thought it was Swahili time (9am) and some thought it was 'European' time (3am)! The government overreacted, unleashing a terrible revenge. All educated Hutus, even teenagers at secondary school and especially anyone wearing glasses, was targeted. About 200,000 Hutus—and a few Banyaruguru Tutsis—were massacred and a further 300,000 fled the country, mainly to Tanzania. Micombero, although he was frequently in a drunken stupor, was aware of what was going on in his name and he did eventually call off the killings, but it was too late. Some people claim that this was not genocide because it was only educated Hutus who were killed, but that is sophistry. The government's revenge was a key moment for Burundi. The venom created in 1972 is the background to all the subsequent history of the country. Melady comments on the hatred that he discovered: 'I had underestimated how deeply rooted it was, like a malignant growth spreading throughout their human relationships.'[3]

Tutsi and Congolese friends remember their teachers being taken away. Hutu friends wonder why they lost their fathers.

Adrien Tuyaga was six years old and at nursery school. 'When soldiers came to arrest my father I could not understand much because other soldiers used to visit us, friends of my father. This time they seemed to have a different, more aggressive attitude. I could not understand why I never saw my father again…'

Athanase Bagorikunda: 'In my third year of primary school I lost my father. He was the head of Kwibuka Primary School. I was there. I

---

2   His father, Mwambutsa, died in Geneva in 1977.

3   Thomas Patrick Melady, op.cit.

saw what happened. My uncle was also killed. I never knew why they were killed. My mother did not say.'

Jean-Marie Nibizi (a Hutu with a Tutsi mother): 'I did not know about the existence of ethnic groups till 1972 when they killed people. At that time there was a friend of my family who was a Hutu soldier and he was willing to buy me trousers, shoes and a shirt— then the killings started. That was the last time I saw him.....I did wonder why my father had been killed in '72. He was a lieutenant in the army. We started living a poor life, so coming back to my past brought hatred in my heart towards Tutsis to the point of deciding not to marry one...later I got healed by Jesus Christ. This enabled me to marry a Tutsi.'

Samson Gahungu, a Hutu, had finished his teacher training in 1972: 'I discovered I was of a certain ethnic group because they started taking people to prison. I was 20 and I began my work as teacher in Mutaho. As some of the 7th year kids were bigger than me, they did not notice me and I escaped. As it was my first year as a teacher I was not known by the administrators.'

Aloys Ningabira: 'My father was not taken in 1972. He was a peasant. He talked to me about the goodness of the traditional chief because this chief had protected all the *colline*....My elder brother could have been killed. He was coming from his school, the *Athenée de Gitega*. He had not been killed at school but when he returned home there were people in the next village who suggested he should be taken hostage, but the chief said, 'No I cannot kill that person'. I grew up and got to know that there was an ethnic problem.'

Osias Habingabwa was head of a primary school near Kayanza, near enough to run to the Rwanda border. Luckily the soldiers who had been told to arrest all Hutu civil servants never reached his school which was very remote.

Thérence Mbonabuca was 15 when his father and his elder brother, a teacher, were taken away.

37

Domitien Ndayizeye, who was later to become President, was able to flee to Belgium and later to Rwanda. He stayed outside the country for 21 years.

Perpétue Kankindi was at school and managed to go home to her father who, as a bishop, was able to protect her until she could be sent off to school in Switzerland where she met her future husband, the politician Charles Karikurubu.

Melchior Nzigamasabo, a Tutsi with a Hutu mother, ran away with his Hutu friends when soldiers surrounded the school. He was taken back and the school was told he was a Tutsi.

Dismas Hicintuka, a Tutsi from Mwaro, was in the fourth year of primary school: 'I saw neighbours who came to our place who spent the day at the house and sometimes they came to sleep under the beds and I wondered why this was. I did not understand at all but only later I learned that there were some people who were being pursued and were being killed...My father and grandfather tried to hide the neighbours. The neighbours were saved and they considered my father to be like a brother. When they had something at their place they always invited us at their *rugo* and they used to come to us when they had a jug of beer. I don't know if the relationship had been so good before...In 1993 when Tutsis were being pursued all over the country they said, 'Ah. It's our turn to hide you! We cannot forget what you did for us in '72'.'

Margaret Sweeney was a British VSO volunteer teacher at the Catholic secondary school at Ijenda in 1969-70, a time when there was already tension and insecurity. There were three young Hutu teachers at the school. One was a political activist. Another was a remarkable man, a lover of poetry who had adopted the six orphaned children of a Tutsi teacher who had helped him in his studies. All three were killed in 1972.

Among the many Hutu victims of 1972 were the fathers and uncles of most of those Hutus who joined the rebellion in the 1990s, notably President Pierre Nkurunziza's father, Eustache Ngabisha, who was a Member of Parliament. Other eminent victims included the 'Pele' of Burundian football, Meltus Habwawihe, who was tortured in front of his family, and the priest and writer Michel Kayoya. The Minister of Public Works, Marc Ndayiziga, who had been on a mission to Chile, had been asked to buy some things for the Micombero family on his way through Brussels. He was arrested as he got off the plane. He, along with the parcel for the president's family, ended up in the huge ditch in Buterere which had been specially dug for the 100,000 victims in Bujumbura The Chevrolet trucks which collected them were known as *'pfakurira'* ('Just get up on the truck').[4]

No-one in Burundi was punished for the massacres of 1972. This was another step towards a culture of impunity. Nor did the international community take any notice of what was going on.[5] However, the trauma of 1972 continued to burn in the memory of the Hutus

---

4   These and other victims are described in fascinating detail in *Burundi, terre des héros non chantés* (Land of unsung heroes) by Herménégilde Niyonzima (Switzerland: Editions Remesha, 2004).

5   It seems that Melady's reports were not passed on to President Nixon by the State Department. A fascinating tape of a conversation between Nixon and Henry Kissinger has recently been released by the US National Archive (this was the time of the Vietnam war):

Nixon: I want State's ass reamed out on that for not, for not—Henry, ah, in the whole Burundi business—I've been watching it in the press—did you know that State has not sent one *memorandum over to us on it?*
Kissinger: Absolutely!
RN: Or have they? Or have you had something I haven't seen?
HK: No, no, they have not.
RN: Well, how do you feel about it? Don't you really feel—just be, let's be totally honest, isn't it a person a person, goddamn it?…You know, there are those, you know, they talk about Vietnam, about these people far away that we don't know,…Well, now, goddamn it, people are people in my opinion… I'm getting tired of this business of letting these Africans (kill) a hundred thousand people and do nothing about it.
HK: And when they have—and all these bleeding hearts in this country, who say we like to kill yellow people.
RN: That's right.
HK: There haven't been as many killed in eight years of the war as were killed in three months in Burundi.

who fled into exile. To these many thousands who fled to Tanzania, 'the people of 72', fear of Tutsis was a constant trauma. This was a 'cultural fear' that the clever Tutsis would somehow still threaten them even in the refugee camps[6] or in Dar es Salaam where many of them lived illegally. This fear also caused mutual suspicion between refugees. For example, Hutus from the Imbo region distrusted those from Muramvya and vice versa. Refugees feared that government agents were lurking near them. Stories of the nightmare of 1972 were passed on to children born in Tanzania who had never met a Tutsi in their lives. Hutus in Tanzania, especially the minority from the Imbo region, still felt that there was discrimination. The UNHCR was denying them secondary education: were they not agents of the Tutsi government?[7]

The first concrete result of 1972 was the creation of Palipehutu (Party for the Liberation of the Hutu People) in 1980, a first step towards eventual revenge.

---

6   Most of the post-1972 refugees were in camps at Ulyankulu (near Tabora), Katumba and Mishamo (near Mpanda).

7   Marc Sommers, *Fear in Bongoland,*, a detailed study of Burundian 1972 refugees living in Dar es Salaam (Oxford: Bergbahn Books 2001).

5

DICTATORSHIP AND THE FIRST
SEEDS OF DEMOCRACY 1977-93

Bagaza built the roads, Buyoya made the speed bumps and Frodebu created the potholes. —Burundian joke.

In 1976 Micombero was replaced in a bloodless coup by a new dictator, his neighbour from Rutovu commune in Bururi, Lieutenant Colonel Jean Baptiste Bagaza. I had the chance to meet this man, now a well preserved sixty year old, in 2006. He seemed proud to have reformed the administrative and tax system, prevented corruption, developed industries (coffee, sugar, cotton) and created infrastructure (roads, electricity, drinking water, new villages). He was successful in getting aid from Arab states, the Soviet bloc and China as well as from the West. When asked about his policy of banning all mention of ethnic groups and just calling everyone Burundians—in reality a way of disguising Tutsi, or more particularly Bururi, control—he said that his government had seen everyone as Africans rather than Burundians, Hutus or Tutsis. When asked why he had thrown half the Congolese population out of Burundi, he replied that they had simply decided to leave! I was too polite to ask him about the expulsion of foreign missionaries whom he saw as the last relic of colonialism (and a few of them were). From 1981 he imprisoned priests and banned a Protestant radio station and the Catholic newspaper *Ndongozi*. He nationalised church schools, closed seminaries and even stopped catechism classes; 87 churches were closed for a time, including Gitega Cathedral. He closed bars during working hours and tried to stop Burundians spending so much time and money on betrothal ceremonies (*la dot)*, weddings, funerals and *levées de deuil* (gatherings to mark the end of the period of mourning). All this did not go down well. Burundians love their ceremonies and their churches, but Bagaza saw the church as a parallel source of authority and power to that of the party, Uprona, though which he tried to control everything.

This was the worst time to be a Hutu. Under Bagaza Hutus were often prevented from going to school and from succeeding in exams.[1] It was hard for even the few well qualified Hutus to get jobs—and they were still traumatised after 1972. These frustrations, as well as bitterness over 1972, were what drove Rémy Gahutu to found Palipehutu in1980 (see chapter 10). Bagaza's policies, even when they were not ill-intentioned, frightened Hutus. For example, they thought his family planning policy was aimed at Hutu women. At the same time, the Bururi Tutsis were alarmed at the growth of Palipehutu and reacted by intensifying the exclusion of Hutus from school and ensuring that they had the military, political and economic means to control the state. They even excluded, though less thoroughly, the '*Tutsis du tiers monde,*[2] those from outside Bururi. Statistics tell the story: in Bagaza's government 15 out of 18 ministers were from the south and two out of the 18 were Hutu; 5 per cent of children in the 12 worst-off provinces were in secondary school while in Bururi it was 28 per cent.[3] The state was the predominant employer and private investment was discouraged. Elections were held in October 1982. Bagaza was the only candidate and won 99 per cent of the votes.

Herménégilde Niyonzima,[4] while bitterly criticising his education policy, lets Bagaza off lightly, praising his efforts at developing the

---

1   Hutu candidates' papers were marked with a small 'u' and Tutsis with a small 'i' so that Tutsis could be assured of better marks.

2   'Third world' Tutsis. In fact, these were the Tutsis who had looked down on the Hima from Bururi in times past.

3   Figures from René Lemarchand, *Burundi: Ethnic Conflict and Genocide* (Cambridge University Press, 1995).

4   Herménégilde Niyonzima, *Burundi, terre des héros non chantés* (Switzerland:

country and especially his abolition of *ubugererwa*, the system of land servitude described above, and the poll tax, *ikori*, which every man had to pay each year. Bagaza had nothing against peasants, even if most of them were Hutu, as long as they remained peasants and got no ideas above their station.

Whatever good he may have done, few people were sad to see Bagaza go when in September 1987 he was forced out by the army in the same way as he came in.[5] The new man was Major Pierre Buyoya, yet another Tutsi of the Hima clan from Rutovu in Bururi province. Relations with the churches improved immediately, but initially nothing else changed. Tutsis remained totally in charge. Then in 1988 came another of Burundi's periodic convulsions, this time confined to the two communes of Ntega and Marangara on the Rwanda border. In an outbreak influenced by Palipehutu and Rwanda's Hutu government and provoked by repressive local officials and the killing of a Hutu family, 300 Tutsis were killed. *Claudette Manariyo* was at a primary school near Kirundo town at the time and she remembers seeing people arriving in a state of shock. She had to take refuge herself and for the first time she became conscious that she too was a Tutsi. The army's revenge was savage. At least 20,000 Hutus were killed and many more escaped to Rwanda. Napalm was used and Buyoya refused an investigation into the killings.

However, the international climate had changed since 1972. Palipehutu was well established secretly inside the country and well connected diplomatically. All over the world human rights were headline issues and images of slaughter could now be seen on international television. The government of a weak little country dependent on aid could not risk any further massacres of thousands of civilians. Buyoya set up a Commission to Study the Question of National Unity; he appointed a well respected Hutu, Adrien Sibomana, as Prime Minister and an ethnically balanced cabinet. The report of

---

Editions Remesha, 2004).

5   According to Ahmedou Ould-Abdallah, *Burundi on the Brink 1993-95* (US Institute of Peace, 2000), the non-commissioned officers (NCOs) who organised the coup felt threatened by Bagaza's proposal to limit army service to ten years and to abolish soldiers' right to free electricity when living outside military bases.

this commission was not very open about the events of 1965, 1972 and 1988, which was not surprising since some members of the commission were Tutsi hardliners, but at least it admitted that ethnic rivalry was the central problem and that there really was discrimination. It also led to a lot of open debate, something Burundi had not experienced since the 1960s. The result was to draw up a Charter of Unity ('*Ubumwe*'), approved by referendum in 1991,[6] with a special unity flag and anthem. As you travel around Burundi you see a 'unity square' in each town, usually with a crudely painted monument, the paint now fading in the sun. Unfortunately this unity was cosmetic: it did not address the real issue of power sharing. Governors and administrators mouthed the slogans as commanded by the president. The failure to create real unity became clear in the 1993 election result. However, criticism of the government for its 'liberalism' by extremists on both sides perhaps suggests that it was starting to do the right thing.

1991 to 1993 was a period of change and of hope. This was the post-Berlin Wall period when national conferences were being 'cooked' (in Nyerere's words) all over 'Francophone' Africa. The world was a different place and even Bagaza would have bent under the pressure. Buyoya refused to accept the idea of a national conference and a transitional government, but he made it look as if he was sharing power. In fact, cunning politician that he is, he kept power in his own hands and merely handed out jobs. Nonetheless, this did begin to create a visible Hutu bourgeoisie. Hutus were even seen on television, where they had never been seen before! They started getting jobs in town. They were free to get some education. Political parties and civil society organisations started to come into the open, notably the Burundi Democratic Front (Frodebu),[7] led by Melchior Ndadaye, which had been in existence underground since 1983. Buyoya even met Palipehutu members in Paris in 1991. However,

---

6   Eugène Nindorera comments: 'The implementation of the charter was too general. Everyone was to be forgiven because everyone had committed mistakes, whereas many Burundians had done nothing wrong. When you generalise responsibility like that you end up with a fairly meaningless charter…'

7   The party's full name is Sahwanya-Frodebu.

two smaller Hutu revolts in 1991 were repressed in the old style, and sure enough it was in the army that discrimination lingered—right up to 2004.

Some people feared that a multi-party system would boost ethnic tension—and it probably did. To avoid this, parties had to prove they had a mixed membership. Buyoya was confident. He thought he had done a lot for the people and he moved fast towards elections, believing he would win—and he also realised that Frodebu was rapidly gaining ground. It was decided to start with the presidential election and this took place on 1 June 1993. Pierre Buyoya ran for Uprona, Melchior Ndadaye for Frodebu and there was a royalist candidate, Pierre-Claver Sendegaya. In the event, on a 97 per cent turnout, Ndadaye won easily with 64 per cent of the vote. Frodebu's score rose even higher to 71 per cent in the parliamentary elections which followed at the end of the month, giving it just over the 80 per cent of seats, enough to make constitutional amendments.

What went wrong for Buyoya? Clearly a large number of people voted on ethnic lines—but many did not, as Buyoya's support was more than double the maximum Tutsi vote. Ndadaye himself concentrated on broad issues—but some Hutus did play the ethnic card. Land and the army were big issues for Hutus. Uprona was arrogant, being accustomed to the one-party system. Many wore Uprona T-shirts and then voted for Frodebu. Hutus, and many Tutsis, wanted change. Memories of 1972 were still alive. Buyoya had taken some steps forward but he, military man from Bururi that he was, seemed to represent some of the bad things about the past—and Ndadaye had considerable charisma. Buyoya deserves credit that the election went smoothly and peacefully, for publicly accepting the result and giving Ndadaye a big hug, a clip that has frequently been replayed on Burundi TV.

But in reality Buyoya was angry and bitter. Neither he nor Uprona had imagined themselves in opposition and they were not very good at it. Even before the parliamentary elections there had been Tutsi demonstrations against the '*éthnisation*' of power. Buyoya's attitude at this time remains unclear. A small group of soldiers rose in revolt before the parliamentary vote and again before Ndadaye's inauguration. On this occasion the President was saved by his guards, led by

45

Capt. Gratien Rukindikiza. The leader of this coup attempt said, just before his death, that he was only carrying out Buyoya's orders. Buyoya is always very careful not to say anything in public that would compromise him and he claims that he was loyal to Ndadaye, but could he not have stopped the powerful elements in the army, many of whom were his close associates, from trying to overthrow Ndadaye after only three months of power? Did he to stop them? Would most Tutsis in Bujumbura accept the election result? Herménégilde Niyonzima[8] says that the faces of his neighbours in Ngagara told him that Ndadaye's Burundi would be short-lived.

Once he was sworn in, Ndadaye moved fast and carefully, appointing a government of national unity: only just over half the ministers were from Frodebu, others were from Uprona, including a brave Tutsi woman Prime Minister, Sylvie Kinigi, and there were two from the military. He was less diplomatic with his other appointments: nearly all the new provincial governors were from Frodebu; and he made a lot of changes in the civil service. Some corners were cut in recruiting police trainees. Hardliners feared that the same would happen when recruitment for the army was scheduled for November. Pierre Buyoya, in his book, *Mission Possible*,[9] claims that 'the roots of the tragedy are to be found in the clumsy and ethnically biased management of the Ndadaye regime.' If this was the main reason, 104 days were not enough to show how good or bad the management was. True, with the return of many refugees, land disputes proliferated, but Ndadaye insisted that allowing refugees to get their land back must not in turn create new internally displaced persons. Privatisation, which was likely to benefit the Tutsi economic elite, was slowed down and there were other measures designed to help Hutus economically. Some Hutus said Ndadaye was doing too little, but most Tutsis thought he was moving too fast and not trying sufficiently hard to allay their fears. Elite Tutsis, embedded in the civil service and the judiciary (and the army), did much to sabotage Ndadaye. However, even his enemies hesitate to criticise the character of Ndadaye himself. They blame those around him.

---

8   Herménégilde Niyonzima, *Burundi, terre des héros non chantés*, op.cit.

9   Pierre Buyoya, *Mission Possible* (Paris: L'Harmattan, 1998).

On 21 October the short experiment of Hutu-led democratic government came to an abrupt end. The blow was carefully planned. Capt. Rukindikiza, who had saved Ndadaye in July, was away in Mauritius and many non-Bururi soldiers were on leave. Colonel Bikumagu, the army chief, gave the green light for a *coup* and Ndadaye was killed. This was another huge, tragic milestone in Burundi's story.

6

THE CRISIS BEGINS (1993)

Ahari abantu, hari urunturuntu. 'Where there are people there is conflict'
—proverb.

President Ndadaye had insisted on living in the grandiose Presidential Palace in the centre of Bujumbura, the *Palais du 1 Novembre*.[1] On
the fateful night of 20-21 October 1993 some elements in the army
attacked. The President was killed the following morning. So were
the Speaker and Deputy Speaker of the National Assembly. Other
leaders survived. Sylvestre Ntibantunganya, the future president, hid
in Kamenge but his wife was killed in front of their children. Léonard
Nyangoma escaped into the Industrial Quarter. For five days there
was no government. The army, now behaving as if it were in power,
rejected the request of ministers for an international security force.
Fearing for their security the remaining government ministers fled to
the French embassy, having—so it was reported—been turned away
by the Belgians. (Later, some ministers would sleep across the border
in the Congo and commute into Bujumbura.)

As the news of Ndadaye's death spread, violence erupted all over
the provinces. Tutsis (and even some pro-Buyoya Hutus) were targeted and killed. Roads were blocked to delay the army's inevitable

---

1   This had been the residence of the Belgian vice governor-general and of the
    King after Independence. The events of that terrible night are described well
    by Robert Krueger and Kathleen Tobin Krueger, *From Bloodshed to Hope in
    Burundi* (University of Texas Press, 2007).

response. Some claim that this response was pre-planned, like the 1994 genocide in Rwanda. There is no evidence that this was so on a national level, but the speed of the mobilisation suggests that some people had feared this might happen and made preparations. Dr. Jean Minani, the future leader of Frodebu, was in Kigali and many people have blamed him for inciting violence. What he said was, "Rise up as one and refuse the new rulers!" By contrast, President Ndadaye's father and his brave widow strongly advised against revenge. It is estimated that during these first days over 50,000 Tutsis (and some Uprona Hutus) were killed and, as the army began its revenge, up to 700,000 Hutus fled, the majority to Tanzania where they joined the 1972 refugees. Most rural Tutsis ended up in "sites" protected by the army and were eventually settled in more permanent barrack-like villages. Killings of Hutu villagers by the army continued for several years.

These are the bare facts. The trauma of "*La crise*" can be best understood through the reminiscences of the people who lived through it.

The most dramatically terrible incident of 1993 occurred at Kibimba, on the main road between Muramvya and Gitega, where about 70 Tutsi schoolgirls and boys were burned to death in a petrol station. Kibimba was the first mission station of the Friends Evangelical Church (Quakers) and was established in 1934. Friends are pacifists and it is truly ironic that Kibimba gained this terrible reputation. The Kibimba mission is perched on a hilltop, visible from afar, where three provinces, Mwaro, Gitega and Muramvya, meet. There is a small hospital which remained under church control. The primary and secondary schools had been taken over by the government during Bagaza's time. The secondary school was also a teacher training institution, an *école normale*.

Matthias Ndimurwanko, a Tutsi, was born and grew up in Kibimba. "I had already taught for 7 years at Matombo and then I was headmaster near Bugendana for 9 years before the crisis. In 1993 I was still head at Bugendana. I set off for my work very early on the morning of 21 October, too early to hear the radio. On the road I met some small groups of people who I thought were just going to the market. Soon I began to see that things were not normal: there were armed people making barriers. I saw teachers returning home, not going to work, so I returned home. A few hours later some people came. They tied us up and carried us off to the petrol station on the main road. I was held all day outside the petrol station, but God protected me. Around 4pm rain began to fall and they took us inside the petrol station. It looked serious, as if they had a list of the names of Tutsis. There were students and teachers who had been brought there at 10am. I was there all day. They kept bringing more people until there was no room for any more—not only students, teachers and officials but also peasants. In the evening they started drinking beer which they had taken from nearby stores after the traders had fled. They had started to get drunk. They threw stones at us. Those with spears started jabbing those near them. One man brought some petrol and told the others to set it alight and burn us alive. When they had finished counting heads they wanted to do their worst, that is to hit us on the head and make us unconscious or stab us with machetes or spears. Some of us were too tired to stand up and had to lie down. There was a corrugated roofing sheet which they had brought and they poured petrol down it into the crowd and they burned tyres too.

'Around 10pm I was able to escape from the filling station through God's power. There were some windows. We found some old sacks, as the place had been used in the past for selling coffee. We used these sacks to protect us from being overpowered by the smoke. There was also a table inside. Together with a certain Anatole, who later died, I broke a window. My aim was to get to where I could be killed as soon as possible so I would not be burned alive. After breaking the window I got under a table for safety. I grabbed the top of the window with both hands and jumped. I had an iron bar to use against anyone who pursued me. I began to run. Behind me someone threw his spear. God protected me again and I continued running. I had bare feet and no shirt. The first rains had fallen. I slipped in the mud and fell down. I hid somewhere beside the main road. People came looking for me and I had to leave where I was. I slid down on my stomach into a ditch. I was there for several hours. I heard the heavy rain falling on the petrol station roof and I heard the ghastly noise of the killing. There was too much noise. I was desperate to drink and eat. I passed through my native *colline* (Musama), then through the forest and through the Ecole Normale. I wanted to reach Ndava commune to get to Mwaro. I met a crowd of people trying to block the army which had now arrived at Kibimba. I hid in the bush. I took a little path and they did not see me. That night I got to my brother-in-law's place. His family was also about to flee. When they saw me they were surprised. I was bleeding terribly as I had a head wound. I went back into the bush and I met a student from Ndava. Each person had taken his own route. On the morning of the 22nd I heard the sound of gunshots. I spent the whole day there. I was wondering if my family was still alive. Two days later I went to the shops at Kibimba and I saw my family being taken on a military lorry to Mwaro. I thanked God. The only remaining thing was to find out if my eldest son was dead because he was at school at Mbuye where he was staying with another family. I joined my family at Mwaro, all except my eldest son. I finally found that my son was with his uncles in Bujumbura."

Samson Gahungu was a housemaster (*surveillant*) at Kibimba School, a Hutu and, like Matthias, active in the Friends' church. He recalls: "When Ndadaye was killed it was as if the sky had fallen on the people. Many people were behind him and when he died people could not believe it, especially the Hutus. They asked if it was possible that the 1972 crisis was being repeated and that they had killed our dear president whom we had just elected. Hutus feared that the Tutsis would continue massacres as in 1972. They said they should act quickly and avenge the president: *'Il faut les dévancer et venger notre président'*. I remember that on the same day, 21 October, from early morning everyone was glued to their radios waiting to hear if Ndadaye was really dead or still alive. While waiting for the latest news of his death, people were ready to take revenge, but against whom? As the President was Hutu, they assumed he must have been killed by Tutsis. When they learned that the president was really dead, that's the moment they started the massacres. Fearing trouble, the headmaster, Firmato Niyonkenguruka, a Hutu, had called together all the pupils and teachers and told them to keep calm and remain on the campus in case any attack came from outside. Shortly after this, Jérémie Ntirandekura, his Tutsi deputy, had secretly called the Tutsi pupils and told them to flee towards Mwaro where there was a military base. Hutu villagers saw them fleeing and, fearing they were going to call the army in as in 1972, rounded them up and led them to their fate.[2]

"I had not been at that meeting but in the afternoon I was at the school and I remember that there were very few pupils around. There were some Hutu pupils but most of the Tutsis had fled. After taking the register (I was in charge of discipline) I saw a crowd of people coming from Gihinga, Hutu villagers armed with sticks, machetes, spears...I took the risk of hiding some of the Tutsi pupils in the staff room. The Hutus were saying, 'We are taking them hostage until they liberate our president'. I did not take it very seriously, believing the people's fury would soon pass. I hid others in the 'salle de discipline'. I went out to meet the villagers who said they were out to avenge the president and were pursuing Tutsi pupils. (The Hutu pupils had also left the school by this time.) The Tutsis were captured in the woods, trying to flee towards Mwaro where there was a military camp, although it was a long way away. I stayed there and they threatened to beat and tie me up so I would show them where other Tutsis were hiding. I also managed to free some of the Tutsis including children of teachers, and hid them in the refectory. I left the school in the evening but I could not get home. The whole place was deserted. There were a number of people wounded in the head or legs lying by the road and I took them to the hospital to be treated. We still had a doctor, Elysée Nahimana, and he took all of them in. I went up and down between the hospital and the school to see if there were other wounded people. That was just one day with lots of wounded people, lots of terrorism. It was sad. That evening I stayed with some others in an empty house. I was too frightened to go to my home.

---

2   Tutsi students believed that the Headmaster played a more sinister role, as witnessed by the only student to survive the massacre, Olympic athlete Gilbert Tuhabonye, in his book, *The Running Man* (John Blake 2007).

"Early on the 22nd I also ran and fled from Kibimba. When the army arrived that day they found many corpses at Kibimba, especially around the filling station, and they began revenge killings. We fled from one village to another...Things slowly returned to normal. The road was reopened. We did not leave our hiding places in the bush until around Christmas. I managed to get to Gitega once or twice during this period and also to get to Bujumbura to carry out my church responsibilities: I was President of the Friends' Yearly Meeting. In 1994 I was able to leave the country. In 1995 I was appointed as head of a new department for peace and reconciliation at the National Council of Churches of Burundi (CNEB).

"One morning I was arrested at CNEB at work on the grounds that, as I had worked at Kibimba, I must therefore know about what happened here during the crisis and, of course, as I was Hutu, I must have taken part in the killings. They took me to the police; they questioned me. It was a Thursday. On the Saturday I was transferred to Mpimba, the Bujumbura prison, and stayed there (without trial) for close on two years. After the verdict I was cleared. I was released on 1 October 1997. It was not me that got myself cleared, nor even my witnesses. I am sure it was the strength of God, because I was not the only one accused of the massacres of 1993. Others accused of the same crime were executed or imprisoned for life. I was among a very few who were acquitted. While I was inside my case was followed up by friends, by the churches, especially by Quakers in other countries and by Amnesty International.'[3]

---

3   A report of the trial gives some detail and shows that Burundian justice could on occasion be just. There were five 'judges' (*juges d'instruction*). The presiding judge said that Samson had been acquitted because the accusations advanced by the state prosecutor were without foundation. Only one of the six witnesses for the prosecution, all former Kibimba students, turned up at the trial. He said that, while he did not see anything, he heard it said that Samson was going up and down on a motorcycle organising the killing, but that Samson had also saved his child! Samson's witnesses said that the Hutu villagers were trying to threaten Samson but he tried to hide some students and he negotiated for the release of others and for others to be taken to hospital. He did not believe the villagers would kill the remaining wounded students. Samson's lawyer also pointed out that his name did not appear on the list of 119 'guilty people' in a book on the genocide. The name of

Aloys Ningabira was a nurse at Kibimba Hospital. "I hid in the hospital pharmacy with Dr. Elysée Nahimana who worked with me. We took a moment to pray because the President had been assassinated and everyone was terribly nervous and had begun to flee in all directions. I remembered that when Frodebu had won they were singing all night and threatening those who had voted for Uprona. I had not joined any party. They did not know if I was Hutu or Tutsi as I was not a partisan. I was taken by a driver who worked at the school and I told him I was Hutu. He said, 'If I leave you there they will kill you.' We fled into the valley then towards Rutegama where I took refuge. Then I heard on the radio that many people had been killed at Kibimba. When I returned I found dead bodies at the petrol station and all around."

Kibimba has since become a place of reconciliation. Matthias, Samson and Aloys have played a major part in this, as is described in Chapter 14 below.

Further up the road in Gitega, other terrible events were unfolding. Gitega saw some of the worst killings. First Hutus had killed Tutsis, but by 25 October Tutsis were out for revenge. *David Niyonzima*, a Hutu, was teaching at Kwibuka School when a group of Tutsi soldiers attacked. David has written up his experiences and I quote some excerpts: "I ran from the scene of the butchering. I was so nearly overcome by fear and shock it was all my legs could do to carry me across the open space to the building where I thought I could hide, a building that had been used to train young people in auto mechanics. I climbed into the pit. An old vehicle was on top of the pit, so I hoped the soldiers might not see the pit and spot me under the car. As awful as the guns had been, an even more terrifying sound was the shattering of the door as the soldiers knocked it down. I imagined Daniel hearing the sound of the grinding of the lion's teeth as he tumbled into the dungeon. But in minutes I experienced

---

the school headmaster, Firmato Niyonkenguruka, had been on the list and, though Samson believes him to have been innocent, he had already been executed.

a Daniel-like deliverance. The soldiers only briefly looked inside. I stayed there for the rest of the day and the night. I was exhausted emotionally and physically, but there was no way to sleep without knowing the fate of the students and others. I grabbed an old pair of mechanic's overalls and chose to go to my parents' home." David's father hid him in the roof of the house and his family were safe, but after about a week he went back to the school. David continues: "I found a friend to go with me back to the school and our home. As we approached the buildings, things were frighteningly quiet. The strongest sensation we had as we arrived was the horrible smell of decomposing bodies. No one had dared to come and bury the bodies. We entered our home wondering if someone might be there to ambush us. But no one was there, and there were no bodies. Many of our belongings had been taken. Even the curtains from our windows were gone. Wild dogs and hungry flies fought with each other to consume the bodies before we could get them buried."[4]

Frédéric Nsabimana was at the university but he happened to leave Bujumbura on the day of the coup. "Our dad never spoke about ethnicity: our maternal grandmother had known several men so he did not know who his own father was; my mother is Tutsi. We had relations with everyone and were never rejected. Coming through Muramvya I could see that they had started taking Tutsis away. I got home and was warned that we might be killed. I was in total fear. One evening they came to take us. They were arguing as to whether they should or not. My father and I were taken away. Mum was in hiding. Someone who knew us in Bujumbura sent a taxi to look for us. They pursued us as a group. I fled on foot. The taxi man had succeeded in taking our mother. After some time I left my hiding place and ran towards the main road. Immediately I saw a minibus going to Bujumbura and I jumped in."

Levy Ndikumana, a Hutu, was at Musinzira Senior Secondary School:

---

4   David Niyonzima and Lon Fendall, *Unlocking Horns* (Newberg, Oregon: Barclay Press, 2001). David Niyonzima later became the head of the Friends' Church.

"I was pursued because I was a Hutu. Here Tutsi students were the majority and they started killing Hutus. I escaped miraculously. Some Tutsis helped me to escape. I did not finish my studies in Burundi but I had the chance of studying in South Africa."

Pie Ntakarutimana, a Tutsi, was already active in the human rights league, Iteka, of which he later became president. "In 1993 my parents were killed at home on the *colline*, in Gishubi (Gitega province)—my father, mother, sisters, all those who were there. My parents had over a hundred cattle, a vehicle, a shop. Everything was systematically stolen, the vehicle and house were burnt and the shop looted....I went home for the first time to find all this. I was still a bachelor and I took on my sister's orphaned children who had somehow escaped. One died of trauma but the others still live with me."

Phocas Ndimubandi was at school at Mbuye (Muramvya province). His family is mixed but he is "ethnically" a Hutu. Hearing of Ndadaye's death, Tutsis mostly fled from the *collines*. Some Hutus went off to kill Tutsis. Phocas went to shelter in the local church. All the schools closed.

By contrast, on *Samson Munahi's colline* in Mwaro province the few Tutsis who fled returned after a few days. Relations had been good and they had enough confidence in their neighbours. Zacharie Ndabakenga, an evangelist, formed a local association whose members visited displaced families and helped them return home. Similarly the head of the local primary school, Ernest Nibirantiza, went to the children's homes to urge them to keep going to school, and the school never closed.

The coup had failed. No new government had taken over but, as we shall see, Frodebu's election victory had less and less influence as time went on. The loss of the charismatic and moderate Ndadaye was as bad a blow as the earlier loss of Prince Louis Rwagasore—and it had more fatal immediate consequences. Both sides claim that there was genocide in 1993. Many Tutsis, led by extreme groups like Puissance d'Autodéfense Amasekanya and AC Génocide,[5] believe that the killings were prepared and that there was a plot to wipe out the Tutsi people. Hutus respond that a greater number of Hutus were killed by the army, not to mention the hundreds of thousands driven into exile. The UN report notes that "acts of genocide" were committed. The word "genocide" has become almost a slogan and it is time to stop arguing about its definition. Everyone can agree that there were thousands of unjustified killings in 1965, 1972, 1988, 1991 and from 1993 onwards. Not everyone can agree, however, on who was really responsible for Ndadaye's death. Clearly those eventually accused were the "small fish"—and it is true that non-commissioned officers were usually the perpetrators. However, some "big fish" such as the army commander, Col. Bikomagu, and some of the hardline Uprona leadership are unlikely to have been innocent bystanders. And what about Buyoya? He was a bitter man and was reported as having said, "Accept your responsibilities!" at a meeting of the army command. Could this be interpreted as a green light?

---

5   See chapter 10.

7

'CREEPING COUP' TO BUYOYA II, 1993-99

Ces Hutu que vous empêchez de poursuivre leurs études, ce sont eux qui entreront aux FDD pour vous combattre demain. 'These Hutus that you are preventing from studying—they are the ones who will join FDD to fight you tomorrow' —Firmin Sinzoyiheba

The events of October 1993 in Burundi have been described as the most successful failed coup in history. Although in theory Frodebu was still in power with a large majority, the government was headless and the army physically in control of most of the country. The coup had been condemned internationally, but inside the country the army and opposition piled on the pressure which weakened Frodebu still more. The country was in chaos and something had to be done. Talks were held early in 1994 and the resulting Kigobe and Kajaga accords named Cyprien Ntaryamira, a Frodebu 'moderate', as President, with a Prime Minister coming from Uprona and with Frodebu's share of ministries and provincial governorships reduced to 60 per cent. Small extremist parties encouraged young Tutsis, especially university students, to organise '*villes mortes*', total blockades of the city. Some irresponsible leaders of these parties were soon rewarded with government posts.

Burundi did not need another stroke of bad luck but this was to come in April 1994. President Ntaryamira had joined the Rwandan President, Juvenal Habyarimana, on his flight home from Rwanda's peace talks in Arusha in Tanzania. They both fell to their deaths in the notorious crash that launched the Rwanda genocide. Negotiations had to start all over again. After tortuous negotiations which took place in the shadow of the terrible events in Rwanda, which made Tutsis ever more nervous, a Government Convention was agreed in September 1994. The 'opposition' managed to get a few extra posts as the price for agreeing to the accession of the slightly more radical Sylvestre Ntibantunganya as President. The UN Special Envoy, Ahmedou Ould-Abdallah, and the Catholic bishops, notably Simon Ntamwana, played crucial roles in enabling this agreement, shaky though it was, to be patched up.[1] One part of the agreement that did not last was the appointment of Jean Minani as president of the National Assembly. Minani was hated by Tutsis for having encouraged resistance over Radio Rwanda after the death of Ndadaye. Tutsi youth blocked roads and even desecrated a church in protest. They got their way: Léonce Ngendakumana became president of the National Assembly instead, while Minani became president of Frodebu.

All these political power games went on in Bujumbura while the rest of the country, like a different world, was becoming the scene of a civil war. Léonard Nyangoma, who had been Minister of the Interior but did not accept the erosion of Frodebu's legitimate power, left the government and went off to create a new rebel movement, the Conseil National pour la Défense de la Démocratie (CNDD) with an armed wing known as FDD (Forces pour la Défense de la Démocratie). Palipehutu benefited from the events in Bujumbura and its armed wing, the FNL (Front National de Libération), moved into action. Rebel attacks and army counter-attacks caused widespread insecurity.

While displaced Tutsis sheltered in camps in the interior, serious fighting began in Bujumbura in January 1994: young Tutsis organised more days of '*ville morte*' and the army started 'ethnic cleansing' of Hutus throughout Bujumbura. Father *Claudio Marino* had opened the Youth Centre in Kamenge just before the coup. He recalls: 'It started in Kamenge where the rebels came. Ngagara and Cibitoke

---

1   Ahmedou Ould-Abdallah's book *Burundi on the Brink 1993-95* (United States Institute of Peace 2000) gives an interesting account of this confused period.

became fortresses of the military. For four months there were battles between the military and the rebels and on 22 April people from Kinama and Kamenge were driven out and the soldiers looted every-thing that remained. We had to leave for one week and we returned on 1 May when the people of Kinama and Kamenge returned. Many men and youths had either disappeared or were imprisoned, or when they were liberated they went abroad or into the interior to fight. The women and children returned on 1 May…The front line was here between Kamenge, Ngagara and Cibitoke and we had a lot of damage. We were twice attacked by the soldiers. They accused us of having rebels inside the youth centre…the people of Kamenge fled eight times during the war and each time they returned.'

Sylvestre Ntibantunganya, in his book *'Une Démocratie pour tous les Burundais'*,[2] remembers the frequent days of *'ville morte'* and the day the army commander, Col. Jean Bikomagu, showed that he could clear the streets when he wanted to—for the swearing in of President Ntaryamira. He also describes the the terrible night of 6 March 1994 when the army went on the rampage in Kamenge, killing women, children and old people. Some of the corpses were dragged out by the main road where the ministers, who were on their way to a meet-ing in Gitega, could see them. Ntaryamira ordered an inquiry; it reported that there was 'no evidence'.

Alexis Kwizera witnessed the increasing tension in Bujumbura. Apart from the army's actions it was mainly a conflict, led on by politicians, between young people who formed militias, Jeudebu on the Hutu side and the Sans Echec and Sojedem on the Tutsi side. Many young people lost their lives. Kamenge was more politicised than Kinama. The soldiers attacked the Hutu militia and any nearby civilians; and the Hutus attacked the Tutsi suburbs. The Hutus had less impact as they had not enough arms to stand up to the army. 'After this when the many army attacks continued we had the idea of going to the bush because many people would die if fighting continued in the

---

2   Sylvestre Ntibantunganya, *Une démocratie pour tous les Burundais* (Paris: L'Harmattan, 1999).

Hutu suburbs...Palipehutu existed but only abroad in Tanzania and Europe. We had not heard their ideology. They were clandestine. We knew Frodebu through the election campaign and we believed they had asked Nyangoma to form the rebel movement.'

The battle in Nyakabiga began in May 1994. Some Hutu youths whose fathers had been killed in 1972 had hidden their arms in the small market. They attacked in the name of the CNDD. They had no experience of fighting, so, when the army commando arrived one Sunday morning, the Hutus had fled to the neighbouring suburb of Bwiza by the next day. After a few days the military attacked again and people fled from Bwiza either to Buyenzi or over the border to Uvira, in the Congo. The temperature had been raised still further by Radio Rutomorangingo (democracy), based in the Congo, which started broadcasting in July 1994, encouraging hatred and rebellion on the same lines as the better known Radio Mille Collines in Rwanda. At the same time, the founding of a new party, Parena, by former President Bagaza was a focus for Tutsi activists. In March 1995 Tutsis from Nyakabiga cleared the remaining Hutus from Bwiza, burning and looting houses in broad daylight. This only left Buyenzi with its large Muslim population which had welcomed everybody into its crowded streets, but even here, finally, in May 1995, the army moved in.

Ntibantunganya is often criticised for being indecisive and for giving in too easily to army pressure, but in truth he was in such a weak position that perhaps he should be criticised for accepting the job at all. For example, he was forced to dismiss his Prime Minister, Anatole Kanyenkiko, a Tutsi he found easy to work with, in favour of Antoine Nduwayo, who tried to frustrate him at every turn. Ntibantunganya did, however, have a strategy. In June 1996 he had meetings with focus groups representing the *forces vives* of the nation—Catholics, Protestants, Muslims, women, youth, trade unions, civil society organisations, businessmen and the media. On the basis of these contacts he drew up serious proposals to resolve the crisis—but at each step he was undermined by Nduwayo. What finally made the military determined to dump the President was their fear of an international force being brought in. July was the crunch month. An agreement for neighbouring countries to 'cooperate' rather than 'intervene' had been signed in Arusha. Nduwayo had been present at the meeting but as soon as he got back to Bujumbura he wriggled out of this agreement and nothing happened. A further worry for most of the army top brass was the growing popularity of ex-president Bagaza. The last straw for the President was the massacre by rebels of 340 Tutsis, mainly women and children, at Bugendana in Gitega province. The President went there for the funeral and had cow dung and stones thrown at him by angry Tutsis who accused him of being behind the rebels. He rushed back to Bujumbura without being able to make the conciliatory funeral oration he had prepared. He refused to resign, although the Minister of Defence, Firmin Sinzoyiheba, had earlier threatened a coup during a cabinet meeting. However, getting intelligence that his life might be threatened, the President asked for and was offered shelter at the US Ambassador's residence. He was well looked after and remained there for nearly a year.[3] Ntibantunganya's position had become untenable. Neither Ntaryamira nor Ntibantunganya had the means to be truly in charge. Decisions were taken elsewhere, mainly by the Tutsi-dominated National Security Council. 'The government was dysfunctional. It was a catastrophic period with a two-headed government' (*Eugène Nindorera*).

On 25 July 1996 the army staged a real coup and put Pierre Buyoya back in power. A meeting of some of the big men from Bururi had taken place just before the coup to select the future president. Most would have preferred the charismatic Firmin Sinzoyiheba but there were other voices who pleaded for Buyoya, saying that the Europeans would never accept a Tutsi Chief of Staff as President and that it would make the plot too obvious. Buyoya was chosen, though many Tutsis blamed him for bringing too many Hutus into his earlier government. However, given the desperate security situation and the power vacuum, many moderates welcomed Buyoya's return. The immediate response to this coup was the cessation of all aid programmes and an international embargo, masterminded by the former Tanzanian President, Julius Nyerere. (This was still in place

---

3 The US Ambassador, Robert Krueger, has written up his experiences: *From Bloodshed to Hope in Burundi: Our Embassy Years during Genocide* (University of Texas Press, 2007).

when I arrived in the country in 1998.) Coups d'état were not to be encouraged in the 1990s. Maybe that is why Buyoya liked to call it a change (*changement)* rather than a coup. While people crowded into the airport to see the last international flight, life got even harder for the poor majority and Burundi's weak economy was given a further hammer blow.

Buyoya was able to discipline the army and prevent Tutsi militia from killing people—and security rapidly improved. However, he could not stop the Hutu rebellion. People could find safety in the towns, but in the rural areas people were still being killed—and mostly by the army. The new President hurried to launch his book, *Mission Possible*, in which he tried to show how lovable he really was and how much he wanted peace and justice. He produced some ideas for stopping the war, more or less a photocopy of what Ntibantunganya had already suggested, and he did go to Rome for a meeting with the CNDD, but he seemed in no real hurry to negotiate. He wanted a political agreement only on his own terms, with international support, so that he could crush the rebellion. The countries of the region put pressure on Buyoya through the embargo. Further pressure was added by donors, international and national NGOs and the UN. His first step was to make approaches to Frodebu leaders. He would not take part in meetings with Nyerere, who had now been chosen as a mediator, until after he had succeeded in getting Frodebu on board in a restructured government in 1998. Nyerere punished him by holding on to the embargo even when Buyoya had started to negotiate.

1994 to 1998 was the period when it could be said that there was ethnic apartheid in Bujumbura. Hardly a Hutu was left in Musaga, Ngagara, Cibitoke, Nyakabiga or even Bwiza and Buyenzi. Hardly a house was left standing in Kamenge. (When the population fled, the soldiers and their friends removed the roofing sheets and the mud brick walls slowly crumbled.) Hutu petty traders brought charcoal and bananas into town but their bodies were sometimes found dead by the roadside. *Perpétue Kankindi* and her husband, Charles Karikurubu, almost the only Hutus in Mutanga Sud, were forced to move to Mutanga Nord, a prosperous suburb which remained a model of coexistence, rather like the university quarter in Belfast.

Minibuses for Kinama and Kamenge avoided going through Tutsi areas and vice versa. A Congolese friend nearly got killed in Nyakabiga for looking like a Hutu and accompanying a child who looked like a Tutsi. There was a policy of *hakwihenda wokwihekura* (don't hesitate—kill first, ask questions afterwards). Land mines were occasionally found on the town's side roads. The father of *Christophe Hakizimana* was a Hutu and the family lived in Musaga. Christophe could no longer live there after 1994, nor could he visit his Tutsi mother who remained at the family home. When his father died, he was only permitted to visit home briefly to take his father's coffin for burial. He had to find a house for himself in an ethnically neutral suburb known as the *Quartier OUA*.[4]

Emmanuel Hakizimana was appointed as *Chef de Zone* in Nyakabiga in 1995 with two objectives: to impose order and to reconstruct the suburb, which had previously had a mixed population but the Hutu minority had fled. It was still a time of fear and he would often find corpses in the street. *Sans Echec*, Sojedem and university students were still organising '*villes mortes*'. 'By the end of 1996 I saw that we had to bring the population back together. First I tried to re-establish security. I was very strict with the *Sans Echec* and the police obeyed my orders. From 1997 there was security. We dealt with prostitutes, drug traffickers and students who were on drugs too. I tried to meet people who had fled, to encourage them to return to help reconstruct the zone. I explained and explained and accompanied returnees who could convince others to return. The administrator at Gatumba who received aid *per capita* for displaced persons was not keen to see me taking my people home!...Tutsis saw me as a traitor. I was the object of personal attack more than three times....They shot at me when I tried to stop some young people shooting. One time they shot into my bedroom. God protected me.' Later on Emmanuel organised sport and cultural activities and twinned Nyakabiga with Ngozi. The Council of Churches and Christian Aid helped fund these activities, including the reconstruction of houses for returnees. When we

---

4   This was a well laid-out housing project built for an OAU Summit which never took place.

invited a group of British MPs to Burundi,[5] they remembered going through Nyakabiga with Emmanuel as one of their most memorable experiences in Burundi.

By the time I arrived in the country in July 1998 there was already the beginning of a thaw. A few Hutus were moving back to Musaga. Emmanuel Hakizimana's efforts as *Chef de Zone* in Nyakabiga were already bearing fruit. A lot of peace-promoting activities were taking place (see chapters 15-17). In the interior it was still often risky to travel. Urban Tutsis wanted jobs but were reluctant to go up country. They had heard too many horror stories of what had happened to their families. Many Congolese were willing to take the risk. *Jean Marie Badionona,* a Congolese friend who worked for the Ministry of Communal Development and later for Christian Aid, recalls driving a pick-up full of blankets on the road from Gitega to Bugarama, hearing shots and hiding under the vehicle. There were many such incidents, one of the worst being the killing of six staff of the International Committee of the Red Cross back in 1995. But rebel ambushes and assassinations by both sides went on. Among the victims were Archbishop Joachim Ruhuna (see chapter 15) and, as late as December 2003, the Papal Nuncio, Mgr Michael Courtney. When he was still Bishop of Bujumbura, the present Archbishop, Mgr Simon Ntamwana, narrowly escaped death, as did a former Prime Minister, Adrien Sibomana. The Head of information at the Headquarters of the Gendarmerie, Lt.Col. Dieudonné Nzeyimana, a Ganwa, was assassinated in 1996. He stood up to his military colleagues and saved many lives—but he knew too much about the events of October 1993. The killings of Col. Firmin Sinzoyiheba, the Minister of Defence, and of Dr Kassy Manlan are referred to in chapter 9.

Rebel activity was reduced in late 1998 and early in 1999 things seemed to be looking up. The embargo was suspended in January, Buyoya's reward for starting to negotiate seriously. One reason for the pressure at the UN and elsewhere to end the embargo was that the poor state of the economy was fuelling the war (though some

---

5   Des Browne and David Lammy, who later became ministers in Tony Blair's government, and Tess Kingham.

of the Tutsi elite were doing very well out of it). Prices had rocketed and agricultural production had slumped, coffee by 50 per cent. Nonetheless, it was an exciting moment when, within hours of the announcement, the first Ethiopian Airlines plane swooped down. Optimism did not last long. Burundi admitted its troops were fighting in the Congo. CNDD-FDD was still excluded from the Arusha talks. Attacks escalated in June 1999. The government imposed a tax for the war effort. (Traders and bus operators were already paying another 'tax' to the rebels to protect their vehicles and passengers.) The economy went on deteriorating.

Following an intensification of fighting, with the red tracer bullets of night combat often visible in the hills above the capital, the government decided to 'regroup' almost the entire population of Bujumbura Rural province, apart from two communes with a Tutsi majority. Camps were hastily established, usually on exposed hilltops and often far from water or health centres. People were rounded up with no warning, sometimes in the middle of the night. The camps were not fenced, and people were occasionally allowed to work in their fields, but otherwise anyone moving outside could be shot. Families of people working in town piled into whatever accommodation they could find. The population of my house and garden rose to about 20. Aid agencies did not want to show their support for this policy but this was a humanitarian crisis, so what should they do?

On 12 October 1999, a UN delegation flew to Rutana Province to review the humanitarian situation at a *colline* called Muzye, 12 miles from the Sosumo sugar company's airstrip. As they arrived they were suddenly surrounded by assailants, lined up against a wall and shot. Their military escort could do nothing. The dead included Luis Zuniga, the popular head of UNICEF in Burundi, a Dutch World Food Programme official and the manager of the sugar company. The UN Humanitarian Coordinator, the dynamic Kathleen Cravero-Kristofferson, managed to run off and escape alive. The UN in Burundi was stunned. Its security level was increased, effectively closing down most UN programmes outside Bujumbura (except when carried out by NGOs whose staff were apparently expendable). CNDD-FDD denied its complicity: 'It cannot openly attack places where there are civilians'. The Burundi government later blamed Tanzania for harbouring the killers.

Meanwhile in Bujumbura itself, the army took action. 11,000 Hutus who had fled from Kamenge suburb when the army attacked their homes in 1995 lived in unimaginably crowded conditions in two camps, one outside a health centre set up by an amazing old American missionary, Carl Johnson, a man who had saved many Hutu lives, the other, known as Le Gentil, outside the Catholic mental hospital. Without warning these displaced families were driven out, back to the ruins of Kamenge with no shelter and no support. The army said the camps were hotbeds of rebel support. Their treatment was hardly likely to increase their love for the government.

Two stories capture the flavour of the times. Twenty soldiers stole roofing sheets from the homes of some 'regrouped' Hutus, sold them in town and got drunk on the proceeds. On their way home they were attacked by rebels and most of them were killed. The next morning the survivors shot some innocent villagers as they left their camp to go to market. The second story concerns a 16-year-old Burundian boy who was found inside the funnel of a British ship after it docked at the island of St. Helena. Scared and traumatised, he had fled from his village when his parents, grandparents and twelve brothers and sisters had been killed by soldiers. He had somehow succeeded in crossing Zambia and Mozambique before taking a lorry ride to Cape Town and stowing away.

By the end of 1999 the rebellion was at its height. CNDD-FDD was the main actor in the majority of provinces. The FNL was active in the western area and was the main threat to the roads leading out of Bujumbura. Optimism was in short supply.

8

THE PEACE TALKS AT ARUSHA 1998-2001

Umurundi aguhisha ko akwanka nawe ukamuhisha ko ubizi. 'A Burundian hides the fact that he hates you, and you hide the fact that you know it' —proverb

Tanzania's former president, Julius Nyerere, had agreed to act as a mediator even before the return of Buyoya in 1996. In spite of his reputation as one of Africa's greatest statesmen, and although he tried to be scrupulously fair to all parties, *Mwalimu* Nyerere was not trusted by most Tutsis.[1] His country, after all, was the base for refugees and rebels. However, once he had Frodebu on board, Buyoya finally agreed to negotiate with Nyerere as mediator. Proper negotiations started in Arusha on 15 June 1998. Seventeen delegations took part, including some of the minuscule 'Tutsi parties' whose total membership, Mandela later said, could fit into a telephone kiosk. The big weakness was the absence of the rebel groups involved in the fighting. Factions of Palipehutu and CNDD were represented, a CNDD faction by Léonard Nyangoma who had by this time been expelled from the main CNDD-FDD but continued to lead his own wing, and a Palipehutu faction by Etienne Karatasi who was in a similar position. Nyerere was strongly opposed to coups and was probably persuaded by Nyangoma not to invite the main CNDD-

---

1   The dangerous 'Nairobi fly' is commonly nicknamed 'Nyerere'.

FDD, now led by Jean-Bosco Ndayikengurukiye, even though Buyoya was prepared to do so.

Four committees discussed: (1) the nature of the conflict, including definitions of genocide, (2) strategies for democracy and good governance, (3) peace and security, (4) reconstruction and development. Some progress was made but the negotiations at Arusha dragged on for years and, while initial mutual hostility gave way to increasing bonhomie, the slow progress showed up the Burundian political class in a poor light. In Filip Reyntjens' words, 'There were increasing doubts about the willingness to arrive at a negotiated settlement. In a very Burundian way of doing business, characterized by the 'unsaid' and the 'almost-said', there were perpetual retreats and questioning, constant strategic re-positioning...a process in which the Burundians pretended to talk, with the international community pretending to believe they did.'[2] Part of the trouble was said to be that the delegates received generous *per diems* which made them reluctant to return to their meagre salaries (a suburb of Bujumbura where some of these delegates have built their extravagant houses was dubbed 'Arusha'). The small parties also enjoyed spinning out the process because they relished having some influence, although they realised they would lose it once there was an election.

Floribert Kubwayesu attended part of the Arusha process. He felt that the mediators concentrated too much on the ethnic aspect in drawing up a constitution. Some people, especially Hutus, probably saw this as a way to gain power—and power meant a share of *le gâteau* (the national cake). In this context the seven mainly Hutu parties organised themselves into a bloc, the G7, and in response the ten Tutsi parties became the G10.

Nyerere died on 14 October 1999 and Nelson Mandela reluctantly agreed to be the new mediator. With his god-like prestige this was considered to be a huge stroke of luck for Burundi. Inevitably, Mandela saw things with South African eyes and the 85 per cent-14 per cent ethnic statistic put him in mind of the black-white

---

2   Filip Reyntjens, *Burundi, Prospects for Peace* (London: Minority Rights Group, 2000).

percentage in his own country. He trod on some toes, but he was determined to move things on quickly. He forced people to face facts, and for him this was more than anything an ethnic conflict. He saw the importance of international support for the peace process. He addressed the UN Security Council, he persuaded the EU and the US to take an interest, he invited President Chirac of France, King Fahd of Saudi Arabia, President Obasanjo of Nigeria and others. He was not sure of the motives of some of the neighbouring states, so he made use of Gabon and ensured that South Africa invested time and resources. He was determined that all the rebel groups should join in, but CNDD-FDD still boycotted the talks, claiming that Mandela had supplied arms to Burundi. In March 2000 a plane had even been sent to Lubumbashi (DRC) to fetch Jean-Bosco Ndayikengurukiye, the CNDD-FDD leader, but he failed to show up. Later Jean-Bosco made conditions for his attendance—that all 'regroupment' camps be dismantled and political prisoners released, conditions which the FNL also insisted on. The FDD, but not the FNL, finally started attending the talks on 19 July 2000.

Mandela was equally critical of the 'regroupment' camps. With Buyoya sitting beside him he said: 'That is a situation that is totally unacceptable to a person such as me who has spent 27 years in jail.' Buyoya promised to close the camps in January 2000 but in July of that year they were still there. Mandela berated the political parties too, surprising some by saying that the army chiefs seemed more ready than the politicians to find solutions. He worked on the basis of 'sufficient consensus', meaning that if the main protagonists were in agreement it was not necessary to wait for every small party to agree.[3] Although at a late stage he tried to engage the Tutsi hardliners (AC Génocide, PA Amasekanya[4] and the extreme wing of Uprona led by Charles Mukasi), they—and many other Tutsis—found Mandela no better than Nyerere, accusing him of seeing the rebels as freedom fighters and never pleading for the displaced Tutsi popu-

---

3   There is a good description of the negotiations and especially of Mandela's role in Kristina Bentley and Roger Southall, *An African Peace Process* (HSRC Press, 2005).

4   See chapter 10.

lation. All in all, however, Mandela's prestige and the urgency with which he viewed the conflict made people believe that an agreement was really possible, thus encouraging those not yet committed to jump onto the bandwagon.

Visiting Bujumbura in June 2000, Mandela persuaded Buyoya to close the camps and to agree to a 50/50 Tutsi/Hutu composition of the army. He visited Mpimba prison in Bujumbura, commenting that he had 'never been so ashamed as to see human beings living in those conditions'. He also helped define a political prisoner: 'Even people who may have killed a president may be described as political prisoners if they committed that offence in protecting the objectives of their political organisation or their community.' Two days later he asked that all political prisoners should be released in the cause of peace, a proposal strongly criticised by the Burundian human rights league, Iteka, on the grounds that impunity was one of the curses of Burundi. Gérard Ngendabanka, the State Prosecutor (a *Frodebiste*), categorised those who were considered to be political prisoners: a few, mainly Tutsis, accused of the killing of President Ndadaye; a large number, mainly Hutus, accused of massacring Tutsis following Ndadaye's death; some Hutus active in the rebellion after 1996; and Tutsis who had planned a rebellion against Buyoya or were accused of trying to kill him. Buyoya did not agree that all of these were political prisoners.

Buyoya's need to negotiate was propelled by the worsening economic situation in Burundi. The government, not for the first time, was worried that it might not be able to pay salaries. (Burundi, unlike a number of African countries, has always somehow managed to pay its civil servants.) Belgium and France began to say that resuming aid should not wait for a peace deal.

As 28 August, the date for signing the agreement, approached, there was a lot of last minute pushing and pulling. Most 'Hutu' parties, apart from Nyangoma's CNDD, were against Buyoya serving as transitional president, as were most of the little 'Tutsi' parties who wanted Col. Epitace Bayaganakandi—who, as the 'butcher' of Kamenge,[5] would not have been easy for the Hutus to work with.

---

5   He led the army's descent on Kamenge in 1994.

Arguments continued as to whether 50/50 in the army meant 50 per cent of Hutus or 50 per cent of ex-rebels. Threats not to sign came from all directions. Grenades were thrown in Buyenzi market and Jabe market went up in flames (which may have been a simple accident). Soldiers sealed off the university. There was enormous pressure to sign. Mandela had invited twenty-five heads of state. President Clinton was coming with a huge retinue. Kilimanjaro airport had no space for so many presidential planes, so they were going to have to drop their VIPs and continue to Dar es Salaam overnight! The 'Tutsi' mini-parties in the G10 continued playing games on the day itself. The plan was to sign at noon but it took until 9pm and then only thirteen out of nineteen parties signed—and the government still had certain reservations (three more small parties signed within a few days). President Museveni said it was like waiting for the baby to be born, a slow delivery. There was no agreement on who would lead the transition and for how long, how the fighting would stop, the electoral system, the army question and recognition (or not) of genocide. The mediation team continued to try to tempt the rebels to negotiate seriously, and the tone of CNDD-FDD's comments after the signing suggested that they would do so.

The need for peace was highlighted by several events. On 4 December 2000 a SABENA plane was shot at as it descended to Bujumbura airport. No one was killed but the airline, which had only just restarted its service, understandably withdrew from Burundi again. On 28 December the Titanic Express bus, whose very name seemed to be an act of defiance, was ambushed on its way from Kigali, giving Burundi a lot of bad publicity in the UK because a British volunteer teacher working in Rwanda, Charlotte Wilson, was among the twenty people shot by the roadside.[6] Then, on the night of 23 February 2001, the entire suburb of Kinama and part of Cibitoke fell to the FNL rebels who had clearly been infiltrating and hiding arms there for some weeks beforehand. 30,000 fled and were housed by friends and relatives and in makeshift camps. The Christian Aid driver *Pie Ntazina* had 30 members of his church

---

6   There is an interesting account of the story and context of Charlotte Wilson's death in Richard Wilson, *Titanic Express* (Continuum, 2006).

sleeping on his floor. Some reported that the rebels were well armed and well fed and were treating the population kindly. Government forces counter-attacked on 6 March and soon recaptured the suburb, but they had a nasty fright.

Amid all the arguments as to whether Buyoya should stay on for the transition and, if not, who should, two real attempts were made to overthrow the government. On 18 April 2001 a group of junior officers took over the radio station (RTNB). They said they supported Arusha but accused the signatories of just seeking jobs and of having little interest in the greater good of the country—which is what most people were thinking. After a few hours the radio station was surrounded by loyal troops and the plotters surrendered peacefully. This incident in fact strengthened Buyoya as it showed that most of the army was loyal. Some even thought Buyoya might have instigated it himself with this in mind.

The second coup attempt was on 23 July 2001, when other junior officers joined university students and attacked the army headquarters, Mpimba prison and the homes of some senior officials in the small hours of the morning. Again most of the army remained loyal. The plotters commandeered vehicles and drove off towards Ngozi. *Dismas Nzeyimana* and his wife, *Rachel,* had left their home in Ngagara to go to the airport. On the way, Rachel noticed some private vehicles full of soldiers. Suddenly a band of soldiers ordered her to stop. She obeyed and three soldiers got into the vehicle. One soldier commanded her to follow other vehicles, which had also been hijacked. Rachel replied that she could not follow unless she was assured of the destination. She added: 'I sense you are another type of rebels and I can't follow you blindly.' When she reached the roundabout she decided to stop. She managed to intimidate the rebels who were in the car, arguing that she and Dismas were Christians and would rather be shot than led into the bush. 'The rebels were quiet with fear…The rebels suggested that we drop them at the *Gare du Nord* bus stop, which we did.' Others, including some staff of the NGO Search for Common Ground, were less bold than Rachel. They had their cars hijacked and the plotters made their way north, only to give themselves up on the road to Kirundo.

Was the Arusha agreement worth the immense amount of time it took to negotiate? Whether or not Burundi had real ethnic groups, the fact is that the ethnic labels had been used for so long in the struggle for power that they had become a reality, as illustrated by the G7-G10 division at Arusha.[7] A choice had been made by the mediation, without much objection on the part of the political parties, to go for a 'consociative' model of power sharing, building in safeguards for the minority.[8] Arguably, as negotiations moved towards a solution at Arusha the extremists from both sides became gradually marginalised.

In spite of the absence of the two rebel groups, the Arusha accord was accepted as the basis for the constitution which was to be approved in Pretoria in 2004.

---

7   'Everything has become 'ethnic' in this torn society, even if Burundi did not know ethnic groups in the true sense of the term'—J.P. Chretien and M. Mukuri, *Burundi, la fracture identitaire. Logiques de violences et certitudes 'ethniques'* (Paris: Karthala, 2002).

8   Even in 1993 Ndadaye's government did not consist of one ethnic group or even one party, in spite of his large majority. An interesting discussion of the 'consociative' model is by Stef Vandeginste, *Theorie Consociative et Partage du Pouvoir au Burundi* (Institute of Politics and Development Management, University of Antwerp).

9

BUYOYA, NDAYIZEYE AND
THE ELECTIONS OF 2005

You will judge us by our actions and your satisfaction will be our pride.—Prince Louis Rwagasore

It was finally agreed on 23 July 2001 that the transition period laid down in the Arusha accord would start on 1 November 2001, with Pierre Buyoya as President for the first eighteen months and as Vice President Domitien Ndayizeye, who would in turn be President for the second eighteen months. It is a measure of the doubts some had of Buyoya's trustworthiness that the 'regional powers' chaired by President Museveni of Uganda made a list of conditions before they accepted him as transitional president. Museveni disliked Buyoya because he had overthrown Bagaza, who had helped Museveni come to power in 1986.[1] One of these conditions was that changes to the composition of the army were to start straightaway. South African troops were to be invited, initially as bodyguards for returning politicians. Eventually they would become the nucleus of an African Union peacekeeping force. Jean Minani, now leader of Frodebu, finally became President of the National Assembly. He and other returning politicians could be spotted moving around town with their bodyguards.

---

1   Bagaza had facilitated the transit of Libyan weapons to the Ugandan guerrilla areas through the DRC (Zaire).

77

When Mandela's term as mediator finished in August 2001, the Arusha accord was fragile and many of the signatories were still half-hearted, having signed under pressure from Mandela and the international community. It was, however, a basis from which to move forward. No-one else could have pushed the Burundians so far or so fast. Burundi had indeed been lucky to get him. Now the South African Deputy President, Jacob Zuma, took over the role of mediator. He had good experience mediating between the ANC and Inkatha in KwaZulu Natal and was another fortunate choice for Burundi.

Buyoya's eighteen months were spent trying to broker a ceasefire with the various rebel groups. Two lightweight breakaway groups led by Jean-Bosco Ndayikengurukiye (who had been overthrown as leader of CNDD-FDD by Pierre Nkurunziza in October 2001) and Alain Mugabarabona (overthrown as leader of the FNL by Agathon Rwasa) signed a cease fire in October 2002 and were rewarded with government posts. CNDD-FDD continued to resist a ceasefire but finally agreed to one in December 2002. It only lasted a short time before fighting broke out again, provoked in some places by the army. Pierre Nkurunziza started to negotiate but then accused Buyoya of breaking the agreement and suspended all contact. CNDD-FDD insisted on the 1992 constitution rather than the Arusha terms which, it said, institutionalised ethnicity. It wanted special immunity for its fighters and its debt to be incorporated into that of the state. A powerful faction in the army opposed any more concessions—rank and file soldiers were already unhappy to see food supplied to disarmed rebels while they were waiting for their pay packets. CNDD-FDD continued recruiting new fighters, often through ambushes and kidnappings where those who could not pay for their release were press-ganged into the rebel force. Others joined willingly, including some of the *gardiens de la paix* (young villagers armed as auxiliaries by the military), seeing this as a way to an eventual job in the new national army. The FNL continued to refuse to negotiate, insisting on direct negotiations with the army and the Tutsi community.

Buyoya was in no hurry to leave office, hinting that he was needed until there was a ceasefire with the main rebel group. In spite of his suave exterior, Buyoya could be ruthless. At this time he was dubbed 'Gustave', which was the name of an exceptionally enormous crocodile which had eaten a number of people along the shore of Lake Tanganyika. The jury is out on who may have been behind the killing of President Ndadaye but when people refer to the helicopter crash which killed the popular Colonel Firmin Sinzoyiheba, Minister of Defence and a potential rival for power, in February 1998, the word 'accident' is usually put in inverted commas. Firmin usually tried to avoid helicopter flights but this time he thought he was safe because Buyoya's private secretary was with him on the same flight. Although he was at Buyoya's side in the 1996 coup, Firmin had been against what happened in 1993 and was a strong advocate of education for all, in other words for Hutus. He is one of the few leading Tutsis to qualify as a hero in Herménégilde Niyonzima's book.[2] The death of Dr Kassy Manlan,[3] the World Health Organisation representative, in November 2001, was another cause for suspicion.

Buyoya is an enigma and it is hard to evaluate fairly his important role in Burundi's history. In his first term he deserved credit for making changes which, with luck and better management, might have saved Burundi from its bloodbath (a national conference might have been better still). However, he felt very humiliated by Frodebu's election victory in 1993. He thought he had done everything for the Burundians—he felt he had been sincere, improved human rights, brought Hutus into the government, created the unity charter...and felt betrayed. According to Alexis Sinduhije, among others, when he came back in 1996 he wanted to take revenge. This time he was without pity and no longer seemed to care for the people. He also wanted to protect himself from any possible accusations about his role in 1993. In his two presidencies he did little for the development of the country. He tended to surround himself with yes-men. He was adept at causing divisions among

2   Herménégilde Niyonzima, *Burundi, terre des héros non chantés* (Switzerland: Editions Remesha, 2004).

3   Manlan's body was found dead on the beach. A commission of inquiry consisting of senior police officers accused Manlan's secretary. The court of appeal in 2005 found the police officers themselves guilty, but the suspicion of the involvement of senior figures will not go away. A big grant for reducing malaria was said to have been 'diverted' and this had to be covered up.

his opponents. The case of Augustin Nzojibwami, Secretary General of Frodebu, is the best example. An outspoken critic of Buyoya, he was arrested and imprisoned, but then released, and allegedly flattered and well looked after by Buyoya. This was described as feeding him on 'owl soup' (*umufa w'igihuna*). The result was a split in Frodebu with Nzojibwami leading a pro-Buyoya wing. Buyoya managed the same trick with Alain Mugabarabona, whose small faction split off from the main FNL.

Not everyone would give such a negative evaluation of Buyoya. He was as charming as he was cunning. He was never loved by extremists of either side but he sometimes had the courage to negotiate—for example, when his friends were pressing him not to do so for fear of losing their jobs—and he did not give up on the negotiations even when things got tough. Under Buyoya there was a fair degree of freedom of speech. You could say things in a Bujumbura bar that would have got you arrested under Bagaza, or in Kagame's Rwanda. A Hutu friend comments that Buyoya was the first Tutsi to accept that the problem existed and to propose a solution—but he designed the solution in his own interest. In his little book, *Mission Possible,* he is obviously trying to justify his various actions, and he comes across as much more human than the caricature of 'Gustave' would suggest. Finally, we have to remember that Buyoya handed over power fairly gracefully not once but twice. How many African presidents have done that?[4]

Eugène Nindorera accepted a ministerial job for a period under Buyoya and tried to fight for human rights from within the government. He comments that, in spite of Buyoya's influence, 'at times the army committed huge atrocities with complete impunity - and yet Buyoya was commander in chief. It was hard to know if he was weak or whether he was behind some of these actions. There were things going on at this time which were very serious. The conflict was between the army and the rebels but the main victims were the civilians. An army has a duty to its national population—nor can rebels change a system by killing innocent civilians.' (The worst such massacre was at

---

4   The only others are Rawlings of Ghana and Obasanjo of Nigeria.

Itaba in November 2002 where around 1,000 villagers were slaughtered by the army.)

Buyoya did step down as planned on 1 May 2003 and he promised never to seize power again. He said he would take his seat in the Senate and maybe one day stand for election. Domitien Ndayizeye of Frodebu took over as president with Alphonse-Marie Kadege of Uprona as Vice President. Ndayizeye had been 19 years old in 1972 and had survived by getting out of the country, living in Belgium and then in Rwanda. Elected to parliament in the Frodebu landslide of 1993, he spent thirteen months in prison in 1995-96, for allegedly supporting rebellion, before becoming Secretary General of Frodebu. When I met Ndayizeye in May 2006 he seemed proud of the fact that he had carried through the transition successfully. Alexis Sinduhije described him as 'a spare tyre' who did not do great things but wanted to make sure the transition went ahead. The major problems he faced were the return of refugees from Tanzania and the setting up and funding of the international peacekeeping force. He focused on completing negotiations with the remaining rebels and organising the referendum and elections—and that constant headache, the economy. 'I had originally persuaded Nkurunziza to join the negotiations...but he was a tough negotiator. They signed in 2002 but there were violations. There was no follow up mechanism for the first ceasefire, so it failed and the war restarted. I was more determined than Buyoya that there should be no elections until there was a ceasefire. I understood better what were the needs of the rebels. Generally, the regional heads of state were helpful. Museveni never stayed long. Zuma wanted to interfere too much. Mandela was a good listener and he dragged the Burundians into accepting certain things they would not have accepted from anyone else.'

The transition was nearly disrupted by renewed fighting with CNDD-FDD rebels and by a major attack on Bujumbura by the FNL, probably with logistical support from CNDD-FDD, in July 2003. Uganda and Tanzania even suggested bringing in an outside force against the rebels. The tough negotiations referred to by Domitien ensued at two more summit meetings. CNDD-FDD demanded a Second Vice President post, the presidency of the National Assembly and four ministries. The final agreement came at a third summit on 8 October 2003. Known as the Pretoria Protocol, it accepted CNDD-FDD's entry into the government:

- Nkurunziza would become Minister of State for Good Governance, be consulted on key matters and be third in rank in the government.
- CNDD-FDD would provide four ministers, two officers and 15 members of the National Assembly, three provincial governors, two ambassadors, heads of 20 per cent of public enterprises.
- CNDD-FDD forces and the Burundi army would be confined to agreed areas.
- Command posts in new national army would be 50 per cent Hutu, 50 per cent Tutsi, 60 per cent coming from the old army.
- The police force would also be 50:50 with 35 per cent coming from CNDD-FDD.
- The gendarmerie would be absorbed into the army and police.
- CNDD-FDD leaders and fighters would have provisional immunity.

Armed with this agreement, Pierre Nkurunziza made a dramatic return to Burundi on 5 December 2003, covering the last 30 kms to Gitega on a bicycle together with his two sons. He made a rather impressive speech with a message of peace, apologising for the suffering caused by the rebellion. He handed over his bicycle and went on to Bujumbura by helicopter. In May 2004 he joined Ndayizeye's cabinet and then almost immediately staged a boycott to make the government speed up the appointment of the promised governors and other officials. Thus relations with Ndayizeye and other Frodebu members were never close, and they became worse when, after the rebel movement had been converted into a political party, a number of National Assembly members, mostly from Frodebu, crossed the floor to join CNDD-FDD. Relations became worse still during and after the election.

In spite of a meeting with Zuma in Switzerland, the FNL remained obdurate. It denied killing the Papal Nuncio, Mgr. Michael Courtney, in December 2003 but followed this by threatening to kill Archbishop Simon Ntamwana for not believing its denial—which hardly suggested it was innocent. The FNL continued to be unpleasantly active throughout 2004, causing the displacement of thousands in Bujumbura Rural in January and again in July. The worst incident was the slaughter on 13 August 2004 of one hundred and sixty unarmed Congolese Tutsis at a refugee camp on the border at Gatumba. The FNL admitted responsibility but others appear to have been involved, including Congolese Mayi Mayi and Rwandan Interahamwe militia.

Another agreement made in Pretoria in August 2004 led to the drawing up of a new constitution. This was approved by parliament in October and, on the basis of this, Ndayizeye's term was extended beyond the day that the transition officially ended, 1 November 2004. The constitution was finally approved by 90.1 per cent in a referendum on 28 February 2005 in spite of opposition from some of the 'Tutsi' parties who feared, not without reason, that the permitted quota of Tutsis would be filled by Tutsi members of mainly 'Hutu' parties. The 'consociative'[5] constitution tries to provide majority rule with participation by the minority and assumes that the Hutu-Tutsi division is paramount. Thus with a Hutu president, one of two vice presidents must be Tutsi. The cabinet should be 60 per cent Hutu and 40 per cent Tutsi, and at the same time 30 per cent female. The same balance is proposed for parliament, with three Batwa to be co-opted. The senate, like the army is to be 50-50.

The country finally geared up for a series of elections in 2005 and everything went amazingly smoothly. The radio stations collaborated to give technical advice on voting and to allow the different parties a voice. Help, advisory booklets and posters were provided by several bodies including the Centre Jeunes Kamenge, the Electoral Institute of Southern Africa and the National Council of Churches (CNEB), supported by the British Department for International Development (DFID) via Christian Aid. The Independent National Electoral Commission distributed copies of the constitution. All parties promised to accept the results. Observers covered all the 2,190 polling stations—CNEB provided observers in 883 of them. FNL only caused

---

5 Refer to chapter 21 for notes on the 'consociative' model.

disruption in a handful of communes and repeat elections had to be held in four communes in Bujumbura Rural and Bubanza.

With a turnout of over 80 per cent the election for municipal councillors on 3 June gave CNDD-FDD 62.5 per cent of the vote to Frodebu's 20.9 per cent. While most people were expecting Nkurunziza's party to win, the scale of the defeat was a shock for Frodebu which claimed that there had been intimidation. If there was, Frodebu itself was not innocent. It tried to stir up fear and resentment of the FDD and flirted with the FNL to try and burnish its militant Hutu image. It got Frodebu nowhere. The parliamentary election with a 70 per cent + turnout gave CNDD-FDD 59 seats, Frodebu 25, Uprona 10, CNDD, the old rump party of Leonard Nyangoma, 4 and MRC, a 'Tutsi' party led by a former presidential hopeful, Col. Epitace Bayaganakandi, 2. Eighteen of the CNDD-FDD MPs were Tutsis. Frodebu accepted the results after a couple of days' hesitation. There was a general sigh of relief and satisfaction.

The Senate is elected by the municipal councillors and it ended up with a large CNDD-FDD majority. To keep to the rules extra women were co-opted, also three Batwa. The four ex-presidents[6] are also ex-officio senators. For this first election after the transition, the president was elected by the National Assembly and Senate together. Only 9 out of 160 voted against Pierre Nkurunziza, and following his famous victory he was anxious to reassure everyone that his government would be inclusive and violence and division were at an end.

Domitien Ndayizeye handed the keys to the new president. He told me he had been pressed to delay the elections a second time but decided that they had to go ahead. He realised that Frodebu was unlikely to win 'with 10,000 armed demobilised soldiers in the rural areas …and the people desperate for peace'.[7] Town voters, he thought, were more sophisticated: Frodebu won seats in suburbs like Kamenge and Kinama.

---

6   Bagaza, Buyoya, Ntibantunganya and Ndayizeye.

7   CNDD-FDD was accused of setting up a parallel administration before the election in areas it controlled.

Eugène Nindorera commented that he was surprised that Frodebu's performance had been quite so poor. The reason, he felt, was that it had been present throughout the crisis 'and could be blamed for all the contradictions. Even when Buyoya was in power, the vice president was from Frodebu, which was thus to some extent seen as being responsible for all the sufferings of the population during this period. Secondly, Frodebu was not a good manager. People never saw them in their constituencies. Certainly there was a security problem, but they were seen as leaders who cared more about their personal welfare than about the needs of the population which they represented. For example, the member for Kinama (which is inside Bujumbura) only started visiting his constituency the year before the elections. In 2001 when Kinama was occupied by the rebels, where was he? They never saw him...I frequently went to Kinama when I was minister.'

Many rural people's perception of Frodebu politicians was that they were town people who had enriched themselves while in power. A blatant symbol of this is the towering office building which Domitien Ndayizeye constructed immediately opposite the presidential offices; another is a hotel built at Kayanza by Jean Minani, who was to be sacked as president of the party because of the bad election result. Alexis Sinduhije commented that Frodebu had failed to take decisions at important moments. Ntibantunganya should have resigned and helped the rebellion, but he was not a natural rebel and preferred not to be under the leadership of Nyangoma.

For most Hutus the crucial change was the successful integration of the army and the police (see Chapter 11) and people thanked CNDD-FDD for that. But, as Ndayizeye hinted, the most telling reason to vote for the ex-rebels was a desperate desire for peace and the fact that CNDD-FDD was present all over the country. Many feared that if the CNDD-FDD lost, the war might start up again.

10

REBELS AND EXTREMISTS

...faire prendre conscience aux Hutu de leur situation d'opprimés, les amener à rev-endiquer leurs droits et à prendre en charge leur destinée. '...make the Hutus take on board their situation as oppressed people, enable them to claim their rights and take control of their destiny.' —from a Palipehutu bulletin in 1998

The beginnings of the Hutu 'liberation movement' were in Belgium where, in reaction to political events at home—notably the assassination of Prime Minister Pierre Ngendandumwe in 1965—Hutu students formed the Mouvement des Etudiants Progressistes Barundi (Meproba), and it became a focus for all opponents of the Micombero regime. After the 1972 massacres some of these activists came together as a committee to aid refugees. Shortly afterwards a political party in exile, Tabara, was formed.

Rémy Gahutu had been a member of the aid committee and of Tabara. He was very much an action man who liked to work with village people. While working in Rwanda to help Burundian refugees, he famously sneaked a letter from Tabara attacking Bagaza's policy onto the table in front of all the presidents meeting at the Franco-African summit in 1979 in Kigali, causing a furious President Bagaza to walk out and relations between Burundi and Rwanda to deteriorate badly. A year later in Tanzania he founded Palipehutu (*Parti pour la Liberation du Peuple Hutu*)[1] which aimed to raise awareness among Hutus about

---

1   Party for the Liberation of the Hutu People.

their rights and how to claim them, and to work for a democratic system. Gahutu's ideology is contained in his book, *Persecution of the Hutu of Burundi*. He emphasises the existence of Hutus, Tutsis and Twa in pre-colonial times—which, at the time he wrote the book, was contrary to Bagaza's official position that everyone was a Burundian and ethnic groups were not to be mentioned. Gahutu accepted the story of the invasion by Tutsis, suggesting that they overcame the Hutus by presenting them with cows and beautiful women—the 'Delilah syndrome'. Tutsi 'cunning, lies and secrecy' had enabled them to hang on to power. The Hutus suffered from an inferiority complex and were in need of liberation. (It is interesting that on Palipehutu's website the national language is called Gihutu, not Kirundi.) Palipehutu aimed to work without violence. Armed struggle was only to be a last resort.

Gahutu's ideas spread fast among the many Hutu exiles in East Africa, Canada and Europe. Within Burundi itself they were a main cause of the Hutu revolt in Ntega and Marangara in 1988. Shortly after this, Rémy Gahutu was imprisoned in Tanzania and in 1990 he was killed by a medical injection, the prison guards having been corrupted by agents of the Bujumbura régime. Etienne Karatasi became leader. Palipehutu, being mono-ethnic, was excluded when the multi-party system came in but most of its supporters backed Frodebu in the 1993 election. The party included a youth movement (JPH), a women's movement (MFPH) and an armed wing, the Forces Nationales de Libération (FNL). In 1991 there was a split. Most of the FNL members deserted Karatasi and formed Palipehutu-FNL led by Cossan Kabura, which became active after 1997 and has remained so, particularly in Bujumbura Rural, Bubanza and Cibitoke provinces, which are Hutu-dominated areas that directly threaten the capital. The distinct ideology of Palipehutu-FNL is the reason for its continued insistence on negotiations with 'the Tutsi people' rather than with any given government—and for the selective killing of Tutsis when they set up an ambush. The FNL has been responsible for many savage attacks and ambushes, including the Titanic Express incident in 2000. It was also among the perpetrators of the horrific massacre of 153 Congolese Tutsis (Banyamulenge) refugees at Gatumba on the Congo border in August 2004. On these occasions, the attackers arrive singing hymns and shouting 'Alleluia'. Many are said to be Seventh Day Adventists

(I do not know if there is any evidence that fewer attacks have taken place on Saturdays). There have been, however, many occasions when the army has blamed rebels for killings it has perpetrated itself. Hutu residents who remained in Kinama when it was briefly occupied in 2001 were not threatened, though their homes may have been looted, perhaps another sign that FNL treated Hutus better than Tutsis.

Unlike CNDD-FDD, Palipehutu-FNL played no part in the war in Congo. It had bases there but after that it was extraordinarily self-sufficient within Burundi. It raised funds by collecting tax from villagers and residents of sympathetic suburbs like Kamenge as well as from businessmen whose trucks and buses ran through its fiefdom. (Did Titanic Express fail to pay on the day it was attacked?) FNL had some relations with the Interahamwe, the militia who were involved in Rwanda's genocide, who saw Burundi as an easier way back into Rwanda. Some FNL fighters were identified as Rwandan by their language. FNL continued to recruit child soldiers up until 2006.

I was told that Agathon Rwasa, the leader of FNL, was stubborn and secretive. He ousted the previous leader, Cossan Kabura, because he had started to negotiate. Rwasa believed that by holding out God would give him victory. A faction led by Jean-Bosco Sindayigaya organised a 'General Assembly' in October 2005 at which Rwasa was said to have been expelled, but in fact he remained the leader of the main movement and Sindayigaya's group was sidelined. Sindayigaya probably wanted to qualify for demobilisation funding—and it seems he was wooed by Hussein Radjabu, then president of CNDD-FDD.[2] Rwasa agreed on a ceasefire in September 2006 but this took a long time to come into effect. There were reports of fighting between FNL factions as well as continuing attacks on civilians. The FNL finally began to demobilise in April 2009. Rwasa removed his army fatigues and put on a tie, confirming that the war had ended. FNL was recognised as a political party in May 2009 which required first dropping the name "Palipehutu", as no political party can have an overt ethnic label. This was a hard decision for them. Rwasa was appointed Director of the Institut National de Securité Social (INSS) and other FNL leaders were given posts. Pasteur Habima-

---

2   Radjabu is introduced in the section on CNDD-FDD below.

na's appointment as Second Secretary at the Embassy in India did not stop him, together with another FNL stalwart, Jacques Kenese, organising a congress and accusing Rwasa of dictatorship. Rwasa expelled them from the party. In 2010 another party heavyweight. Jacques Bigirimana, opposing FNL's boycott of the elections, split with Rwasa and was expelled from the party. In both these cases that CNDD-FDD was using the tactics used against them in the past by Buyoya. FNL contested the 2010 communal election and won the most votes in Bujumbura Rural but joined the other main opposition parties in their boycott.

CNDD, including its armed force FDD, was, as we have seen, created by Léonard Nyangoma as a split-off from Frodebu in 1994 when the party was being forced to make what he saw as unacceptable concessions. Nyangoma built up the movement fast, the armed struggle began and he soon began to get recognition outside the country. Apart from demanding democracy and human rights, CNDD carried little ideological baggage. The ethnic conflict was seen mainly as a creation of the Belgians, and differences between Hutus and Tutsis were not a matter for endless debate. The FDD was developed as a more formidable fighting force than the FNL and has had links with Laurent Kabila's Congo, where it was a component of the force that toppled President Mobutu. It also had bases in Tanzania and some help from Mugabe's Zimbabwe. These links gave strength to the movement. Had another war not broken out in the Congo in 1998, it is not impossible that the FDD with military support from Kabila might have defeated the Burundian army and imposed a settlement. By the same token, CNDD-FDD was dependent on outside help— and much more susceptible than Palipehutu-FNL to external influence—which was what helped bring it eventually to the conference table.

Alexis Kwizera, whose recollections of life in Kamenge are recorded in Chapter 6, ended up joining FDD. He had decided to finish his schooling first but 'other youths came to see me and said it's not like before, the movement is well structured now. It works well, there are lots of arms.... I went to the bush out of curiosity, to Kayanza and into the Kibira. It was very cold, very hard to see the sun because the forest is dense, closed off, there were only a few rays of sunshine. Life was very tough, army life plus being in the bush.' The ideology at first was that all Tutsis—and only Tutsis—were enemies. Alexis recalls: 'In our attacks against the army, some of my friends were killed, sometimes civilians were killed and some of our men raped women. Sudanese black mercenaries came and helped train us in tactics.'[3]

Nyangoma was deposed in May 1998. (He remained leader of the small CNDD party which is still represented in the National Assembly today, where he provides some of the most cogent opposition to the government.) The new leader was Jean-Bosco Ndayikengurukiye. CNDD-FDD, like the FNL, cannot escape responsibility for many deaths of innocent people, but it is also true that on most occasions when a rebel contingent passed through an area it was more likely to result in looting and the, quite unnecessary, burning of homes, than in killings. In 2001 Jean-Bosco also succumbed to Buyoya's 'owl soup' and was overthrown, but he kept his small faction active so that his supporters could get a share of the benefits from demobilisation and he could qualify for a government post. Hussein Radjabu, already a powerful figure, led the movement into choosing Pierre ('Peter') Nkurunziza as the new leader. When Peter took over there was a new ideology. It was not Tutsis that were the enemy but the system. The struggle was for justice, democracy and development. The movement still insisted on many conditions before it joined the negotiations, but there was no turning back—and the new orientation made CNDD-FDD less frightening for Tutsis, a number of whom, including some soldiers, saw the way the wind was blowing and began to switch sides.

The third and smallest of the rebel groups, FROLINA (*Front de Libération National*), grew out of Ubumwe, a political party mainly consisting of Imbo Hutu refugees in Tanzania and led by Joseph Karumba. It broke away from Palipehutu in 1990 when it made its first cross-border attack from Tanzania. Its armed wing, the Forces Armées Populaires (FAP), was small and largely inactive, but it did make several attacks from 1997 onwards.

---

3   Alexis joined FDD's information team and worked in Congo, in Rwanda and in Kigoma in Tanzania. On an undercover visit to Bujumbura, Alexis met his namesake 'big Alexis' Sinduhije and he joined the staff of the new African Public Radio.

At the other end of the ethnic spectrum are two hardline Tutsi organisations, PA Amesekanya[4] and AC Génocide.[5] Both organisations were born of a revulsion against the mass killings of Tutsis after the death of President Ndadaye. For them this was Burundi's genocide. They do not regard the mass killings of Hutus in 1972 and 1993-95 as genocide, arguing that in 1972 the killing was selective and that in the 1990s the army was carrying out security operations with no genocidal intent. Events in Rwanda in 1994 understandably strengthened these movements and their resolve to combat genocide in the future. When it began, Amasekanya was a youth movement. The youths have grown older now. They denounce, mainly through street demonstrations, the presence in government (and there are quite a number) of those they consider to be genocidal killers, *génocidaires*. Their broad definition implicates most Hutus. They oppose the UN presence, which protects *génocidaires*. They are basically rabble-rousers.

AC Génocide is at first sight a more serious organisation. Its leader, Dr Venant Bamboneyeho, is a don and former rector of the University of Burundi, who, like numerous others, lost many family members in 1993. His status and intellect enabled him to influence his students and to present his views effectively. His views were no different from those of PA Amesekanya and he made a strong case against impunity, something about which he could make common cause with Ligue Iteka and others except for the fact that he was only concerned with October 1993. The unjust killings of Hutus do not appear to have worried him at all. He was, in fact, a boarding master at a school in Gitega in 1972, when many of his students, including most of the sports teams, were carted away to their deaths.

However, as Jan Van Eck[6] has emphasised, Tutsi worries about genocide cannot and should not be brushed aside. Burundi is not so different from Rwanda and minorities require genuine and robust constitutional safeguards.

---

4   Pouvoir pour l'Autodéfense Amasekanya (Power for self-defence…).

5   Action contre génocide (Action against Genocide).

6   Jan Van Eck was based at the Centre for Conflict Resolution in Cape Town and was one of the most respected analysts of the Burundian situation. He made contact with rebels before others were willing to do so.

11

INTEGRATING THE ARMY: DISARMAMENT AND DEMOBILISATION

There were many bad things done. Both parties were responsible. —President Pierre Nkurunziza

Seven hundred South African peacekeepers arrived in October 2001, using the old presidential palace ruins in the centre of the city as a base. Initially their role was to be bodyguards for returning politicians. In the first months there was some tension with the Burundi army, which had always opposed outside interference, but the South Africans kept to their prescribed role and relations quickly improved. More South Africans arrived in April 2003 and were soon joined by Ethiopians and Mozambicans to form an African Union force (AMIB) with a mandate to oversee the ceasefire, support disarmament, demobilisation and reintegration (DDR), assist stability in the country and prepare for an eventual UN deployment. Demobilisation was problematic. How were combatants to be defined? Many were new recruits who had signed up to provide extra negotiating power and in the hope of receiving demobilisation payments. Others were reluctant to hand over weapons which could be used later for stealing cattle and goats or for self defence. What was the status of the *gardiens de la paix,* the youths originally recruited as auxiliaries by the Buyoya government? Nonetheless, movement to the assembly areas started in December 2003 and demobilisation got off to a good start. In spite of a shortage of funds and the problem of monitoring different ceasefires simultaneously, AMIB counted as a success and a model for other African peacekeeping missions.

The UN Security Council authorised a peacekeeping force to support and implement the Arusha agreement.[1] UN Operations in Burundi (ONUB) took over from AMIB in June 2004 and AU forces became part of it. ONUB was responsible for: ensuring respect for the ceasefire agreements; disarming and demobilising combatants; monitoring the quartering of the soldiers of the national army (the FAB); helping with security during the election period; protecting civilians who faced possible threats to their lives; helping and advising the government on reform of the army, police and judiciary and on the protection of human rights. Its mandate would run until the end of 2006. It took some time to get established but by the end of the year the integration of the army and the DDR process were going ahead.

Once the main rebel group had stopped fighting, security increased greatly. The presence of ONUB did not, of course, discourage the FNL from its continuing attacks, but its presence did help ensure calm during the elections of 2005. ONUB's relations with CNDD-FDD got off to a bad start. Before the election there had been more contact with Frodebu and Uprona. ONUB officials did not believe CNDD-FDD would win.[2] Even after the election ONUB did not always consult with the government.[3] It was no surprise that the new government was soon to ask for ONUB to withdraw, which it did by December 2006. It was not the government's plan to chase away the UN altogether and, at its request, ONUB was replaced in January 2007 by BINUB (Integrated UN Bureau in Burundi). The UN system loves acronyms.

Demobilisation continued successfully, with the credit going both to ONUB and to the Joint Ceasefire Commission. Over

---

1 Resolution 1545 of 21 May 2004.

2 They must have had poor intelligence. It was clear to most observers that CNDD-FDD had a fair chance of winning.

3 Action Aid's report *BINUB: Good Governance, Security Sector Reform and Enhancing Human Rights—Establishing Priorities* provides interesting detail.

40,000 combatants from both sides had been demobilised by 2006, as well as the *gardiens de la paix*. Over 3,000 child soldiers had been demobilised in a special effort supported by UNICEF and the World Bank. Pierre Nkurunziza presented himself for demobilisation just before being sworn in as President. Demobilisation of the FNL may, however, be more of a problem.

There was, however, more of a question mark over disarmament.[4] It appears that the former armed groups hid caches of weapons in case they were needed in future. Around 100,000 households in Burundi are thought to possess small arms. Only 6,000 arms were recovered from all the demobilised fighters. The army lacks the means properly to destroy obsolete arms. Armed crime is on the increase.[5]

Restoring the ex-combatants to civilian life was complicated and expensive. This was the main work of the government's National Commission on Demobilisation, Reinsertion and Reintegration (NCDRR). The ex-combatants were given 18 months' income and five options: help to reintegrate into their home communities; vocational training for self-employment; continuing education; training in business; or direct help in getting employment.[6] Reintegration has not gone well: a UN study estimates that 80 per cent of armed robberies and violent crime are committed by ex-combatants. There was not enough in the budget to help the communities who received the returning fighters or to deal with the real problems, psychological as well as material, of the returnees.

Nkurunziza had wanted the army to be reformed before there was a ceasefire, but in the event this did not happen. Yet the integration of the army, always seen as the country's most intractable problem, has gone ahead remarkably smoothly, perhaps partly motivated by a common desire to eliminate the FNL. The composition of the new Burundi National Defence Force allows

---

4   About 6,000 weapons had been handed in by mid-2006.

5   Details can be found in Stéphanie Pézard and Nicolas Florquin, *Small Arms in Burundi: Disarming the Civilian Population in Peacetime*, published jointly with Ligue Iteka (Small Arms Survey, Geneva 2007).

6   There is also a modest programme to rehabilitate and reintegrate war wounded.

a maximum of 50 per cent to be from one ethnic group. CNDD-FDD has been allocated 40 per cent of the senior posts.[7] The force will have been reduced to 25,000 by the end of 2006. Of course there are problems: various ceasefires have given temporary immunity, which means there are some members of the force who have committed war crimes—and, judging by some recent reports of torture and rape, they are not all reformed characters.[8] It has also been difficult to harmonise the ranks of the different forces. Young rebel officers tended to get promoted faster than those in the army. Training is crucial and this has begun, but so far it has not included much on human rights. Incorporating FNL fighters will create new tensions. The army's role in a peaceful Burundi will be very different and there is always a danger that it will be used as a repressive force by the government.

For the police, a force of 20,000 has been agreed. This new force is an amalgamation of the old police force, the old gendarmerie, now abolished, and ex-rebel fighters. The old force had been frequently accused of corruption and of inflicting torture. Ex-rebel elements joining the force are likely to have even less training and less understanding of law. The police thus face all the same problems as the army, including the presence of men who may be guilty of genocide or war crimes—yet the daily interface with the civilian public requires a certain level of professionalism. A number of donor agencies realise the seriousness of this problem. Belgium has offered to support the training of every police officer. This will include behaviour, investigation and human rights. France is paying for the establishment of a police officers' training institute.

So far the changes in the army are significant. If this process proves to be irreversible, it means that the old army dominated by Bururi Tutsis is no more. This army had committed atrocities in its time, the last being the killings at Itaba in 2002, but it was the

---

7   The 50 per cent rule is in the Constitution. CNDD-FDD's share was agreed at Pretoria and could cause problems when FNL has to integrated too. The remaining 10 per cent are Hutus in the old army and the splinter rebel groups.

8   ONUB soldiers also got a bad reputation for rape.

army that the Tutsi community saw as their ultimate safeguard.[9] The process also neutralises the FDD rebel army—and will, if all goes well, neutralise that of the FNL too. These changes give serious cause for hope.

---

9   In an article published in 2007 René Lemarchand suggests that there is still enough Tutsi power in the army to be that ultimate safeguard and that it is for this reason that the FNL proposal for further reform was not accepted at the Dar es Salaam negotiations in 2005: René Lemarchand, 'Consociationalism and Power Sharing in Africa: Rwanda, Burundi, and the Democratic Republic of the Congo', *African Affairs* Vol. 106, no. 422, January 2007.

12

TALES OF 'ETHNICITY'

Physical differences, yes, they exist, but they are not general or constant enough to allow us to conclude that there is a neat and always real racial differentiation.
—Albert Gille, 1937 quoted by Jean-Pierre Chrétien

Considering the damage caused in the name of 'ethnic conflict', it is remarkable how young children were generally kept unaware of their own ethnicity except when there was an obvious crisis, as in 1972 and 1993. Adults may be very conscious of it but, even so, it is not normal to ask a stranger or even an acquaintance which group he or she belongs to. Only when you know somebody well can you ask this question, or more often you find out through a third party. Here are edited extracts from some people I interviewed about this in 2006.

Alexis Sinduhije. 'You do not discover it, you learn about it at home. When I was six in 1972, all kids felt fear. Parents took advantage of that moment to tell us. It frightened me because the kids I played with were Hutus and they were apparently from the group that wanted to kill me. I liked them and they did not want to kill me—but the fact of my parents' feeling the fear, plus the anxiety of other kids who had lost their parents, made me very frightened at the age of six. I grew up in a very poor milieu where children ate only once a day, where they had real problems of food, sleeping, clothing. To add this ethnic contradiction was too much for us. This was fear which you could not remove, fear of your mate which you hide from him: you didn't tell him what your parents had said in the house and you played in a situation which was not honest, where you were in a permanent state of fear. Sometimes parents would say, 'Don't trust those Hutus too much, they could kill you'. And I imagine it was the same thing among the Hutus—'Don't trust those Tutsis, they are cunning, they are hypocritical, they can kill you any minute, they are brutal, they are not kind to us. They can get together to exterminate us...' This is the context in which we grew up. Young Tutsis got together because of these negative remarks of parents, as did young Hutus. All these negative influences have an origin which is that there was bad management of the country, there was blood, people killed each other and where there is blood, bad people play on fear and profit from it to keep themselves in power.

'My childhood was like that, but my adolescence was even more difficult. Things calmed down. People explained that the Hutus had wanted to kill the Tutsis and therefore the government had killed Hutus—and the government was associated with the Tutsis. Thus there was a gulf. There were teachers taken away in the middle of the class...It was not yet a war, but the state sent militia and police to take people away and kill them...Those who lost relatives were labelled *umumenja* (cowards, traitors, *génocidaires*) and kids grew up classified as victims or as executioners...according to each person's interpretation.'

Louis Marie Nindorera. 'I was not familiar with the divisions which created the crisis. I learned about these questions at secondary school. Another student in my class put a note on my desk asking if the boy next to me was Hutu or Tutsi. I knew that there were Hutus and Tutsis but naively I turned to the boy to give him the note. The one who had asked me the question saw what I was doing and jumped on me in the middle of the class and snatched the note from me. That's when I started asking myself what this was all about. That's the first time I knew about this. We had grown up in the late 70s under the one party system where there was no freedom of expression, a total blackout. In the Tutsi milieu in Bujumbura where I grew up such questions were not asked. Children were educated to be ignorant of such things. I'm not sure of the motivation—perhaps parents wanted to protect us.'

Alexis Kwizera. 'As a child in Kinama in the late1980s people some-times said, 'That family is Tutsi, don't go there'. But we played foot-ball together. I had Tutsi neighbours and we went there sometimes. We did not know why we were told not to go there. In 1993 we saw that some neighbours went away. As I was staying, I assumed I must be a Hutu.'

Adrien Tuyaga. 'After my dad was taken away in 1972, I was not aware that there was an ethnic conflict because in my family we never spoke about it, perhaps because we were ethnically mixed and my parents had married for love and had never had a problem about it. It was later when I was older and at primary school that I became more aware. My dad had always driven me to school and I had never attended any funeral. I was at Stella Matutina, a school for fairly well off kids. In fact, in class I was sitting next to the daughter of Presi-dent Micombero, the man who had ordered my father's death. We had good relations, but I noticed that after my dad's death my name had been changed from Bandyatuyaga to Tuyaga. I later discovered that all the children whose fathers had been killed in 72 changed their names so that they could not easily be identified as the sons of those killed, as a way of protecting us.

'In 1979, when I was at Collège Notre Dame at Gitega, we went to the refectory after our classes and then had 30 minutes rest be-fore going for sports. In the dormitory I was shocked to find insults written on my suitcase. I don't know how they knew I was a Hutu because I have all the characteristics of a Tutsi, but if they knew that your father died in 72, they guessed. (If your father died of an illness you had to explain that.) I went home for the holidays. I did not understand much. I told my mother about it and I asked her about my father. I had seen his photos—he was better looking than me. All I knew was that he had died due to some political problem. My mother, who was a Tutsi of the Rwanda royal family, and because it was part of her culture, found it very difficult to talk about it. ...but I wanted to know who I was. She finally explained that he was a

Hutu and that my grandfather had been an important counsellor of Prince Baranyanka who had sent my father to the Collège Royal at Bukavu. When I was at secondary school it was a fairly calm period and we did not talk about ethnicity. Bagaza threatened that anyone who talked of Hutu or Tutsi would be prosecuted. This was a way of maintaining Tutsi power...I left school without completing the course. I had been brought up in a fairly well off home and I could not stand the food in boarding school'.[1]

Aloys Ningabira. 'I knew the 1972 conflict in Karuzi province—I was five years old. I saw people coming with big lorries to take some of the people away and I asked why. They said they had come to take Hutus and explained what Hutus and Tutsis were. I asked, 'What are Tutsis like?' There was a Ganwa (a member of the royal clan) who lived near us and I was told that Tutsis looked like him. I asked why they killed people. My father was not taken in 1972. He was a peasant. It was he who told me all this.'

Athanase Bagorikunda. 'In 1972 I was in my third year at Kwibuka Primary School, near Gitega.[2] My father was the head of the school and he was taken away to be killed. I was there. I saw what happened. My uncle was also killed. I never knew why they were killed. My mother did not tell me why. I grew up in this climate. I remember always fearing that they could chase us from our government house a couple of kilometres from Kwibuka. I remember one thing they said: that whenever we saw a vehicle at the school we should run away. During the exams, when I saw a vehicle arriving, the women and teachers were the first to run. We saw teachers even jumping through the windows to run away. That's what we saw, but we did not really understand what was going on. I asked about these things when I was at secondary school at Buhiga. I asked a fellow pupil what ethnic group I was. He thought I was stupid. He said, 'Mr Athanase, your ethnicity is clear.' That's the first time I knew I was a Hutu. And I began to ask how people could be identified—by their noses?...I spent

---

1   Adrien's story and that of JAMAA continues in Chapter 16
2   Where David Niyonzima was teaching in 1993, see chapter 6.

six years at Matana High School and never had any trouble. I was well disciplined and kept out of politics. I was a scout and tried to get to know everybody and not to get involved. There was a bad climate between people from Muramvya and Bururi. The Hutus from Bururi did not show themselves. We thought they were Tutsi. The first time I knew they were Hutu was later at the university. In a way this was lucky because if we had known we were in a class with a majority of Hutus we might have behaved differently. The fact that we thought we were alone made us be polite to each other.

Dismas Nzeyimana. 'I discovered my ethnicity when I was six years old in 1972. I was at the village and I heard that the security services were searching for Hutus who had tried and failed in an attempt at genocide. Soldiers were combing the villages for suspects and I had learned that Hutus had an ideology which aimed to exterminate the minority using machetes. As a young Tutsi I felt lucky to escape from the danger of being killed.'

Fidele Kanyugu. 'I heard my parents say in conversation that such and such were Hutu or Tutsi but I was not aware of any problem till I was at school. I come from Gisozi district, Mwaro province, which is a Tutsi majority area and there was only one Hutu at the school. In 1988 I was at a boarding school in Gitega and lost some friends. I found this hard to understand.'

Jean-Marie Nibizi. 'My father was a Hutu, my mother a Tutsi. I did not know about the existence of ethnic groups till 1972. At that time there was a friend of my family who was a soldier. He had promised to buy me trousers, shoes and a shirt—then the killings started. I came to know he was a Hutu because that was the last time I saw him. A few months later, my mother told me he had been killed. At secondary school I learned a bit more: each time I got good marks the teacher cancelled the test. I discussed this problem with my friend, another Hutu, from the same village. He said, 'Don't you see that when you and I have good scores he cancels the test.' That's how I came to know about prejudice. I did wonder why my father had been killed in 1972. He was a lieutenant in the army. We started living a poor life. This brought hatred into my heart towards Tutsis and I decided not to marry one. When I was at university I was filled with such hatred and anger. The way I have been healed from that hatred is that I believe in Jesus Christ and, when the time came to marry, my fiancée was a Tutsi. I remember seriously discussing this later with my wife. She told me she was so surprised when I courted her because she thought I would never marry a Tutsi girl. I told her that the Lord brought her to me as a cure. Now I love Tutsis because I have now understood that we are all Burundians, made in God's image. In fact, biologically two out of four grandparents of my children are Tutsi, but Burundian society classifies them as Hutu. These thoughts brought me to engage myself in reconciliation even before the crisis began.'

Alexis Ndayizeye. 'We lived in Rutana where all three groups lived. At primary school we did not know what we were. Children were not told. When we ate or drank and when there was a party, everyone was there. In 1972 I was six and I knew nothing, but as I grew up, people said that so-and-so's dad had been killed, and, when I was at secondary school, Hutus said they had suffered and that their fathers had been killed. I also noticed that those who went to join the army were Tutsi. I thought maybe it was because they were the cattle owners! But I learned that before 1972 there had been a majority of Hutus in the army. We always knew about the Batwa because they used to come to the house to sell their pots. Thus I began to understand what I was—but I refused to join the army.'

Juvenal Ntakarashira. 'I was a Baptist from birth. After 1972 I knew I was a Hutu. In the family we did not speak much of the events: my father was not very interested. I did all my schooling at Kayanza, a Hutu dominated area. Where I lived at Musema everyone was Hutu and we were not much aware of the problem.'

Samson Munahi (Hutu): 'I was not conscious of ethnic differences until 1988, apart from the Batwa with whom my family exchanged bean seeds for pots. I used to play football with them but some people accused them of stealing.'

Perpétue Kankindi was the daughter of the first Burundian Anglican bishop. She had not been aware of ethnicity until, when at school at Kibimba in 1972, Hutu boys and even girls began to be threatened. She fled home to the mission station at Buye where she was protected. She was later sent to school in Switzerland where she met her husband, the future Frodebu politician, Charles Karikurubu.

Pacifique Ntawuyamara (Hutu). 'I was living in Rwanda in October 1990 when the war broke out with the invasion by the Rwanda Patriotic Front and ethnic tension increased. I knew I was Burundian by nationality because, when there was an inspection at school, they first asked all the Hutus to raise their hands, then all the Tutsis and finally all the foreigners, meaning us refugees. In April 1994 after the shooting down of President Habyarimana's plane (with Burundian President Ntaryamira on board), I had just returned from a visit to Burundi. In June, due to the genocide and war we had to flee back to Burundi, as the situation was becoming impossible. I departed with my mother and three young brothers in torrential rain. Heaps of corpses were lying everywhere in the streets of Kigali. We stopped for the night at Gitarama, the next day in Butare and then Gikongoro. The worst moment of my life was crossing the Nyungwe forest. There was an Interahamwe roadblock. They made me get out of the bus. Someone came and took off my shirt and started to count my ribs, saying that Tutsis had more ribs than Hutus. Suddenly I was knocked over as in judo and fell on the ground. I could not move and one foot was in a pool of warm blood from someone who had just been killed. My mother managed to save my life by handing out a 5,000 franc note. The militia men said that I would never get past the next two roadblocks. I was totally traumatised for two weeks and it nags me still today.'

I was told the story of a Tutsi who had spent eight years training in Canada and had a moderate, balanced outlook. He came home in 1994 and lived in a *quartier* that was not badly affected by violence. His first shock was that his home province, which had not previously been affected, was suddenly attacked. Parents and relatives took refuge with him, upsetting his home life. His opinion moved 20 degrees.

Then he had another shock. His suburb was attacked one day during the daytime. He was out of town. The place was encircled by the army and no one could go home at midday. His youngest daughter was at home with the maid. A rocket hit the roof of his house. After this, the man's opinions changed totally. He started to think he had been naïve before. He only wanted mix with his own people. Everything changed—his way of speaking, his perceptions, his behaviour. Terrible experiences changed many people's attitudes.

The divisions between different regions are seen by many people as being as deep as the ethnic division. This comes across clearly in Athanase's description of life at school. In pre-colonial times these differences had led to fighting between the *banyaruguru* royal family based around Muramvya and the Hima princes of Bururi. It has been suggested that the Hima, a distinct Tutsi clan, had arrived in the region much later than other Tutsi settlers, that there was little land left in the fertile centre and north of the country, and so they were directed to the south. Realising that the land they had been allocated was much less fertile, they felt resentful. At the same time they were socially ostracised: it was an unspoken rule until around the time of Independence that members of other Tutsi clans should not marry Himas. Thus the tensions between the south and the centre existed long before the political divisions of the Micombero and Bagaza years, when the tables were turned and your chances in the national competition for secondary school places, even if you were a Tutsi, were greatly reduced if you were not from Bururi. Discrimination in education created an effective 'old boy network' ensuring that the best jobs in the civil service, the state enterprises and especially the army went to people from Bururi. President Ndadaye was from Muramvya. Might he have been spared if he had not had the double curse of being Hutu and being from Muramvya? Léonard Nyangoma, Hutu rebel though he was, may even have been protected because he was a Bururi man.[3] Anglican Archbishop Bernard Ntahoturi is from Bururi and he agrees that since power lay there, investment and other priorities did go south. At least, he says, in Burundi, unlike Rwanda, you can talk as freely about regionalism as you can about ethnicity.

---

3   Tutsi politicians at Arusha were very kind to him when his father died.

13

THE TWA—ORGANISING THE MOST MARGINALISED[1]

We were the king's hunters and sacrificers. We would hunt leopard for the King. Neither Bahutu nor Batutsi had the courage to do that, only us Batwa.[2]

It is reckoned that there are less than 60,000 Batwa in Burundi, under 1 per cent of the population, with a greater concentration in Cibitoke and Karuzi provinces and almost none in the south. They are the descendants of the earliest inhabitants. Batwa ('Pygmies') are not exceptionally short. Many are of normal height and one or two are tall, owing to intermarriage. When the country was covered with forest they lived by hunting wild animals and gathering wild fruits and honey, as they still try to do in parts of the Congo. They were the experts on the forest where Hutus and Tutsis might fear to go. They were also, and still are, potters. In the past they had easy access to sources of clay and a ready market for their pots. Some were black-smiths and others were fishermen on the shore of Lake Tanganyika. They were nomads: when someone died, the whole family would move on from the 'cursed spot' to another place where clay was to

---

1   In this chapter I will refer to them as Batwa (singular Mutwa), which they are more commonly called in Burundi. The Twa form part of the population known as pygmies, see chapter 3.

2   The words of a Mutwa interviewed at Nyangungu in 1999 by Jerome Lewis, *The Batwa Pygmies of the Great Lakes Region* (London: Minority Rights Group 2000).

be found or where the local Hutus or Tutsis would let them settle in their temporary grass or banana leaf huts.

As the forests were gradually destroyed for farming, the Batwa had to adapt. Mostly they had no land of their own so they moved around, offering their services as labourers and guards and often held in a kind of slavery by the Hutus and Tutsis, while the women made and sold pots. They had lost their status as expert foresters and, with the demise of the monarchy, they lost the traditional role they had at the court as entertainers, messengers and hunters. Pottery became their main source of livelihood. As women were the potters, their role in Twa society grew stronger. Today, however, clay is increasingly hard to get and people buy cheap enamel pots. This leaves the Batwa with no means of livelihood, unless they can obtain land and learn to farm, or get an education.

The Batwa have suffered greatly from prejudice, abused as 'savages', 'smelly' or the butt of jokes. Dr. Harold Adeney, a missionary in the 1940s, recalls asking a Burundian friend, 'What person is that?' The friend answered, *'Si muntu, ni mutwa'* (It's not a person, it's a Mutwa). They have been, and sometimes still are, pushed to one side in churches, markets, village festivals, health centres and schools. Others would not sit down to a meal or a drink with them. The only relation that the others had with them was to buy their pots. If an animal died, it would be given to the Batwa, as they ate 'impure' meat. They were also traditionally the only ones to eat mutton or lamb. They were discouraged from going to school and were unlikely to be able to afford to do so. When they did get there, they were teased and ostracised, so they usually dropped out. *Vital Bambanze* recalls that he was often beaten when he was in school, so he ran home. When he got home his father beat him, so he went back to school again, and again. He ended up as the first Burundian Mutwa to gain a university degree.

Libérate Nicayenzi, a Senator since 1998, is probably Burundi's best known Mutwa. She had advantages that others did not. Nonetheless, her story is fascinating. 'Our family was self-sufficient, as we had some land to cultivate and my mother did pottery. This brought enough income, together with the pigs she sold. We also had a cow and I grew up drinking milk. Maybe that's why I lived 40 years—they say pygmies do not live more than 40 years! The prince, the Muganwa, who gave the land to our parents had ordered them to be baptised and to send their children to school. My elder sister was at school till the ninth year, my elder brother too, and me and my younger brother, but I was the only one that succeeded. The school was run by sisters at Kibumbu in Mwaro province. It was a well organised school and I did not suffer from exclusion because my elder sister worked for the Soeurs Immaculées and she had friends among the teachers.

'I finished primary school with no trouble but I had problems when I entered the national competition to go to Kiganda Secondary School in Muramvya. In that province Batwa were not treated as they were at home. There they were very much excluded. Before they sent me to that school my uncles and aunts and all the family had a meeting. Some said, no, I should not be sent there. After I had been there a week and the other children knew there was a Mutwa there, they started to tease me. Groups around started to jostle me and in the dining room they shouted, *'Ah, voilà un Mutwa, un Mutwa, un Mutwa.'* So someone took me out of the dining room to the headmistress, a Belgian, Soeur Noella, who asked me what had happened and whether I was ill. I said I was not ill. Then she questioned me and asked if I was Hutu. I said no. Tutsi, I said no. Twa, I said no. She asked me why the kids had teased me. She asked who had started it. There was a girl called Silvana who had been at the same primary school as me and it was she who had inflamed the other girls...I felt frustrated and wounded. My intelligence deserted me. I became a lazy girl who did not lift a finger. I came back to Kibumbu school (*Ecole normale d'économie familiale*) where I did 8-10th years: They transferred me again to Kiganda; but this time it was in the final year. I was in a group of six girls from Kibumbu, the best ones, and they were my friends and I felt at ease and we were always together and they helped train me.'

Batwa are not the only Burundians who lack rights but they are the least likely to be aware of what their rights are and the least likely to get a fair hearing. In the past they had no identity cards, probably because they hid from the tax man. Although they had no part in the conflict, they were blamed by Hutus for siding with the Tutsis and by the Tutsis for siding with the Hutus. If they fled from an attack with the Tutsis, the Hutus took revenge on their return, while those that did not flee were targeted by the Tutsis. Some were accused by one side or the other of making pots containing poison. In the village of Kizingoma (Karuzi) Tutsis blamed the Batwa for helping the Hutus and killed almost all of them—out of twenty households, only one person survived. Some Batwa have looked after the land belonging to Hutus who had departed as refugees but they fear, as do others who have been granted land, that the demands of returning refugees will have precedence. In order to fight successfully for legal protection and political rights, it is necessary that some Batwa have good education. Their experience of trusting others to speak on their behalf has not been encouraging.

In this context, the continuation of Libérate's life story is relevant. The man she married, Stanislas Mashini, was himself an outstanding Mutwa. He had studied at the *Ecole Pédagogique* and committed his life to working for the Twa community. He was a member of the human rights league, Iteka, which he had represented at a conference in Germany. 'In 1993 I was already married with children and living at Gitega. I saw how Hutus were ready to avenge the death of Ndadaye...we took refuge near the centre of Gitega. My husband hid after hearing of the death of Ndadaye. He had been on a delegation to Germany and when he got back he had been imprisoned for his political activities, so when he heard of the assassination he feared the whole delegation team would be seized. One thing Ndadaye did was to appoint Mashini as head of an agricultural school. He continued to hide because the Tutsis had made a black list of all those they wanted to kill in Gitega and he was on the list. Mashini was a militant who defended many Batwa. At any meeting people would say, 'Oh, now you'll hear Mashini going on about his Batwa.' He had started court cases to defend Batwa who were trying to escape from servitude to some of their Tutsi neighbours. So they felt bitter towards him and they did seize him some time later. He went to the school each day and one day they arrested him and put him in Gitega prison... He was condemned to death. He was transferred to Bujumbura. At this point they stopped my salary and I could not even travel to Bujumbura. I went on working. The only news I had was from the radio which announced that they would hang him on 31 July 1996. I went to Gitega to check if this was correct and I found that they had already hanged him...

'I was nominated senator in 1997. It was nothing to do with Buyoya. They saw that the crisis had resulted from exclusion and that there ought to be a Mutwa in the transition. The priests at Gitega said I should go down to Bujumbura and when I got there I was given this news. They said it was not so much to do with politics as to help me pay for the kids, as Mashini had been innocent.'

Nominating one senator was a small step, but Burundi was ahead of its neighbours. Recently there have been more advances, resulting from the determination of some educated Batwa to campaign for their rights. Uniproba (*Unissons-nous pour la promotion des Batwa*)[3] was founded in 1999 with Libérate as its president. It campaigns for Batwa to have the same rights and duties as all citizens, to be allocated an agreed proportion of seats in parliament, to participate in government, in the army and the police, to have extra help in education and training and to have a role in civil society. It has also helped communities to obtain land, to pay school fees and obtain health care. There have already been some successes, due to lobbying by Uniproba and others. Batwa are now accepted as citizens. Batwa are mentioned in the Constitution and there are now three Twa senators and three nominated Twa members of the National Assembly. Nationally, there are several at university, over 100 at secondary school and over 3,000 at primary school. Vital Bambanze, Libérate Nicayenzi, Emmanuel Nengo and others have represented the Burundian Batwa at numerous conferences. Vital represents the minorities of Central Africa at the World Bank. Batwa issues get an airing on the radio. Visiting Burundi in 2014 I was picked up by Emmanuel Nengo, now a member of the Assembly of the East African Community, in his air-conditioned 4x4 to go for a drink by the lake shore.

Yet the reality for most Batwa is that they are still at the bottom of the heap, lacking land, schooling and any regular income.

---

3   'Let us unite for the promotion of the Batwa'.

Where some funding has been found, Batwa have proved themselves capable of progress. Land has been granted in some areas, motors have been provided for fishing boats on the lake, houses have been built and some funding has been provided for school expenses. (In theory Batwa are excused primary school fees, but often this is only in theory.)

Innocent Mawikizi and his wife Beatrice are Congolese Pygmies who got to Gitega in 1994 and began to learn about the problems of the local Batwa. Together with Salathiel Nzibariza, a local Mutwa, they visited many of the Twa settlements in the central part of the country and began raising awareness among them. They established the Union Chrétienne pour l'Education et le Développement des Désherités (UCEDD)[4] in 1998. It aims build up the confidence and capacity of the Batwa, as well as enabling them to improve their standard of living, creating 'a holistic transformation'. The first projects were literacy classes for which classrooms were built. At Nyangungu, this developed into a primary school for the whole community. It is now a secondary school as well. Thus, instead of being deprived outsiders, it was the Batwa who were welcoming others, as they did most successfully when they hosted the workcamp described in chapter 15. National reconciliation has to include the Batwa. At the literacy classes the parents of the Hutu and Twa children, who were all illiterate, started meeting and making friends. UCEDD has also provided school fees and run short training courses for adult Batwa.

Equality has to be fought for. At one school where the Twa children were being segregated, Innocent would come each day to stop the teachers allowing this discrimination. UCEDD has been instrumental in helping obtain plots of land. Many people who had not farmed before are now successfully growing potatoes, maize and vegetables and rearing goats, chickens and even cattle.[5] Uniproba has similarly countered discrimination and advocated land rights in other parts of the country.

4　Christian Union for the Education and Development of the Deprived.
5　Christian Aid reported that UCEDD's agricultural project was among its most successful.

Minority Rights Group International has been a pioneer in advocating rights for the Batwa of the Great Lakes region. In Burundi, I am proud that Christian Aid led the way in supporting the Batwa. A number of other international aid agencies have also been involved including CARE International, Oxfam, ActionAid, Dan Church Aid, Norwegian Church Aid, the Mennonite Central Committee, and Catholic Relief Services (CRS) which supports a local association, Action Batwa, run by a Ugandan, Father Elias Mwembebezi.

MAKING PEACE

14

PEACE COMES TO KIBIMBA

Ijambo rigukunze rikuguma mu nda. 'The word that's bothering you—keep it inside you; in other words "stay buttoned up"' —a proverb illustrating a very Burundian characteristic

Kibimba is notorious for the atrocious slaughter in 1993 which has been commemorated by converting the old petrol station where it happened into a monument with the legend, *'Plus jamais!'* (Never again!). Sadly, the opportunity was missed to make this a monument to all who died in 1993, not just the Tutsis.

After listening to *Matthias Ndimurwanko's* account of his experiences (in Chapter 6), I asked him if he had forgiven those who tried to kill him. This was his reply: 'I think personally that we Burundians have a character that I cannot really pin down: if you meet someone whom you know who did certain things you should forgive in order to live in peace. Pastors, priests and bishops preach love to the Christians, but truly I do not know if they understand. I should try to put myself in the place of the other. As you love yourself, you should love your neighbour. If there is the blood of an enemy who is a Tutsi and another who is a Hutu, no doctor can tell you whose blood is which. It's only perhaps politicians who wanted a place in politics who taught such things, that you should kill a Tutsi or kill a Hutu. We could live in a paradise. Many countries have many tribes. In Burundi can't we live together with only three and share our peace together?... As an educator [Matthias was head of the reopened

Kibimba Primary School] I have to start with the young. At this school at first the Tutsi kids wanted to treat the Hutu kids badly. I tried to show these children that they should never think of revenge. It's not the remedy for those who have done wrong. If you forgive those who've done wrong, that is already something important. They can perhaps realise that they should not have done it. In his heart he would realise. And if you meet the one who did wrong, forgiveness is a way of healing the wound. And their children become friends.'

Burundian Friends (Quakers),[1] following the ways of the American founding missionaries, do not worship in silence as in the UK. However, a central tenet for all Quakers is the Peace Testimony, that 'war and preparation for war are inconsistent with the spirit of Christ'. With this conviction, the Friends have succeeded in making Kibimba a haven of peace and reconciliation instead of a place of slaughter.

Kibimba hospital only closed briefly. After the killings, the staff trickled back but at first few patients dared show their faces. Fear only abated slowly. Susan Seitz, an American volunteer nurse who came through the Mennonite Central Committee, arrived in 1994 and Aloys Ningabira, who had been working as a nurse there in 1993, returned to Kibimba. These two heroes of Kibimba Hospital, together with the other hospital staff, called to a meeting Matthias and all the displaced Tutsis who were living in the secondary school buildings, as well as the headmen of the surrounding *collines* (Hutus), and the Tutsi soldiers guarding the displaced persons. 'We were frightened at first,' Aloys remembers. 'Those from the *collines* feared the soldiers and fled. We discussed what activities we could organise—we started by organising football matches, the population vs. the army.' The Kibimba Peace Committee resulting from these activities was born late in 1994. Matthias was elected chair of the committee and he proposed that the primary school should be reopened. Tutsi and Hutu staff were recruited and, as Matthias described above, the children soon came to accept each other. The peace committee encouraged everyone, Hutus, Tutsis and Twa, to come for treatment at the hospital and, to give them still more chance to meet, they opened the Restaurant Amahoro (Peace Restaurant). Thus the hospital became

---

1   The Friends Evangelical Church or *Eglise Evangélique des Amis*.

a peace project in itself. Patients sat together in the sunshine or lay in the same ward, at a time when people normally feared to meet each other. 'If I am ill and he is ill and we are put in the same room we become friends.' The hospital later had the idea of running mobile clinics. Sick people were frightened to travel to the few hospitals that were still working. Others had been destroyed or looted. A tough second hand vehicle was obtained which toured to churches and schools in a wide area. Medicines and running costs were provided by CRS and Christian Aid. As at Kibimba, treatment was for all and only minimal fees were charged.

There were still people bitterly opposed to peacemaking. Matthias received a letter threatening him with death, and his car was stopped twice by people wanting to kill him. Luckily on both occasions he was not in the car. In spite of these threats, the peace committee expanded its work. The sports club organised matches with mixed teams, including soldiers, and mixed spectators came to cheer the mixed teams. They helped reconstruct houses and built ten houses for homeless Tutsis and Hutus. They distributed goats, run many reconciliation seminars, village festivals, theatre performances—and the women's mat-making project.

After 1993 Tutsi women had fled from their *collines* and were living in 'sites' or in the school classrooms at Kibimba, while Hutu and Twa women remained at home. In 1993-94 most of the Tutsis never ventured out for fear of their lives. They could not cultivate their fields and had sold the few cattle they had. Anne-Marie Hakizimana, a Tutsi, had taken refuge in the church in 1993 and stayed on in the camp for displaced persons. Josephine Nyambikiye, a Hutu, had fled to her *colline*. Susan Seitz had sent out word that women who wanted peace could come together. Josephine plucked up courage and came to the hospital and talked with people there. She and others started coming to meetings with the Tutsi women. At first all the Tutsi women sat on one side and the Hutu women on the other. Susan tried to mediate, showing that they could cooperate to feed their families. As confidence grew, more and more women came to meetings. Josephine and Anne-Marie were elected to the committee and it was decided to start a project. Traditional mats are made by women from banana leaves and they are important for

119

sleeping, for sitting, for preparing dry food, for sick people and for wrapping bodies after death. The women created a co-operative with over 200 members, divided into six teams containing equal numbers of Hutus and Tutsis plus a few Batwa. Each month the women were to produce four mats, made of banana leaves and sisal. At the end of the month the women would gather together to deliver the mats for sale to the co-operative. The mats were bought by Christian Aid to be donated to displaced people in other parts of the country. Out of the cash received for the mats, each woman paid 50 francs (£0.03 or US$0.06) as a fee for a weekly literacy course. Two local teachers, a Hutu and a Tutsi, offered to teach the women to read. After a short time the Tutsi women were no longer frightened to cultivate their fields and all the women had some income—and they could read and write. I attended a ceremony when the women received their literacy certificates. They put on a very moving and humorous little play showing how the crisis had separated them and how they were now friends again. For example, when there was a security problem they would secretly inform the other group. Anne-Marie and Josephine became the firmest of friends.

The women's play was just one among a number of theatre performances organised by the peace committee. Plays to promote forgiveness and reconciliation were performed in many centres around Kibimba. Each performance was followed by a three-day workshop and dialogue.

By 1998, when I first visited Kibimba, life was getting back to normal except that the secondary school was still occupied by displaced families: five hundred people were sleeping in the classrooms, the dining hall and even in the church. They had used the desks for firewood and the classrooms were black with soot from years of cooking. The government had been eyeing Kibimba School as a possible military training base. The Quakers were naturally horrified. They requested the government to return the school to the church, as a few schools had been recovered by other churches. I offered to write a letter to the Minister of Education to support the request, indicating that Christian Aid was willing to fund the rehabilitation. (I don't remember asking permission from my manager to make such a promise!) Others wrote supporting letters, including American

Friends, who wrote to the Burundian Ambassador in Washington. The minister at the time, Prosper Mpawenayo, happened to be a Baptist and a veteran of the Hutu political struggle. He was sympathetic and somehow managed to convince the government to hand over the school. The displaced families were moved, some to their homes, others to other 'sites', and the military presence was removed. Fortunately, the school was solidly built and no major structural works were needed. The school reopened in 2000 with Thaddée Nizirazana, a Hutu, as headmaster and with staff and students both Hutu and Tutsi. I visited the school in 2006 and 2014. It is totally restored and painted, with over 500 pupils, girls and boys, and what seemed to be a warm and friendly atmosphere. Training sessions on peace and reconciliation have been organised in the school. It has already restored its academic reputation with a full curriculum offering *normale* (teacher training), *économique* (arts) and *scientifique* (science) options. I was told that if Tutsi and Hutu children can study again in friendship at Kibimba of all places, it means there really is peace. You could compare it to Germans and Jews going back to school at Auschwitz.

There is no doubt that the work of the peace committee and the peace mission which the hospital and the primary and secondary schools set themselves has had a big impact. Aloys Ningabira commented, 'If you had tried to visit Kibimba in 1994, you could not dare to—it was really a desert.' Writing in 2003, he described how, at first, the military would not distinguish the rebels from the population and killed indiscriminately, but as a result of including soldiers in the peace committee and organising activities such as football matches, these attacks became rare, one exception being when a drunken and irresponsible commander was posted there in 1995 and two churches were bombarded and 50 people killed. Fewer young boys were attracted to join the rebel forces or the army's *gardiens de la paix*. People were no longer imprisoned by their prejudices: Tutsis no longer saw Hutus as rebels and many returned to their homes. Parents collaborated at school events. Although they realised that it was poverty that fuelled conflict, the only thing the committee could not do, for lack of resources, was to invest in economic development.

121

Of course some people are still traumatised, but Kibimba is now a happier, more normal place. As Aloys said hopefully: 'Some people appreciate what we have done.'

15

ACTION BY CHRISTIANS: PEACE EDUCATION AND TRAUMA HEALING

Churches and other faith groups are often the only networks that have sufficient credibility and reach to deliver. —Rowan Williams, Archbishop of Canterbury, after his visit to Burundi in 2005

The great majority of the population consider themselves to be Christians, so it is obvious that many Christians were involved in the killing of innocent people in 1993 and in 1972. David Niyonzima, former leader of the Evangelical Friends' Church, considers that this was mainly due to fear being a stronger motivation than faith. (He has also done some research which suggests that only 30 per cent of Burundi's Christians are real believers.) Jean-Louis Nahimana, Secretary of the Catholic Diocese of Bujumbura, reminded me that in Burundian culture people obey the leader or head of family and that the violence was provoked by leaders, mainly political ones. The church had not tried to build up strong leaders, concentrating rather on evangelising the 'small people, not the big'. The political leaders may have been nominal Christians but their political, clan, regional or ethnic prejudices were dominant. In Burundi, however, there was less evidence than in Rwanda of churchmen committing atrocities. Churches always remained places of sanctuary.

Could the churches have spoken out sooner or louder against violence? Could they have influenced politicians more? Do the churches actually oppose violence? Many Burundian Christians find no biblical position for saying that killing as such is wrong, just as Western 'Christian' leaders go to war. FNL fighters sang hymns on their way to battle. The Anglican Archbishop, Bernard Ntahoturi, feels that the church should take a consistent moral (but not party political) position, working normally at grass roots level but also investing more energy at the middle level—civil servants, teachers, business and professional people, those who influence decisions. He was happy with the efforts of the National Council of Churches (CNEB), in good collaboration with the Catholic Church and the Muslims, to be observers at Arusha and to talk from time to time with the government.

After 1993, the Catholic Church started to be more active in social affairs. It took steps to protect and welcome survivors of the violence; it organised *Nduwamaroro*, a space for displaced people to meet with their former neighbours who had remained on their *collines*. A research centre[1] was established as a forum for the discussion and publication of issues such as reconciliation. One problem is that each diocese is independent and some are more deeply involved in reconciliation activities than others. Catholic Relief Services (CRS), the American relief and development agency, has been in Burundi since 1961. It played an important role in relief efforts during Burundi's worst moments and it has worked with those in the Catholic Church who are active in peace building. A project supported by CRS[2] to promote a culture of peace includes: inputs in schools, including sport; listening centres; a special synod for reconciliation involving workshops and discussion sessions dealing with conflict and trauma; measures to help the priests themselves to cope, as they have also suffered physically and psychologically during the crisis; and the strengthening of the Justice and Peace Commission. The church also has its own radio station, La Voix de la Paix, and a studio where pastoral broadcasts are prepared and recorded. Church youth groups with their mixed membership have also been active in promoting reconciliation. These include the Mouvement Xavéri which aims to help young people live Christian lives and incorporates African

---

1   *Centre de Recherches pour l'Inculturation et le Développement* (CRID).

2   Funded by USAID.

values and traditions. The movement organises work camps, literacy projects, youth work, cultural and spiritual events.[3]

Some leading Catholics used their influence for reconciliation. Among these, Joachim Ruhuna stands out. Bishop of Ruyigi from 1973, he became Archbishop in 1988. He worked hard to bring young people into the church and supported the building of new schools. After 1993 he took great risks and suffered opprobrium from many fellow Tutsis by demanding an end to violence and the protection of innocent people whoever they were. He would walk towards a group of armed killers and ask them to question their actions and to join him in prayer. He welcomed to the church complex in Gitega everyone who sought protection and he was not afraid to criticise whichever group perpetrated violence. His harsh words for those who committed the slaughter at Bugendana in July 1996[4] cost him his life. Rebels killed him on the road two months later. Ex-President Ntibantunganya wrote of him: 'Nobody dared take the responsibility for the assassination of this man whose sense of conciliation was without equal in Burundi.' Ntibantunganya also recalled telling a new provincial governor to be advised by Archbishop Ruhuna because he was 'armed with truth', a rare commodity in Burundi.

A peace education project with a Catholic inspiration is the Centre Ubuntu, established in 2002 in the centre of Bujumbura and run by Dominican Fathers. It is a drop-in centre where people can use a library. The centre has the services of several psychologists and provides trauma counselling. It has also trained young people in counselling and theatre techniques. Publications include books on human rights and the representation of the people as well as a magazine. There are regular broadcasts on RTNB and on the Catholic Radio Ijwej'amahoro.

The National Council of Churches of Burundi (CNEB) coordinates the old-established Protestant churches—Anglicans (EEB),

---

3   The Mouvement Xaveri was founded by Father Georges Dufour, a very
     learned and charismatic character who was still alive in Bukavu at the time
     of writing.

4   Refer to the fall of President Ntibantunganya, chapter 7.

Baptists, Free Methodists, United Methodists and Friends, along with the Kimbanguists.[5] Ethnic and political tensions existed between churches and between church leaders and here CNEB served as a neutral meeting place and a force for reconciliation. The Anglican church (Eglise Episcopale du Burundi) has tended to have the reputation of being the 'Tutsis at prayer'. This is perhaps unfair, as the first Bishop of Burundi,[6] Nkunzumwami, was a Hutu and a majority of church members are Hutus. It can be a surprise to see Land Rovers driving around labelled in English, 'Mothers' Union'. In fact, this Anglican agency is very active in promoting women's rights, literacy, health education and reconciliation. The Baptists, Methodists and Friends have a mainly Hutu leadership and membership.

To provide more dynamism for peacemaking, Samson Gahungu, whose painful experiences at Kibimba are referred to above, was asked to open a CNEB department of peace and reconciliation. He worked there for eight months until he was imprisoned early in 1996.[7] The department continued in the hands of Juvenal Ntakarashira and Alexandre Sinzikayo who attempted to incorporate reconciliation, non-violence and conflict resolution into all the council's evangelising, educational, relief and development programmes. For example, its women's programme, run by the dynamic *Perpétue Kankindi*, daughter of Bishop Nkunzumwami, has involved breaking down barriers of fear and prejudice by organising visits between Tutsi and Hutu dominated parts of town; running micro-credit schemes; training girls in vocational skills; and in 1998 organising a successful women's peace festival. CNEB has also run youth seminars and has cooperated with the Scouts, Guides, the Mouvement Xavéri and Christian Aid in organising youth workcamps. A good example of this was the project at Nyangungu in Gitega province in 2001. The volunteers who took part were young Hutus, Tutsis and Twa from Bujumbura and from rural areas plus a few from Rwanda, Uganda

---

5   The Kimbanguists are described in chapter 2.

6   In 2005 an Anglican Hutu priest, Pascal Benimana, who was led to believe he was in line for a bishopric, was turned down in favour of a Tutsi. He has caused a mini-schism and set up a new 'Moravian Church' in the north of the country.

7   Details in chapter 5.

and Congo to add to the mix. The work project was to build houses for local people of all ethnic groups. The Batwa hosted the camp at the literacy centre and primary school belonging run by the local Twa association, UCEDD[8] and the Twa were in the unusual position of being proud hosts and beneficiaries at the same time. The ambience at the camp was wonderful. Perceptions changed and prejudices were reduced. Peace has to be built with hundreds of small steps like this.

The church which has been the most active in promoting peace is the Evangelical Friends' Church (EEA). The Quaker Peace Testimony calls for action rather than just prayer. This church has aimed to change people's mentality, to educate and train people to create a non-violent world. They have been helped enormously during the years of the crisis by the Mennonite Central Committee (MCC) which has provided key workers and occasionally funding. The Mennonites are another 'peace church' but do not have their own churches in Burundi. The three projects described below all grew out of the Friends' church.

Trauma Healing and Reconciliation Services (THARS) is a response to the shattering of community life through war and its side effects—rape, debilitating injury, the breakdown of families and AIDS—which have caused traumatic stress in many thousands of Burundians. By nature people tend to be reticent and when suffering from terrible psychological wounds they fear to speak and often fail to realise what is afflicting them, believing it to be demonic attacks or the work of ancestral spirits.

David Niyonzima, when he was the leader[9] of the Evangelical Friends' Church, was already aware of the problem of trauma. In exile in Kenya in 1997, he organised a workshop on trauma healing with participants from all over eastern Africa, including Rwanda where there was some good healing work being done. Having returned to Burundi, David became passionate about the need and the potential of trauma healing. An American counsellor, Carolyn Keys, was invited to Burundi to train local staff and David meanwhile

---

8   See chapter 13.

9   The leader of a church in Burundi is known as its Legal Representative.

completed a Masters Degree in counselling in the USA. Together with *Jean-Marie Nibizi* and others, David founded THARS, which began as part of the Friends' Church but after a short time became separate and independent. It has a number of related programmes—raising public awareness about the existence of trauma and thereby encouraging traumatised people to come forward; training workshops and seminars on counselling including the development of listening skills; training in non-violent ways of resolving conflicts (AVP—Alternatives to Violence Programme); therapy with victims of torture. THARS set up 'listening centres' in six provinces which are staffed by the best available counsellors. The next step after listening is to provide ongoing support, and this is also based at these centres. THARS has also teamed up with another organisation, SBVS (Burundian Synergy for the Struggle against Sexual Violence), to try to respond to the enormous increase in rape and sexual violence. Soldiers and rebels had been blamed for this, but as the conflict ended the problem may even have got worse, perhaps a sign of the breakdown of tradition and community generally. Two shelter houses were created where families are helped to welcome back traumatised women relatives.

THARS' latest report quotes several examples of healing. A woman had been raped by rebel soldiers and had a child. Later, government soldiers attacked her family compound and one soldier killed her parents, her brothers and her sisters. She was the last one left alive and the soldier assigned to kill her said, 'I'm tired. I have been killing people all day…', so she escaped. She and many others with terrible experiences have been given support and therapy. Another woman was attacked with a machete by her husband, who blamed her for his poor sexual performance. She had a huge scar on her head, another on her back and a thumb which was nearly cut off. She was persuaded to go to the listening centre where, at first, she could only cry but finally was able to tell her story and even to open up to others during a training course. Then there was the case of a pastor who quarrelled with his church and founded a new one. The leaders of the former church had him denounced as a rebel. He was arrested, tortured and strung up all night and his teeth were torn out of his mouth; the soles of his feet were beaten till they bled. After his trial and release he chanced to attend a THARS training session where he realised how badly he needed healing. He had therapy and extra medical attention.

Levy Ndikumana began to involve himself in reconciliation activities each time he returned home while studying in South Africa. In 1997 when he returned permanently he started youth work for the Friends. 'Each time there were troubles we thought of activities which could bring the country towards reconciliation and development...we wanted to resolve conflicts peacefully and work for integrated development and the idea grew up inside me to create something.' South Africa had many good examples of reconciliation projects, and during Levy's first visits home he discussed the concept of a peace centre with his friends. The result was to set up Mi-Parec[10] in 2000 with some support from the Mennonites in the form of volunteer 'experts' in peace education and some funding. Starting small, Mi-Parec grew fast and gained a good reputation for training, targeting five main categories of people: those who never left their *collines*; demobilised soldiers from both sides; returning refugees, especially from Tanzania; internally displaced people; and political prisoners who have been liberated. Mi-Parec tries to target all these groups together, integrating Hutus, Tutsis and Twa, including members of all the different churches. Training covers every possible aspect— peaceful resolution of conflicts, human rights, the struggle against HIV/AIDS, community development, leadership. 'We help people to understand the need for, and then to demand and lobby for, restorative justice, reconciliation, tolerance, social justice and social reintegration. We try to convince ex-combatants and those holding arms illegally of the bad effect of possessing arms and to give them up voluntarily.'

I asked Levy how he can evaluate the effect of Mi-Parec's work. He gave the example of the commune of Mutaho, an area where there was terrible destruction. It was like a ghost town. People there, he said, were in the process of asking each other for forgiveness. Lots of arms have been given up voluntarily. This gave hope to the popu-

---

10 Ministry of Peace and Reconciliation under the Cross.

lation. There was now mutual confidence and trust. New schools had been built, where returnees were welcomed and reintegrated. Internally displaced Tutsis were only slowly gaining the confidence to return to their *collines*—and in some cases were settled at their new *sites* but even here mutual confidence was growing.

A successful example of Mi-Parec's work was a youth programme in Makebuko commune, Gitega province, funded by German Co-operation. The aim was to help integrate young returnees and displaced persons and at the same time to work for better understanding among the settled people of different ethnic groups. The conflict left young people traumatised, brutalised, unemployed and lacking in skills. They were strongly tempted to keep their weapons. To make these people agents of peace meant first addressing fear, suspicion and lack of trust and then planning a better future. Mi-Parec organised three work and study camps with returnees, displaced persons and ex-combatants taking part alongside settled Hutus, Tutsis and Twa. They helped construct the venue for the camp, took part in training for reconciliation, lobbying for rights, leadership, community development and combating HIV/AIDS—using active games and audio-visual aids—and they organised the domestic routine and social, cultural and sporting activities. The camp participants have now demanded more vocational training so that they can find jobs, and a good number of guns have been handed in voluntarily.

Mi-Parec set up as an NGO independent of the church but still working in close partnership with it. They were able to buy a plot of land and build a permanent centre which brings in some income to add to what is earned from providing training activities for various organisations. Some of the community training is done in the centre; there is a good little library, specialising in peace and conflict (a problem being that it is easier to get such books in English than in French).

After his release from prison, *Samson Gahungu*, whose story was told in Chapter 6, wanted to continue doing peace and reconciliation work. The post at the National Council of Churches had already been filled, so 'I began to write. Burundians do not buy books, but I began to write and distribute free pamphlets written in Kirundi. After leaving prison, a friend had given me a sum of money and I decided to use most of this to start printing leaflets, asking if we can forgive those who did wrong, or whether we should avenge them. When, outside the country, I submitted this project to Friends in Kansas and they provided some funds. I brought out four such leaflets, some referring to reconciliation in the Bible…I gave talks in the central region, especially in churches…'

Samson was invited to a seminar on the Alternatives to Violence Programme (AVP). This is a method of dealing with conflict which began as an initiative by prisoners in the USA in 1975 and it has been used by Quakers in many countries. It grows out of the belief that there is good in everyone and that this can be nurtured so as to overcome tendencies to violence. Through a series of workshops it enables people to know themselves, to communicate, collaborate and manage inter-personal conflicts; to understand deeper causes of conflict, fear, anger, prejudice, frustration; to explore forgiveness and thus to cut out violence as a solution.

After his return in 2002 he ran the first seminar on AVP in Gitega. Other American Quakers also helped run training seminars including the training of trainers—leadership techniques and methods of training. AVP in Burundi, which is now a recognised association, aims to change people through a 'structured experience' so that people, even those in detention, can learn new attitudes and ways of behaviour and can lead fuller lives. Samson considers that the impact of these activities has been positive. AVP has targeted *gardiens de la paix*, ex-combatants and prisoners and its has run training programmes for members of the staff of Search for Common Ground, THARS and others.

16

PEACEMAKING ON THE GROUND

Béni tous ceux qui ont à coeur la reconstruction humaine, morale et matérielle de ce pays. 'Bless all those who have at heart the human, moral and material reconstruction of this country.'—part of a prayer written by Dona, a young member of the Centre Jeunes Kamenge

This chapter describes the work of local non-government organisations which have worked for peace and reconciliation; and also some attempts at coordinating these activities.

Centre Jeunes Kamenge

Young people constitute over 50 per cent of the population of Bujumbura, and even before the crisis they lacked any kind of community facilities. Gangs such as the *Sans Echecs* existed already, and informal meeting places (*ligara*) were the only social centres in the suburbs. To meet this challenge the Catholic Church asked the Xaverian Fathers to take an interest in the youth of Bujumbura's four northern suburbs, Kamenge, Kinama, Cibitoke and Ngagara. *Father Claudio Marino* had worked in Burundi from 1964 as a parish priest. He was one of the 600 priests and missionaries expelled by President Bagaza. A few years later, Father Claudio returned on condition that he was not given a parish, since there were enough Burundian priests. So in 1991 he took up the task of establishing a centre where young people could mix in situations—sport, culture, education—sufficiently normal for a generation to grow up in an atmosphere where being

Hutu or Tutsi was the same thing, so that one would never take up arms against the other. This was the vision, but the experiences that Claudio Marino and the staff of the Centre went through in the early days severely tested their faith—and showed that there really was a need for such a centre.

In the chaotic situation described in chapter 7, Claudio Marino and his team had to shelter elsewhere. During this period Médecins sans Frontières used the Centre as a field hospital, treating sick and wounded Tutsis and Hutus from Kamenge, Kinama, and Cibitoke. Claudio recalls: 'Sometimes we were able to clear a space between the military and the population in order to give a chance for people to pick up the dead to avoid an epidemic breaking out. We lived through the most terrible time. The centre was closed. No-one could get in because of the fighting. We survived because we had shown by our actions and our presence that we were not for one side or the other. Sometimes we were accused of being pro-Hutu, at other times pro-Tutsi. We understood that the way to operate was always to work with all the suburbs and to make clear we were for peace and reconciliation.'

When Claudio and his colleagues returned and tried to reopen the Centre, they found the grounds, which had been occupied by the army, scattered with cartridges, military equipment, guns, cows' carcases…'It was incredible. It required courage to return. At such a moment you think you are crazy. We began immediately to say that the Centre was open to all—we never closed the gate…and people could come in from different directions depending on where the fighting was taking place. When dozens of young people started coming in, we began to take those from nearby Cibitoke (Tutsis) to play together with those from Kamenge (Hutus). When Kamenge became a bit more peaceful we took youth from Ngagara (Tutsis) and we always tried to make this an island of peace. You could hear the noise of war outside but with football, basketball and films you could think about other things.' As time went on more young people began to come to the centre and the facilities were improved. The football and basketball pitches are of a high standard, there is an excellent library, computers and meeting rooms of all sizes.

'In 1997 local administrators, heads of school, *chefs de zone*,[1] presidents of associations came and congratulated us. They said we should not just target youth but work with the community in all the northern suburbs: 'We live in the suburbs which are ethnically polarised. If you do not help us we will remain divided.' So work started outside the centre on four projects—awareness raising on AIDS, peace and reconciliation, setting up local clubs and literacy classes. Activities were based within one suburb or preferably two, so that there would always be an ethnic mix. Competitions could be between all four suburbs. Staff from the Centre worked with primary and secondary schools, religious communities, health centres and the local administration. Peace building activities were prepared and tested at the Centre before being tried out in the suburbs. Claudio remembers: 'We continued from crisis to crisis. I remember at the end of the occupation of Kinama (in February 2001) some young people organised themselves to prevent looting. When extremist groups arrived to loot, the youths from the Centre asked them: 'Why do you want to loot Kinama? They are poor like you.' Then they took shovels and started to open the roads.'

Many people have said that if the northern suburbs were partly saved it was due to the presence of the Centre Jeunes Kamenge which had never taken sides in the conflict and which was well known because it was often visited by journalists and other foreign visitors. In 2007 the Centre worked in six suburbs (Buterere and Gihosha had been added), with 95 schools, with the Catholic religious community, with 27 health centres and with several local associations, and helped set up new local youth centres. Drugs had become an increasing problem. About 50 people worked in the centre, plus a further 20 community workers in the suburbs, most being unpaid volunteers. There were some volunteers from France, Switzerland and Italy who come for a month or up to a year. The Centre got funding from Misereor, the Italian Bishops Conference, Carème in Switzerland, from Canada and from the Belgian, Italian, US, Austrian and Ger-

---

1   *Chefs de zone* are the chief administrators in each neighbourhood or *quartier*.

man governments. Users of the centre must be aged 16-30, though over 30s can use the cyber cafe and library.

Claudio comments, 'It is good to be able to stay away from adults because in the local culture adults always command, teach, make young people fight or make peace. It is important for young people to be together in groups, play games, go to shows to help make them into responsible adults, a new generation for the country...We are an open project, flexible. Each day we decide how to react to situations...thus everyone feels at home. We make people self-reliant.' To help the young people who are still traumatised by the war, a psychologist comes to the centre; also a legal adviser (from Avocats sans Frontières) who can advise on problems of land law, rape and violence. 'The most beautiful thing,' Father Claudio comments, 'is the recent coming together between Muslims and Christians. We work with the 16 mosques in the suburbs, four Catholic parish churches with their local churches and many Protestant communities...The Quakers are close friends as we saved their nearby church during the war in 1993. There was chaos for a day and a half. After the looting of the market they came down to the church and then towards the Centre and then the army intervened. The Uprona party hall was destroyed by the military who stole everything.'

JAMAA

Adrien Tuyaga, whose childhood reminiscences we have encountered already, dropped out of school because his mother had lost her job and could not pay the fees in Bujumbura for all four of her children. So in 1983 Adrien found a job at Savonor, the local company making soap and margarine. He earned 180 francs a day (nearly £1 in those days), working eight hours in a factory full of smoke. 'I went all over town and could not find any other work. I took tests. They said I had been accepted and then found someone else had started work instead. I became totally discouraged. One day at the factory one of the workers had his hand cut off. There was no protection. I used the same machine. For 180 francs a day this was not worth it. I had saved up US$50 and the factory manager, a German, had given me a bicycle. With what I got for selling the bicycle plus the $50 I went off to Tanzania. When I reached Dar es Salaam I hoped (in vain) to get a boat to Europe. I spent several months there and met by chance some Burundian Hutu exiles. I never knew such people existed and I learned from them a bit about the problems of Burundi. I came home and found the same situation. Without someone to help you there was no chance of getting a job.

'In 1986 I became a drug addict. I spent many years as an addict, sleeping anywhere. I dropped from 89kg to less than 50kg. I took heroin, crack, synthetic cocaine mixed with marijuana. One day I was with some other addicts in an abandoned chicken-house in Buyenzi. I did not stay at home. I did not want to show myself to my young brother. I woke in the middle of the night and my conscience was aroused while the others were sleeping. I thought of my father. I asked myself if I had been born just to die like this, because if I continued I would die. My sign is Aries. I am a fighter. That day I had stolen a hair clipper in Buyenzi. I sold it to buy a ration of heroin which helped me to think clearly. There and then I decided to stop and I finally went back home.

'I found my room had been cleaned, with clean sheets and a pot of hot tea, bread, butter and *paté de foie* ready for me and presents that my sister in Europe had sent me were on the table. I changed out of the filthy clothes I had been wearing for years without changing. I called my mother and said I was ready for a detoxification course. I took a taxi direct to the clinic. After two weeks of treatment I stopped on 25 February 1992 and have never taken drugs again. My mother said I had no job and risked going back to my old friends and starting again. I said there was no risk of that. She said I must look for work but I said if you don't know someone you never get work in this country. I told her I would never go begging to someone to ask for work. I would do something to help people who are in the same situation as me.'

That is how Adrien Tuyaga thought of creating JAMAA, and he explained his idea to Alexis Sinduhije, who promised to help, and to another friend, Abdoul Niyungeko, who played a big role in the early days but later died in a road accident. Alexis introduced Adrien to Louis-Marie Nindorera, then at Ligue Iteka who helped write the Constitution, and who provided some credibility for donors. The

Kiswahili word *jamaa* really means a family or an assembly of people, but in the street in Bujumbura it means 'young people out of school and out of work'—'These were the people whom we helped to survive and whose expectations we tried to satisfy.'

JAMAA was registered as a non-profit making association (ASBL) in 1995 with the aims of creating solidarity and reconciliation between Burundians of all ethnic groups through work, study, sport and leisure activities; raising awareness about the problems of youth; and creating opportunities for training and work for social integration. Abdoul and another friend, Tino, were well known among the youth as 'rastas' whether or not they had dreadlocks. JAMAA used the influence that these two had on young people to influence them against the use of violence. They started off by organising football matches. Branches were started in several suburbs, with meetings always held in neutral zones like Buyenzi. In 1996-97 their first project was to train some of these unemployed youths as barbers. The project was to be funded by French Cooperation but after Buyoya's coup in 1996 official aid stopped and this project was rescued by a grant from Christian Aid. Some of these barbers are still in business. One of them used to cut my hair.

JAMAA had Canadian funding for two years for the promotion of literacy, information sharing, communication, an office, a computer, a vehicle, and audio-visual equipment. Loans were given to young people so that they could earn their own living. JAMAA claims to be a pioneer in resolving conflicts through job creation.

The tough context in which JAMAA started working was Bujumbura in 1996 where there was incredible hatred between Hutus and Tutsis. 'The only contact,' Adrien remembered, 'had been violence and death...there was no law and order, no policing. We decided to get in touch with the groups involved in this violence, bring them together to spend a night together so that they could reflect on the situation and be convinced to stop fighting. This gave them enough time to create friendships and then to create mixed football teams who would play against other mixed teams.' JAMAA mobilised young people at the risky time of the *'villes mortes'* demonstrations[2]

2   See chapter 7.

when the situation was bitterly polarised, identifying people who had taken part in violence. Real friendships were created and people who felt they had no future found a new purpose.

Another big success was the first comic book (*bande dessinée*), *Le meilleur choix* (The best choice), which was funded by Search for Common Ground and published in French and Kirundi. It shows how young people turned to violence under the influence of bad politicians and how they learn to make…a better choice. This book received a prize from UNESCO. A second comic book was produced entitled *Oeil pour oeil, oui ou non?* (An eye for an eye, yes or no?) A video of the first book was produced and another video telling the stories of three child soldiers, one a *gardien de la paix* in the national army, one from the FNL and one from the FDD. They collaborated on the film and are now good friends. Their message is: don't do it!

JAMAA's biggest project is a youth centre, mainly funded by Christian Aid, which was built in Kwijabe, in a fairly central location near to Buyenzi, Bwiza and the northern suburbs. It consists of an attractive meeting hall and an all-weather basketball court which doubles up as an open air performance space. It is a place where youth can mix and have fun. The centre has never been used to its full potential and it is looking shabby due to lack of funds. With full time staff and a good programme of activities it could have an important role in the future.

SHINE

Jean-Marie Nibizi is of mixed parentage and his late wife, Sophie Kamikazi, was a Tutsi. In 1993-94 they were living in Musaga on the boundary between the mainly Tutsi and mainly Hutu areas where they were able to stay together. 'During that time I called on Hutus and Tutsis to see how we could continue to live together.' They succeeded at first but after some time the Tutsis concentrated in Musaga and the Hutus moved off to Kanyosha; 'At the end the pressure was too much. We moved to the Hutu side for a week, then to Buyenzi where there was still peace.' In 1995 two white South African Christians visited Burundi for a youth seminar on peace and invited Jean-Marie and Sophie to go to South Africa. 'I was keen to learn about the South African experience and I tried to convince church leaders, black and white, to come to Burundi for a church leaders' conference. I had even written to Mandela to ask him to stop supplying weapons to the Great Lakes Region and instead to teach us about the South African experience. He never replied but they did stop selling arms.' Jean-Marie and his wife went to South Africa in 1996 and he trained as a pastor and community development worker. He returned to Burundi in 1999 when I first met him. Sadly, Sophie had died on her way home. Apart from having an active role as a pastor in Kanyosha and Ruziba, Jean-Marie started Shine Jesus Ministries, shortly afterwards renamed SHINE (Services to Humanity for Integration, Neighbourliness and Equity)—but the acronym came first! 'Shine' is also symbolic of the conviction that a divided people can share together in a common witness of peace, healing, reconciliation and development. Like all small organisations, in spite of having lots of interesting ideas for projects, SHINE has been very limited in its action owing to the difficulty of attracting funds.

SHINE's aims are conflict transformation and community development through social enterprises, including child development and training for leadership. SHINE started by training youth, women and church leaders to work for reconciliation, including how to manage fear, suspicion and rumour and how to welcome returning displaced people and refugees to their villages of origin. SHINE ran workshops targeting church leaders and also officers of the army and police, many of whom are former rebels. In 2007 the main project was for primary schools in Bujumbura and the provinces of Cibitoke and Bujumbura Rural, with the title 'Raise up a new generation: our children for peace, development, human rights and reconciliation.' Teachers are trained, first, to learn about 'our true identity, understand our wounds, pain and suffering', then 'forgiveness, repentance, reconciliation', and finally conflict transformation. The teachers go back to their schools and train other teachers and then their pupils. At the end of this programme a cultural and sports competition is organised and the teachers and pupils feed back the peace message to their communities. Trees are planted in a 'peace garden' as a living reminder of this learning process. This project was further developed by including discussion of the relation of poverty to violence and illustrating this by starting income generating activities at the schools. SHINE also organises education on HIV/AIDS in primary schools. SHINE believes that the most effective way of breaking the cycle of distrust, hatred, stereotypes and violence is to cultivate values of reconciliation, human rights and community well-being among children of 7-10 years, the most formative period of their lives.

SHINE has also organised conflict resolution training with church leaders. It has been active in pointing out to politicians the relevance of the South African experience to Burundi's situation and had close contact with South African troops in the peacekeeping operation. In addition, some small social community enterprises were set up to help Hutu and Tutsi widows and orphans, including those with HIV. They were given small loans to start their own businesses, such as making handicrafts and selling tomatoes. This gave them an extra income to pay for school fees, uniforms, food and medicine and it is done in a spirit of reconciliation. There was a similar scheme for young unemployed people to make bricks which they could sell to the community to earn a living, rather than waiting for a job that they would never get.

A very imaginative initiative was the Sangwe (Welcome) project. In 2002 the number of refugees returning from Tanzania increased greatly, some organised by the UN High Commission for Refugees (UNHCR), others spontaneously. SHINE, along with JAMAA and others, felt it a priority to help with the peaceful reintegration of refugees who usually returned without any proper psychological preparation and, finding Tutsi soldiers and Tutsi UNHCR staff dealing with them, felt nervous, even though these Tutsis were not usually unfriendly. So, to put new arrivals at their ease, SHINE set up a transit centre near Ngozi. The UNHCR agreed to fund this pilot project. The returnees were helped to unload their possessions from the lorries and warmly welcomed by volunteers, both Hutu and Tutsi, men and women, young and old. They were given useful information to help them adjust to life in the old country, especially concerning their rights as citizens and how to contact the authorities over matters such as their land, health and education. They were also given a presentation on HIV/AIDS. Children's games were organised and drummers drummed. In the words of one returnee: 'This welcome

141

seems a very simple act, but very profoundly meaningful, because to be welcomed by a mixed group of Burundians and to be cared for tremendously touched our emotions, perceptions and behaviour. This gave us joy and hope for the future. It prepares us to go back home with confidence.' This experiment influenced others to improve the welcome given to the many returnees who have followed.

New Generation (NG)

Each of these peace initiatives has a 'moving spirit', a person whose strong vision and determination has led to action. The man behind New Generation is Dieudonné Nahimana. He started working with youth in Nyakabiga in 1998 and went on to build up an effective association which aims at a 'spiritual, cultural and economic' awakening of young people, including street children, ex-combatants, and youth in school and out of school (*jamaa*). This means working for reconciliation, training, solidarity, recognition of artistic talent, and a culture of peace, and against HIV/AIDS, drugs and delinquency. The number of activities is impressive: thirty-five youth leaders are trained each month, fifteen street children are helped each day, computer training is offered, including a cyber café, library and video. Every Sunday afternoon NG organises youth meetings throughout Bujumbura; it has held conferences in various provinces, run youth camps, handicraft workshops, small music festivals and presented radio and television broadcasts. A daily programme at all the 30 centres where NG works provides in the morning literacy classes, skills training and a communal meal to which street children, former child soldiers and young unemployed people are welcomed, while in the afternoon different discussion groups and cultural clubs have their meetings. New Generation has been successful in raising funds for most of these activities from foundations, the US Embassy, World Vision and UNICEF.

Youth movements

My own first contact with Burundi was with leaders of youth movements who took part in an international exchange in 1993. Before this programme ended, the crisis had begun and we got a grant from

142

UNESCO for an international workcamp to help with reconstruction. It turned out to be too soon to think about reconstruction, but we were able to use the funds to organise a study tour to peace projects in Northern Ireland for five leaders of youth organisations.[3] This visit opened minds to new ideas, as did later exchanges with South African youth groups.

The Scouts and Guides had always tried to be non-ethnic and their faith was tested during the crisis. They helped sick and wounded people in hospital, distributed aid in camps for the displaced, helped bury the dead. Because they were seen to be ethnically mixed and neutral they could go where others were frightened to go. Where the Burundi Red Cross was seen as too Tutsi, the Scouts were not. They never allowed soldiers in their vehicles. The Burundian culture of discipline and obedience to the leader has had bad effects at times, as when town youth organised '*ville morte*' demonstrations, but it can be turned to a good purpose through organised, uniformed youth organisations. The popularity of the Scouts, Guides and religious youth movements is evidence of this.

Maison Shalom

Everyone calls her Maggy and everyone in Burundi has heard of her. Marguerite Barankitse is definitely a 'celebrity' and her fame is well merited. Daughter of a wealthy Tutsi family in Ruyigi, she witnessed at first hand the horrors of 1993. Local Tutsis attacked Hutus who were sheltering in the bishop's compound. Some of them were her own students and she tried to stop them, but they saw her as a traitor and they humiliated her in every possible way. Seventy-two people were killed before her eyes, including women and children, though she somehow managed to save twenty-five of the children from slaughter. She also lost most of her own family.

Those twenty-five children became the seeds of Maison Shalom—the Hebrew word for peace, *shalom*, was chosen by some of the children in preference to the Kirundi word *amahoro*, which they thought had got debased by the events in the country. Now, literally

---

3   Muslim Youth and the *Mouvement Xavéri* as well as Scouts and Guides.

thousands of orphan children are living a full life without hatred, eating well, being trained and socially integrated as a result of Maggy's vision. When I met her she was resplendent in a brightly coloured costume. ('They see we have vehicles and I have nice clothes and they say I am a rich woman but they are all gifts.') She is obviously a great extrovert and with her energy and determination she has been able to charm funding—and clothes and vehicles—from the toughest donors.[4] Children come or are brought to her. An effort is made to find their families and to reintegrate them but, she says, 'The children who come remain children of the house. Even if we cut the umbilical cord, we follow them when they marry and we visit them and we create family ties.' She does not see Maison Shalom as an NGO but as an extended family. Children have come from far and wide—from all parts of Burundi, even from Rwanda and Congo. Those who have no surviving family have the option of getting one of the houses which Maison Shalom has built in a kind of village. 'I try not to ask donors for things that make our children dependent, so that one day when we have no donors our work will survive… we shall soon be able to pay 50 per cent of the present staff from what we earn. That is the strength of the Maison. What annoys me is that the government does not support us. Rather, we have become donors by paying fees at secondary schools.' Apart from producing food for the children in Ruyigi, Maggy built a hotel restaurant as a revenue earning and job creation project.

The problem of orphans is enormous. There are estimated to be up to 900,000 in Burundi; about one third of this number is due to AIDS. Maggy may have helped up to 30,000 in 13 years. In addition to the school, farm and village in Ruyigi, she has developed the Cité des Anges, a sparkling community centre which stands out in the rather dull little town of Ruyigi. There is a swimming pool, a library, a garage where young people learn motor mechanics and Burundi's only proper cinema since the closure of the Cine Cameo in Bujumbura. Reconciliation happens informally here in the Cité, as in the JAMAA and Kamenge centres. A hospital was also under

---

4   Donors include Caritas and the UN (World Food Programme, UNICEF and UNHCR).

construction at the time of my visit. The work of Maison Shalom also spread beyond Ruyigi. Amani House[5] opened in Bujumbura in 2005, a centre for orphans and street children. Fees, clothes and food are collected for 10,000 schoolchildren, and another centre was opened close to the Tanzanian frontier to cater for the needs of returning refugees.

Maggy has been awarded numerous international prizes. These give her more fame and enable her to raise even more money from donors, but, in the spirit of the Heroes Summit[6], she asks, 'What about the Hutu women who ran to protect Tutsi children—or the Tutsi mum who hid Hutu kids? Burundians' vision needs to change and Burundians should be proud of their country. The new regime should invest in such people'. Maggy toured Europe to promote her book, *La Haine n'aura pas le dernier mot* (Hate won't have the last word). She says she is proud of being a Christian, part of one human family. Her doors are always open and so many children come that occasionally when she feels overwhelmed and annoyed she says to God, 'Seigneur, today you have nought out of ten.'

Networking for peace

When I was working in Burundi I arranged a small 'day of reflection' in October 1999, bringing together different national and international NGOs and church people to compare and coordinate our small projects. It was the right moment. The situation in the country was deteriorating badly at that time and this little initiative grew rapidly into a network and gave rise to many suggestions for action. The first major result was that nearly 5,000 people took part in a march for peace through the streets of Bujumbura on 29 January 2000. The Scouts, the *Mouvement Xaveri* and Chiro[7] led the march, with the band of the Kimbanguist Church. The same weekend Search for Common Ground organised the *Sangwe* Music Festival. The UN Humanitarian Office (OCHA) saw the value of this networking and funded a full time worker. Some synergy was created and few

5　*Amani* means 'peace' in Kiswahili.

6　See p. 150.

7　Another Catholic youth movement.

joint projects resulted: one such was the Sangwe project for returning refugees described above, another was a directory of peace organisations and their activities.[8]

---

8   Major players in this network were Search for Common Ground, Africare, Christian Aid, JAMAA, SHINE, Ligue Iteka, Oxfam, the Canadian Centre for Study and International Cooperation (CECI), Catholic Relief Services and the Scouts.

Belgian-style art-deco architecture in Bujumbura.

Cyclists hitching a lift on the main road up country.

The Anglican "village church" at Buhiga (Karuzi province).

Renaissance Italy or modern Africa? The enthronement of a new Anglican archbishop in 1998.

What was left of the petrol station at Kibimba after the massacre of 1993, with the monument under construction.

Displaced persons at a camp at Musongati (Rutana province) in 1998.

A widow who lost all her family in the crisis (Mpinga-Kayove, Rutana province 1998).

Batwa women and their pottery.

Women join in a workcamp to rebuild their homes in Kanyosha, Bujumbura.

A tea plantation in Bururi province.

A literacy class in Mutanga Sud, Bujumbura.

A roadside barber's shop in Gitega.

A Twa man
making a pot.

Bananas are a
major crop.

Typical cultivation patterns up country.

Village children dancing.

17

THE MEDIA

Le dialogue vaut mieux que la force. 'Dialogue is better than force.' —Radio Isanganiro slogan

This chapter describes the media scene in 2007. Chapter 22 looks at more recent developments.

Burundian traditional culture is oral and the only important 'medium' is the radio. In spite of poverty, an estimated 85 per cent of Burundians somehow manage to listen to the radio—on the most remote hills as well as in every suburban home and commuter minibus. Radio can be an influence for good but also for evil. Radio Mille Collines had a big part in encouraging genocide in Rwanda. A small Kirundi radio station, Radio Rutomarangingo, based in the Congo from 1994 to 1996, stirred up inter-ethnic hatred at a time when the only station inside the country was the official one, RTNB.[1] What happened in Rwanda showed Burundians the power that radio could exert. Private radio stations could be used to promote understanding and educate the public about tolerance, democracy and much else. Eugène Nindorera commented to me that the media had had the greatest impact on the political landscape because it reached almost everyone in the country. As the quality of the private stations improved, so, faced with competition, did RTNB. During 2005 the radio stations collaborated effectively and were partly responsible for

---

1   Radio Télévision Nationale du Burundi.

147

the success of the elections. In 2006, however, things began to go wrong. The new government became over-sensitive to criticism and began arresting journalists and intimidating the media.[2] It remains to be seen whether this tendency will continue.

Radio Umwizero (Radio Hope) was the first independent radio station with a mission to promote reconciliation and to provide unbiased news. It was set up in 1996 following a visit by the well-known French humanitarian and politician Bernard Kouchner. He visited Rwanda and Burundi and, horrified by the effect of Radio Mille Collines in Rwanda, supported a joint venture between the Association Radio Umwizero and the French Association pour l'Action Humanitaire (AAH) with funding from the European Union's humanitarian budget (ECHO) and some second-hand equipment. AAH had promised to build up the local association but it only provided technical training for the journalists. It broke its promises by neither providing management capacity nor being open about the funding. Antoine Ntamikevyo and other journalists decided to create a different association, Radio Bonesha, which successfully competed for support. Nonetheless, Radio Umwizero remained a strong voice for peace until 1999 when it lost its funding. The association still exists but has no resources. Bonesha, on the other hand, continues to broadcast. Led for some years by Antoine Ntamikevyo, it is a reputable radio station, perhaps more cautious in its reporting than some of the others, but fighting the same battle for freedom and reconciliation.

Search for Common Ground (SFCG) is a groundbreaking American NGO which works for reconciliation mainly through the media. As its first initiative in Africa it set up Studio Ijambo at the height of the crisis in 1995 to promote dialogue, peace and reconciliation. The studio produces radio programmes which examine all sides of the conflict and highlight things that can unite rather than divide Burundians. In Burundi, the absence of dialogue is a breeding ground for rumours and misinformation.

---

2   And yet the Minister of Information from 2005 to 2007, Ramadhani Karenga, used to work for the BBC in London.

Christophe Nkurunziza was one of the Studio Ijambo team of Hutu and Tutsi journalists, themselves a symbol of the unity and understanding that the programmes aim to foster. As a journalist, he recalls, it was hard to know who would tell the truth. Some people hesitated to speak for fear of rebels, others for fear of the army. On one occasion in Bujumbura Rural province, 'We arrived and it was strange—there were bodies of children aged three to five there. While we were investigating, soldiers were frightening the people. We asked what really happened. Two persons took us aside and said that it was the soldiers who had done this, saying it was because rebels had been hiding in their houses—when there clearly were none. They had also killed the father and mother.' After this, the provincial governor, Stanislas Ntahobari, denounced journalists as 'bringers of evil'. On another occasion in Gitega, 'The population trusted us because of what we said on the radio. We talked with the people and they said there were at least 100 bodies buried in a ditch. We could not believe it. The soldiers were surprised that we knew of the burials. They said they were dead rebels. We knew they were innocent civilians. We were able to dig up some bodies—they were all women and children. Only the media could expose such things...' and fortunately the media were free enough to report such things in spite of the governor's strictures. Nonetheless, some accused Studio Ijambo of encouraging 'criminals' by interviewing them, and the opinions of rebels were only allowed to be broadcast in paraphrase. In Bujumbura another problem for a mixed team of reporters at the height of the crisis was that some could not safely enter certain parts of town.

Apart from news magazines, Studio Ijambo has produced radio drama, live interactive programmes, round tables, documentaries, music and children's programmes. A particular success was a popular radio soap opera, *Umubanyi niwe muryango* (A neighbour is part of the family), based on the daily challenges of two neighbouring families—one Hutu and one Tutsi—where listeners can identify with problems faced by others and understand positive, non-violent ways of resolving conflicts. Another wonderful series of programmes, *Inkingi y'ubuntu* (Heroes), recorded real life stories of people who, during the crisis—and even as far back as 1972—had risked their own lives to save the life of someone from another ethnic group, rather in the spirit of the commemoration of the 'righteous among the nations' at Israel's Yad Vashem memorial in Jerusalem. At first some of the interviewees were frightened to talk, even though they were interviewed in their own homes. In Karuzi, for example, some people had been hidden in the roof of a house. It was possible to trace those who had protected neighbours such as these and the story was confirmed by those who had been saved. There was at first some cynicism in Bujumbura as to whether these reports were true, but many people could demonstrate that their children were alive thanks to such good neighbours.

A special Heroes Summit was organised in April 2004 to give recognition to those, some Tutsi and many Hutu, who had taken part in these broadcasts: out of the 200 who were honoured there were nearly 50 women. Leading personalities made speeches, and the popular singer Kidumu and other musicians played in their honour. Some heroes from Rwanda and Congo were also present. Adrien Sindayigaya, the impressive director of Studio Ijambo, gave me an example of a typical story: a man was on the run. The villagers turned over a dugout log of wood used for making *urwarwa* (banana beer) and hid him underneath. The soldier who was pursuing him sat on the log and asked where the man was. The villagers invited him to drink lots of *urwarwa*, which had as it happened been brewed in the same dugout. He drank his fill and staggered off, forgetting why he was there. There were other cases where people were hidden covered in banana leaves in holes where bananas are stored to ripen to make *urwarwa*. Had she lived longer, Perpétue Kankindi's mother, Marianne Nkunzumwami, should have been among the heroes, having saved the lives of many Tutsis. Some of those taking part in the Summit feared being branded as traitors, but nothing of the kind happened. Even extremists recognised that these were people of good faith, though the hard line Tutsi organisation AC Génocide still refused to recognise that many Hutus, not just Tutsis, died in the crisis. The head of a local secondary school wrote to SFGC after the Summit: 'Previously, to say that someone had saved your life during the crisis meant exposing him to dangers from people of his own ethnic group, who would consider him as a traitor. These people of good will had to live in the shadows until now, even though their country needed them. The Summit has thus had an immeasurable impact. The world is full of people famous for their bad deeds. But there are others who act with their heart and faith but we hardly know them. What Studio Ijambo has done is to take these numerous heroes from the shadows and present them in front of the nation as the genuine flames of peace and reconciliation in Burundi.'

The results of all Studio Ijambo's productions have been evaluated through the setting up of listeners' clubs where questions about the content of broadcasts could be raised and discussed. Sadly, in spite of the studio's success, SFCG had to reduce its work in 2005 due to a shortage of funds, but it still survives.[3]

Alexis Sinduhije is one of Burundi's most charismatic and dynamic personalities and a brilliant journalist and now leader of the MSD. He was involved with Studio Ijambo at the time of its foundation but he wanted it to be totally independent and not a project of Search for Common Ground. So he decided to set up an independent radio station, African Public Radio (RPA). The station, on the air since 2000, has sought to inform, educate and amuse the public, and to promote peace by hiring both Hutus and Tutsis, including training up young ex-combatants from both sides as journalists. 'One will tell the other, 'So you were fighting in this area? I was on the front line just opposite you, so we could have killed each other'. Now they are friends...I wanted to humanise relations between the ethnic groups in Burundi and set an example of former enemies working together to build peace.' The station's courageous investigative reporting and grassroots approach to issues affecting ordinary Burundians has earned it the nickname *iradiyo y'abanyagihugu* (the people's radio). It has developed a network of correspondents at a very local level throughout the country: 'We try to give a voice to the voiceless who have had no medium through which to express themselves.' Broadcasts are in Kiswahili and French as well as Kirundi and, although the struggle

---

3   SFCG also set up a network of women's centres and supported youth
     reconciliation initiatives, including JAMAA, see chapter 16.

for funding meant that there were still corners of the country not yet covered, RPA had the biggest audience in the country. It was the radio most likely to be blaring out of crowded minibuses. RPA has played a daring and critical role during the transition. Having had the best contacts with the rebels, it helped both sides to see their opponents in a rational way and rebels to understand that their enemy was the system and not the Tutsi population as a whole. RPA was frequently critical of abuses by the army and the police, of corruption and of human rights violations, and for this it was harassed by the pre-2005 government, which earned Sinduhije the International Press Freedom Award in 2003. The courage and willingness of RPA to criticise the regime when it got some of the same things wrong meant that RPA has been seen as hostile and has been persecuted by the government.[4] Apart from the radio station, RPA built a state of the art recording studio, one of the best in Africa.[5]

A more recent arrival on the scene and another strong voice for peace is Radio Isanganiro ('meeting place'). Janine Nahigombeye, then head of programmes, explained to me that Burundian staff working for Studio Ijambo had for some years suggested that a full radio station, rather than just a studio, would have more impact, but only a few of the staff wanted to take the risk involved. With some funding from Search for Common Ground and the use of Studio Ijambo's facilities, the station was launched in 2002 as a non-profit-making association. Its programmes would concentrate on straight reporting, emphasising concern for human rights, good governance—which includes questions of justice, freedom of expression and land rights in particular—and other real problems that impede reconciliation. Its broadcasts have had an effect on reconciliation, though this is not easy to measure, and on policy. They claim, for example, that their broadcasts led to Burundi's recognition of the International Penal Code. As with RPA, their honest reporting has made them enemies within the government. Matthias Manirakiza, the director, was

---

4   Two RPA journalists were imprisoned and Alexis Sinduhije spent some months in exile.

5   Alexis Sinduhije retired from RPA in December 2007 to found a new political party, the Movement for Security and Democracy (MSD), aiming to promote peace and development.

arrested and imprisoned in 2006. Isanganiro has trained up young journalists and it has built up its audience. Its superior funding and equipment (it was digital from the start) enabled it to be available via the Internet outside Burundi. Its television programmes were available via the Internet. It has an impressive website.

The government radio and television service, RTNB, has changed with the times. Before 1991 it was a government mouthpiece with scarcely a Hutu to be seen or heard. It slowly began to change. Antoine Kaburahe describes it in 1993: 'During this pre-election period it is a veritable nerve centre. In a country where the majority is illiterate...the battle will be fought above all on the radio...The Uprona men guard jealously the only medium and the new political parties find it hard to get onto the air...At the RTNB the weight of the one-party system is still evident, but some journalists display real democratic openness.' He recalls the programme 'Cards on the table' where politicians such as Ntibantunganya and Mukasi battled it out on the air.[6] During the crisis, RTNB tended to support whichever party dominated,[7] but it never became a mere mouthpiece for the army. During the *villes mortes* Celsius Nsengiyumva, a Hutu himself, and his team of journalists managed to maintain a level of objectivity. It has responded positively to the competition provided by the new radio stations. It has been broadcasting some of Studio Ijambo's productions since 1998 and it has its own very popular television soap opera, *Ni nde?* (Who's that?), which has had a positive influence on people's attitudes to each other. RTNB broadcasts in Kirundi, French and Swahili, with a short news broadcast in English. It has also developed a website. Given the present government's heavy-handedness with the private media, RTNB has little chance of maintaining a balance in its reporting.

There are several other radio stations, most of which also promote reconciliation to some degree: Radio Culture, which has been running since 1999 and broadcasts programmes made by Studio

6   Antoine Kaburahe, *La mémoire blessée* (Paris/Brussels: La Longue Vue, 2002).

7   For example, Antoine Ntamikevyo, who was later to run Radio Bonesha, was suspended by RTNB at the end of 1993 for broadcasting more detail about the killings in the provinces than the Frodebu ministers wanted.

Tubane; Radio Ivyizigiro, a religious station which started in 2001, on which CNEB has a weekly spot; Radio Renaissance, run by a former RTNB director, Innocent Muhozi, which began broadcasting in 2003 and was the only private station to have a television service; Radio Ijwi ry'amahoro (Vatican); and Radio Nderagakura (for schools' broadcasts). TransWorld Radio has a studio promoting religion and peace.

A good example of cooperation between different media groups was the creation of a national network to ensure accurate and professional coverage of the constitutional referendum and elections in 2005. This 'Media Synergy', initiated by Studio Ijambo, comprised five radio stations (Bonesha, Isanganiro, Renaissance, Culture and Nderagakura) as well as the Agence Burundaise de Presse and Studio Ijambo itself. The five radio stations broadcast special news broadcasts simultaneously. Over 50 journalists stationed throughout the 17 provinces enabled far more comprehensive coverage than any single radio station could manage.

The BBC broadcasts for 30 minutes six days a week in Kirundi and Kinyarwanda. The service began as a support for Rwandan refugees after the genocide in 1994. The BBC African service and Radio France Internationale are both available on FM in Bujumbura.

If there are too many competing radio stations, the same cannot be said of the press. This consists of one extremely boring government daily paper, *Le Renouveau* (and its Kirundi version, *Ubumwe*), which is mainly distributed to subscribers in offices in Bujumbura. It pedals the government line and advertises available posts. It has recently smartened up its layout and introduced coloured photos. The oldest established journal is the fortnightly Catholic paper *Ndongozi*, which has been going since before Independence. It was, in its day, a strong supporter of Prince Louis Rwagasore and has retained its balanced outlook ever since. By far the best journal is the weekly *Iwacu* which also has an excellent website and produces online reports and interviews. Otherwise the only press tradition has been a number of weekly or fortnightly journals, frequently scurrilous and libellous. For example, at the height of the crisis a leading article in a Tutsi-controlled publication offered a large sum of money for Léonard Nyangoma's head. Another had a headline asking, 'Do Hutus have a soul?' Many journalists have been better trained since then but the current crop of fortnightly and monthly papers represent the various political parties and contain more opinions (and often insults) than facts. The most readable are *L'Aube de la Démocratie* (Frodebu), *Intumwa* (CNDD-FDD) and *Umuco-Lumière*. It is not surprising that Burundians who travel to Kampala or Nairobi are envious of the lively daily newspapers on sale at every street corner. There are several press agencies: the government Agence Burundaise de Presse (ABP) and the traditionally very pro-Tutsi Netpress, which has been an effective critic of all regimes. There are also an increasing number of websites which carry news, true and false, and opinions of all shades. All these printed and on line media can only reach a tiny minority. Radio will remain the dominant medium for many years to come.

18

GOVERNANCE, HUMAN
RIGHTS AND JUSTICE

The culture of impunity and the culture of fear justify and perpetuate each other.
—Ahmedou Ould-Abdallah, UN Special Envoy to Burundi 1993-95

Lasting peace requires justice, not impunity. The judicial system in Burundi was weak and ethnically very one-sided before the crisis and needs thorough reform. The failure to convict the real culprits in notorious cases such as the killing of President Ndadaye, but also in thousands of low-profile cases, has created a culture of impunity. There is no trust in the system: to be convicted is seen as bad luck, victimisation or ethnic prejudice rather than just retribution. Torture, though illegal, is frequently used to obtain evidence or confession. Judges are under political pressure. In 2006 the Supreme Court ordered the release of detainees but the state prosecutor reversed the decision.[1] There is little consistency: similar crimes do not lead to similar sentences. Corruption pervades the system.[2] The failure of justice has resulted in increased violence, especially against women. Many cases of rape by soldiers and rebel fighters were reported dur-

---

1 This was in the case of the alleged coup plotters including ex-President Ndayizeye.

2 An international NGO has no chance of winning a case over (for example) dismissal of a worker. The fact that an international organisation is sure to pay up ensures good rewards for judges, lawyers and litigants.

ing the crisis but they continue, perpetrated by civilians as well as ex-combatants and police. There are also many cases of household violence, a sign perhaps of the breakdown of family tradition and authority. As elsewhere in Africa, this 'modern', though dysfunctional, national judicial system with its 'written' law exists in parallel with the old system of customary law, which is still influential, especially over rights to land and cattle, succession and marriage. The two systems ought to be properly integrated into a judicial system which is comprehensible to all and which answers the real needs of the people.

Burundian and international NGOs have worked hard to improve things. In this chapter I have tried to include a few of the actions and initiatives taken in this context.

The doyen of Burundian NGOs is the human rights league, Ligue Iteka, founded in 1990 with Eugène Nindorera as its first President. It was able to establish itself during the brief flowering of liberty and peace before 1993 and it has tried, and usually succeeded, to hold the line through a very difficult period, speaking for Hutu, Tutsi and Twa, fighting human rights violations and promoting a just society. It has attracted outstanding leaders, including Eugène and his brother Louis Marie Nindorera, Christophe Sebudandi, Pie Ntakarutimana and Jean-Marie Vianney Kavumbagu.[3] Iteka has been active as part of the Human Rights League of the Great Lakes (LDGL)[4] and of the International Federation for Human Rights (FIDH). Its reputation has attracted good funding[5] and this has enabled it to work seriously for justice and human rights.

Details of Iteka's activities can be found on its website. They have investigated human rights violations, listening to those who have had their rights violated, and trained the 'listeners'. They had a team of

---

3 The presidents of Iteka have been: Eugène Nindorera (1991-93), Albert Mbonerane (1993), Gervais Havyarimana (1993-94), Tharcisse Nsavyimana (1994-95), Christophe Sebudandi (1995-99), Pie Ntakarutimana (1999-2003), Jean-Marie Vianney Kavumbagu (from 2003). Louis Marie Nindorera was General Secretary.

4 Ligue des Droits de la Personne dans la Région des Grands Lacs.

5 Main funders have included the Belgian NGO 11.11.11, *Développement et Paix*, NOVIB, USAID, UNHCR, the Canadian Episcopal Church, CECI, Christian Aid.

observers in different provinces who, among other things, reported cases of torture or sexual violence, and ensured that returnees' rights were observed. An important initiative was to transport witnesses and litigants, paying for fuel to enable hearings to go ahead. They organised visits to prisons and police stations to examine conditions and to check whether detentions are legal. They assisted torture victims and tried to convince the police at local level not to use torture. Iteka has also produced a manual to create awareness about good governance and the struggle against corruption.

Pie Ntakarutimana, who became president of the league in 1999, described to me how he got involved in Ligue Iteka. He finished at university in 1990, just as the multi-party system came in, but found joining Iteka, which was led at that time by Eugène Nindorera, more congenial than joining a political party. It was 'a balanced organisation, it suited me…and things eventually conspired to bring me to be head of this association!' After 1993 'it was difficult…the majority of Hutus in the league had fled, but it managed to continue to do extraordinary work. Christophe Sebudandi was running it at this time. I was president of the Youth Commission. I was persuaded to join the committee and was later persuaded to become President. I had worked on setting up clubs in schools when I was in the Youth League. …it was tiring work. We were attacked by the military, by rebels, by the public. You make a statement and you are threatened by the military, you make another and you are attacked by either by Tutsis or by Hutus, or threatened by rebels.' Pie considers that Iteka has made a real difference: people now have more confidence to stand up for their rights, there is more of a culture of open criticism. 'Now,' says Jean-Marie Vianney Kavumbagu, the president after 2003, 'you can speak about human rights without people thinking you are a dreamer.'

Ligue Iteka is not so strong and active in 2015 as in the past. Association pour la Protection des Droits Humains et des Détenus[6] (A.PRO.DH), has become the leading promoter of human rights in Burundi. Led by the highly respected Pierre-Claver Mbonimpa,

---

6   Association for the Protection of Human and Detainees' Rights.

it works for good treatment of prisoners and detainees and assists with psychosocial rehabilitation and reintegration into society and provides information, for example about the international convention on torture, on a very active website. The association collects complaints and testimonies about violations of rights and publicises them in the media.[7] It has put prisoners in touch with lawyers and given them food and medical aid. Micro-credit has been provided for released prisoners to help them integrate into their communities.

Responding to the incidence of torture and sexual violence, a Burundian section of the international organisation, Action by Christians for the Abolition of Torture (ACAT), was established in 2001.[8] Its main aim is to campaign for changes in the law on torture and for changes in the penal code on sexual offences. ACAT members visit detained prisoners and organise focus groups on issues of torture and sexual violence. A study of sexual violence in the suburb of Kinama has recently been produced. ACAT has run a training course on international law and human rights in the course of which police officers were reminded that torture was not permitted. The debate became very lively when the officers learned that in no case could they avoid punishment by claiming they were obeying orders. The president and founder of ACAT Burundi is the young and dynamic Chantal Mutamuriza who has undertaken consultancies for the Human Rights Law Group and International Medical Corps. She has collected and analysed the decisions made by Burundi courts from 1975 to 2000 regarding women and children, in order to make a compilation of law cases.

Christophe Sebudandi was for six years president of the Observatoire de l'Action Gouvernementale (OAG). This watchdog was created by an initiative of Ligue Iteka. About 30 civil society organisations wanted to follow the peace process by monitoring, evaluating and following up government actions, especially those relating to the re-

---

7   In 2005 A.PRO.DH reported 1224 cases of violence, some leading to death, and including many cases of rape. Many incidents took place in broad daylight as the perpetrators have little fear of retribution.

8   More details can be found on ACAT's web site, see Annex 4.

form of the army, institutional reform and the economy. OAG has member organisations including the teachers' union, Ligue Iteka, the Maison de la Presse (Press Club) and also some independent journalists and parliamentarians. OAG publishes well researched studies on all aspects of government. A recent one was on the role of the Constitutional Court on the question of the president's third term; others are analyses of laws, follow up on budget expenditure and treatment of women and minorities. It also lobbies for better governance, makes declarations on important issues[9] and publishes news items relating to Burundion its website. It is hard to measure its influence but, Christophe believes, it has certainly helped the development of a culture of responsibility in the political landscape and the possibility of evaluating individual ministers' or civil servants' decisions on an objective basis, taking no account of ethnic or regional cleavages. OAG has mediated in conflicts such as that between the government and the nurses' union and even that between President Domitien Ndayizeye and Vice President Alphonse-Marie Kadege.

Presidents Buyoya and Ndayizeye accepted the OAG, but the new regime in 2005 was at first highly sensitive even to very constructive criticism. Christophe remarked in 2007 that the government was elected because there was freedom for people to express themselves but 'it is strange that the new regime is trying to deny the system which gave it birth...We hope it's a question of time, of experience. Maybe they will become more open...the position of being a friendly critic of any government is not easy.' To change governance it is necessary to try and influence the government and to do this public opinion has to create pressure. The population has to be informed. This is difficult when the media are muffled and when civil society is attacked as it has been in the CNDD-FDD newspaper, *Itunga*, and on a website which is said to be government-backed. 'Before the election we faced a regime whose legitimacy was challenged and for us it was easy to take advantage of the weakness of this system to increase our freedom, but now we are up against a regime which has the legitimacy of having been elected. And they ask what right we have to criticise them...I have suggested a meeting with all the active actors in civil

---

9   Its voice was heard when Bob Rugurika of RPA was imprisoned.

society so as to debate in a positive way how we can adapt ourselves to the new context, to work for rights and for peace and to help the regime go forward and not isolate itself, so that we do not become its enemy.' Sadly the government has remained very hostile to criticism, however constructive, but at least the OAG has survived.

The national civil society organisations are backed—and in many cases directly aided—by a variety of international organisations which either have representatives in the country or follow events closely from outside. The United Nations office which changed from ONUB to BINUB, then BNUB and now simply the UN country team, along with the UN High Commission for Human Rights, has kept a close watch on human rights and governance issues. NGOs active in this field are the US-based Human Rights Watch, the Belgian Avocats sans Frontières (ASF), RCN Justice et Democratie[10], International Alert and Global Rights. Amnesty International follows events in Burundi closely but has no local representation.

Global Rights is a US-based international NGO working for human rights and especially women's rights. Its policy, where possible, is to work through local civil society organisations to push for legal reform.[11] In Burundi its main concerns are: land and inheritance rights; accountability for war crimes; women's role in government and issues of governance generally. A number of promising, but not necessarily highly educated, individuals have been trained in 'legal clinics' as 'paralegals' on the same basis as paramedics. They learn a little about the law and receive training in listening, counselling and resolving small conflicts—or just become informed citizens. Some of them take on the role that used to be (and often still is) that of the *bashingantahe*, the traditional wise men, who these days sometimes expect payment for their wisdom. Whoever is involved, 80 per cent of the cases in Burundi's courts are about land.[12] Often the courts

---

10   Citizens' Network—Justice and Democracy (Belgian).

11   See Annex 5 for the web site.

12   Law relating to land is unhelpful to the small man. The 1986 Land Act grants legal title to whomever occupies it for thirty years unless claims are made in the first three years, regardless of how the land was obtained. Most such cases relate to land which previously belonged to families who left to become refugees or IDPs.

fail to resolve the issues fairly and most people cannot afford the costs—or the bribes. The paralegals can often help the two parties arrive at a fairer solution. Global Rights works closely with Burundi's active Association of Women Lawyers.

RCN Justice et Democratie[13] has become a major player, also working through local partner organisations for justice and democracy. In 2007 I met the head of RCN in Burundi, Sylvestre Barancira, Burundi's foremost psychologist and a man of varied talents. He ensured that RCN has made good use of the media, using radio to provide digestible information on the law and to retail legal opinions—and villagers' opinions—on the practical problems faced by rural people: divorce, polygamy, child abuse, rape, inheritance, land rights. RCN took as its starting point the dual origin of Burundi's laws, the traditional royal system and the very different colonial apparatus. To create an *Etat de droit,* a state which fully respects legality, involves unifying the two systems, not just by rewriting the law book but also through wide popular education. As with the 'heroes day' organised by Search for Common Ground, RCN has built up a collection of 260 'praises of just actions'[14] from which 19 stories, most dating from the time of the crisis but some traditional, were selected, dramatised and broadcast on Radio Isanganiro as a way of spreading understanding of the law and linking human rights to traditional Burundian cultural values. RCN also promoted a theatre troupe of ten professional performers, men and women, from all ethnic groups, drummers, dancers, poets, writers. Some did not speak French. Some had gone through unimaginable experiences. They would develop a drama through discussion among themselves and with the people of the rural communities where the play was to be performed. *Si ayo guhora* ('Don't keep your mouth shut!') and other dramas deliberately stirred up memories of the bad things that have happened as a way of confronting the problems honestly. Traumatised people need to talk and theatre is a way of healing by unblocking the memory.

When Uprona was the sole party it contained a large number of local development associations, many of which still exist even if they

---

13 See RCN's website for more details (Annex 5).

14 *L'éloge des actes justes.*

have lost their links with the party. These were the type of small rural association that RCN chose as partners, provided that they were now non-party, ethnically mixed and non-discriminatory and had a democratic structure. A major aim was to empower rural people who tend to be socially passive and lacking in influence compared to the civil society organisations based in the capital. RCN collaborates with the women's network CAFOB[15] which includes rural women's groups. Its 2014-16 programme prioritised women's access to justice at a local level. RCN supplements the work of Iteka and A.PRO. DH in trying to improve the quality of justice, especially in the local tribunals. Decisions need to be harmonised, less time wasted on adjournments, fewer people detained, more magistrates trained and appointed. RCN has given direct support to the legal study and documentation centre (CEDJ).[16] From 2010-12 it had a project to protect albinos who suffer discrimination in Burundi.

The work of all these organisations has enabled justice to be done in many cases and it has undoubtedly made the general public more confident of their rights and better informed. Despite many training opportunities for magistrates and civil servants, it is too early to say whether the judicial system has begun to evolve positively—and for the moment impunity still reigns supreme.

---

15 Collective of Women's Associations and NGOs of Burundi.

16 *Centre d'Etudes et de Documentation Juridiques.*

19

POVERTY AND DEVELOPMENT:
THE ECONOMY AS A KEY TO PEACE?

Munda harara inzara bwaca hakazinduka inzigo. 'When someone has nothing to eat, he hates easily.'—proverb

The density of population in Burundi, as in most of the Great Lakes region, is far above what is usual in Africa. This concentration of population was due to the exceptionally favourable conditions in the region—good rainfall through most of the year, fertile soils, a moderate climate, absence of serious disease on the plateau and the fact that the tight and well organised kingdom of Burundi was able to defeat the Zanzibari slavers in the nineteenth century. By the mid-twentieth century most of the forest had been cleared and by the end of the century the demographic pressure was starting to destroy the formerly beneficial ecosystem, even in supposedly protected areas such as the Kibira Forest. Family plots were constantly subdivided, steep slopes were cultivated, soils were getting exhausted and erosion became serious. Pressure on land thus became a cause of conflict and the effect has been that the peasantry, previously fairly contented and well-fed, has become poor and hungry, struggling to survive.

A 'modern' economy developed during the colonial period. Coffee production—by peasants, not on plantations—was established and provided Burundi's main export income. The Belgians also developed the port and some light industries in Bujumbura, which acted as a commercial entrepôt not only for Ruanda-Urundi but also for the huge eastern part of the Congo. Investment in development after Independence and especially during the Bagaza period (1976-87) included the sugar plantations and refinery in the interior (Sosumo); cotton plantations and the Cotebu[1] factory; and increases in the production of tea and tobacco. Other industries included cigarettes, matches, blankets, shoes, batteries, furniture, pharmaceuticals, glass, paint, insecticides, metal piping, nails, barbed wire, toiletries, fruit juice, palm oil, beer and soft drinks. Thus in the 1980s Burundi was showing modest economic progress, though this was soon to be threatened by the instability of world prices for coffee and tea, the relatively high costs of production in a landlocked country with a small market, and the pressure on land and environment mentioned above. The major industries were state controlled. They included coffee and tea processing and packaging, sugar, cotton and the brewery. There was a constant balance of payments deficit which was made good by development aid, mainly from Belgium, France and China, and which led the IMF to impose a structural adjustment programme in the 1980s. The IMF's medicine reduced inflation but led to government cutbacks which—the usual story—hurt the poorest people most.

The twelve years of civil war from 1993 and the nearly three years of embargo imposed after Buyoya's coup of 1996[2] severely battered this already fairly fragile economy. The flight and displacement of a large part of the population affected food production. Coffee bushes were not tended and many were burned in the course of the war. Cattle and goats were killed. Key personnel were killed or emigrated. Development aid began to dry up due to the prevailing insecurity and then stopped entirely during the embargo. From 1993 to 2005 the GDP dropped by an average of 3 per cent per year. In 2005 it was US$700 per capita and by 2012 it had only risen to US$737. Annual investment dropped from 15 per cent to less than 6 per cent. In a good year imports are double the value of exports and in a bad year the gap is much wider. The government has had to borrow from

---

1   *Complexe Textile du Burundi.*
2   See chapter 7.

banks and beg for outside help to survive. Of course, it has also spent a big proportion of its budget on the army and an increasing amount on servicing the debt, which stood at US$1.2 billion in 2003. Unlike some countries, however, Burundi is not a failed state and has always managed to pay government salaries, meagre though they are.

Other indicators show how things got worse by 2004-7. The percentage living below the poverty line increased from 33 per cent in 1990 to 68 per cent in 2004.[3] A large majority of the population lacked real food security and 16 per cent were seriously at risk. Half the population had to walk a kilometre to fetch water. School attendance had reached over 70 per cent but dropped by half during the crisis. Most primary schools lacked drinkable water and any kind of toilet. Literacy was estimated at 60 per cent for males and 45 per cent for females. Malaria spread even into the highland areas, where peoples' resistance is much lower. Health provision and the supply of drinking water deteriorated. The movement of soldiers and rebels infected many villagers with the AIDS virus, though the level of infection in the towns was worse. Over 250,000 were thought to be infected and a similar number of orphans lost at least one parent through AIDS. The majority of hospital beds were occupied by sick people who were HIV positive. Life expectancy dropped to 39, lower than the African average. 20 per cent of children died before their fifth birthday. In 2011 Burundi was 166th out of 169 countries in UNDP's Human Development Index. Thus an elderly widow was unable to cultivate her garden, having lost most of her family through war and disease. An elder child, head of the household, with the children in rags and a very small plot of land, would depend on food aid. Those living in displacement 'sites', which in many cases have turned into permanent villages, were dependent on food aid. People living there, far from their original homes, had no cultivable land. They ended up just waiting for handouts. Families who have land will have to subdivide their plots to an average of 0.3 hectare within 15 years, insufficient to feed a family. Already peasant farmers only scrape a living. They cannot afford seeds and tools and credit

---

3   41 per cent in town but 83 per cent in the rural areas. Figures from various sources, mainly the Poverty Reduction Strategy Paper.

schemes are few. They cannot afford health care. Their voice needs to be heard. It was their votes that brought the new government to power in 2005.

With the peace agreements and ceasefires signed and a legitimate government is in place, more aid began flowing in and the economy began to recover from the low level to which it had fallen. UN figures in 2012 show that life expectancy has risen to 54. The number with HIV is now below 100,000, yet the total number of orphans is over 600,000. 73 per cent have access to drinking water. Burundi qualified for debt relief from the African Development Bank[4] and more widely under the HIPC scheme.[5] It is obvious that future peace and stability depend on a stronger economy and the new government announced how it aimed to reduce poverty and develop the country. For this there needed to be a growth rate of around 7 per cent for a sustained period. The government's ability to succeed depends to a great extent on its ability to obtain enough help from international donors. This in turn will depend on how it is perceived by donor countries—its democratic credentials, its human rights record, its financial honesty, its management capability.

Over 90 per cent of the population is engaged in agriculture, including livestock rearing. Half the GDP and over 90 per cent of export earnings are from this sector. For this to be 'a motor of development', as the government hopes, a lot needs to be done. Coffee, nearly all Arabica, is still by far Burundi's main export, 72 per cent of sales. The country seldom earns less than US$20 million each year and it supports over half a million peasant families. However, production has dropped because many of the bushes are too old and badly maintained, crops have suffered from bad weather conditions and parasites, from war and insecurity—and the world price has been low. Too much of Burundi's output is smuggled to Rwanda where producers have been able to earn up to four times as much. Privatisation of most of those parts of the industry which were state owned

---

4   US$226 million over 38 years (18 per cent of Burundi's debt).

5   The World Bank-IMF Heavily Indebted Poor Countries debt relief mechanism, whereby the country agrees to use the money saved for health and education.

has cut out middlemen and in theory gives a better price to producers, but it is a market price and not guaranteed, so small producers may suffer in bad years. An encouraging development has been the growth of a network of coffee growers' associations determined to fight for a fair deal for the producers. Ocibu, the main state coffee company, is now only involved in quality control and taxation.[6]

Tea has become an important export: production has doubled and provides 16 per cent of exports but investment is badly needed in the processing plants. Most tea is also grown on family plots in areas of high altitude unsuitable for other crops. Good prices are paid and this has discouraged smuggling. The war had a particularly bad effect on cotton growing, but with investment in inputs and irrigation, farmers can be expected to revive this crop. Whether the loss making state textile industry, Cotebu, originally set up with Chinese aid, can stay in business is another question. Once a very successful producer of the brightly coloured cloth worn by women, the factory has been running far below capacity, faced with competition from Asia and from imports of cheap secondhand clothes.

Sugar suffers from the same problem as coffee. It sells for more than double the price in Rwanda. If the state sugar firm, Sosumo, exported the sugar directly, the state would benefit, but it is private people[7] who make money buying sugar and exporting it, while Burundi is sometimes forced to import from Zambia. With irrigation there is potential to enlarge the area of sugar plantations, but private investment would be needed.[8]

Food crops can also be increased with some investment in seeds, back up and irrigation. Wheat production has already increased. There are big possibilities of expansion of rice paddy cultivation as well as other crops such as tomatoes on the Imbo plain. The other

---

6   International Alert has produced an important and excellent report, *Reform of the Coffee Sector in Burundi: Prospects for Participation, Prosperity and Peace* by Jean-Paul Kimonyo and Damase Ntiranyibagira (London: International Alert May 2007), which explains the complex structure of the industry and the options for privatisation.

7   Big exporters of sugar included Mme Buyoya and more recently leading members of CNDD-FDD.

8   I understand the Mauritians may be interested.

main crops are bananas, beans, maize, sorghum, cassava, sweet potatoes, groundnuts, taro (*colocasia*), millet, garden vegetables and fruit. There are two long rainy seasons which allow two crops a year and this is supplemented by irrigated cultivation, mainly of beans and other vegetables, in the drained marshlands along the river valleys. Recent droughts and floods have caused serious damage to these valleys and diseases affect cassava, bananas, and taro.[9] These risks to production require the revival of the agricultural extension service and more appied research.[10] It is tempting to start exporting vegetables, fruit and flowers but the economics of doing this by air are very dubious in the longer term.[11] A balance must also be kept between the food requirements of the whole population and the need for foreign exchange. Properly managed, the export of coffee, tea, cotton, fish, and certain manufactured goods ought to provide a realistic amount of foreign exchange, but not enough for wasteful expenditure on military equipment, government vehicles and presidential aircraft.

The shortage of land, already the subject of dispute as refugees return, is a continuing problem as the population grows. It has the potential to re-ignite conflict. It is a factor that must inform nearly all the decisions taken on rural development. There needs to be strict planning of land use. Exploitation of very steep slopes and marginal land must also be controlled in order to combat erosion. During the crisis, cattle, goats and sheep were stolen, killed and eaten. Cattle are still treated as wealth even though they often serve no economic purpose. It would be better to improve breeds by crossing with foreign stock, but also to control the number of cattle and goats in order to prioritise food and cash crops—and small livestock such as poultry and rabbits should be given priority. The veterinary service needs to be revived. In cooperation with the other states which share Lake Tanganyika, well managed fish production could be greatly in-

---

9 Cassava (manioc) is suffering from mosaic infection, bananas from withering caused by bacteria. These infections are spreading rapidly in the region. Taro has been decimated and new strains are being produced.

10 It is good news that IRAZ, the research institute near Gitega, is returning to full strength under the joint management of the three Great Lakes countries.

11 Flowers are already grown just above Kamenge and flown to Belgium.

creased, as could fish farming in the interior. In the years before the crisis, a programme of planting increased Burundi's forest cover to 8 per cent. After 1993 forests were set on fire to destroy rebels' hideouts and caches of weapons, trees were chopped down for charcoal or to clear land for planting with little state control, and the forest cover is now down to 5 per cent and still falling.[12] To counter this, a tree planting week has been introduced, and efforts are being made to save what remains of the forests. Burundi's environment is fragile and under serious threat.

Burundi's landlocked position means that imported raw materials are expensive, as is the cost of exporting goods. However, labour costs are low and there are good possibilities to export to the Congo and to the south via the lake. Some industries have survived, the strongest being the partly state-owned Brarudi,[13] producing beer and the Coca Cola Company's range of drinks. Soaps, blankets, pharmaceuticals, matches, cigarettes and fruit juice are still produced. Other industries, especially those concerned with processing agricultural products, can and should be developed. Due to World Bank and IMF pressure the government plans to privatise the water and electricity company (Regideso[14]), the telephone group Onatel[15] and two banks, Bancobu[16] and BCB,[17] as well as Sosumo and the tea and coffee processing industry. Workers fear job losses but, if they cannot prevent privatisation, they want at least to be able to become shareholders. Privatisation may lead to better management: the current heads of all state enterprises are political appointees, many of whom lack business experience and are thus often incapable of preventing corruption even when they are not corrupt themselves. Political pressure and unpaid government bills have killed airlines all over Africa, and Air

---

12 A side effect of this is the lower water level in Lake Tanganyika. Another cause was the destruction of a natural dam on the Rukuga River in the DRC where water flows from the lake towards the Congo River. Bujumbura port is badly affected by this drop in the water level.

13 Originally *Brasserie du Ruanda-Urundi*.

14 *Régie des Eaux* (Water Company).

15 *Office National des Télécommunications*.

16 *Banque Commerciale du Burundi*.

17 *Banque de Crédit de Bujumbura*.

Burundi with its one plane is no exception.[18] The belief that political power is the best route to economic power leads to corruption and incompetent management. By contrast, Interbank Burundi, run by a dynamic entrepreneur, Calixte Mutabazi, is making a healthy profit.

In theory it should be good news that Burundi, along with Rwanda, has been accepted as a member of the East African Community, but Burundi's industries need protection. Burundi is also in the Common Market of Eastern and Southern Africa (COMESA), a large grouping stretching from Libya to Angola but excluding Tanzania. Burundi, with its small output, has gained little from this.

Mineral wealth seems more often to be a curse than a blessing to African countries, yet Burundi still dreams of it and the first ambition is to develop the known nickel deposits around Musongati, in Rutana province. Along with the nickel is some vanadium, gold, cassiterite and colombo-tantalite. It is rumoured that CNDD-FDD made promises about these deposits to a foreign business, perhaps Chinese, when it was still fighting in the bush. The main problem is that Musongati is inaccessible, so huge investment would be needed in transport as well as mining. Shorter term ambitions include quarrying to produce cement and ceramics.

Burundi is beautiful, but to develop a viable tourist industry will take time and money. Lake Tanganyika and the hills of the interior would have to be the main attractions. Burundi's few hippos and crocodiles can hardly compete with Kenya or Tanzania or with Rwanda's gorillas, but some beach resorts on the shore of Lake Tanganyika are already developed and are very popular among the Burundians and expatriates working in the country. With some imaginative planning, Burundi could organise joint packages with Rwanda, Tanzania and Zambia, including scenic cruises on the lake.[19]

---

18 When President Nkurunziza went to Uganda for the swearing-in of President Museveni, he commandeered Air Burundi's only plane, taking it out of business for most of the day. He needed to stop at Kigali on the way home. Air Burundi had passengers waiting at Kigali but the President would not share the plane, so it had to go to Bujumbura and then back to Kigali. A company cannot survive in such conditions, although this is not an argument for a presidential jet!

19 The recently published *Petit Futé* country guide to Burundi (in French) describes all the existing tourist attractions and gives a very positive and

A solid transport infrastructure existed in the past. The main roads, which were in many cases well built, were in need of repair and many have now been greatly improved. Tarmac has reached Karuzi and a big new road built between Gitega and Ngozi. Electric power also requires investment: power comes from Bukavu in the DRC and from eight hydro-electric plants, mostly small, but owing to increasing demand the country suffers from frequent blackouts.

The best scenario for Burundi would be to develop a service economy taking advantage of the lake, the airport and a tax-free industrial zone. This was one of Bagaza's proposals. It is a bigger challenge today than it was in 1980. For such a project to succeed, the port would need to be improved, the legal system reformed and banks persuaded to provide better service at lower interest. In the meantime the government must enlarge its tax base.[20] The budget is over-reliant on donor funding, though it is hard to see where enough funding could be found from other sources.[21]

Peasant agriculture will not be able to cope with a population, 10 million in 2013 which is likely to grow to 16 million within twenty years. Burundi is one of the least urbanised countries in the world, but with the increased pressure on land, it is likely that there will be a massive move to the towns where there is already high unemployment.[22] Small enterprises and the informal sector are likely to develop and this process can be assisted by an increased programme of micro-finance—small loans to traders, especially women; dressmaking cooperatives; carpentry workshops; motor repair services. In fact nearly 300,000 people have already benefited from micro-credit schemes.

Education, health services, housing and safe drinking water are the four greatest priorities in the fight against poverty. The formal education system was quite well developed before 1993 but it fell

---

detailed picture of the country.

20 Study visits have been made to Rwanda, whose planning for the future is more advanced, and to Kenya.

21 The auditor-general's comments on the budget as well as other details can be found in the *Burundi Country Report*, Economist Intelligence Unit, 2006.

22 Less than 10 per cent of the population currently live in the towns.

apart during the worst years of the crisis and up to 200,000 children missed out on their education. At least 500 teachers were killed and others fled. One in four primary schools were destroyed. Things started to improve in 1996: primary school enrolment had already recovered even before the new government abolished fees in 2005, which doubled the numbers (but reduced the quality in the short term, with enormous class sizes, until more teachers could be recruited). Kirundi had been the medium of instruction in the first four years, but French is now to be started in the first year with English and Kiswahili added later. At secondary level, schooling was very elitist and, as we have shown, it mainly benefited the Tutsis before 1992. The building of new basic community colleges all over the country gave more of a chance to Hutus, though the standards in these schools are low. There has also been a big increase in the number of private schools, mainly in the capital. Some of the older schools have been rehabilitated, as in the case of Kibimba. However, there are still imbalances. Bururi, Gitega and Bujumbura are better served than other provinces; boys still get more chances than girls; the poorest people, especially the Twa, can now take advantage of free primary education (though they still need to find money for clothing and exercise books), but they have to pay fees at secondary level.[23]

The number of students in higher education has also increased, partly due to a proliferation of small universities, some of which are more like senior secondary schools. The University of Burundi, which has several campuses at Bujumbura and Gitega is more balanced ethnically than in the past. Unfortunately the quality of education provided has declined as a result of a serious brain drain of academic staff, who can earn much more in Rwanda—or have fled overseas.

There are some literacy programmes for those who have missed out on the formal system and the overall adult literacy rate has risen to 86 per cent but it is much lower among women and Batwa. At all levels, equipment is lacking and teachers are badly trained or not

---

23 Girls in school in 1999 were 44 per cent at primary level, 30 per cent in secondary and 25 per cent in higher education. The situation of education in Burundi in 1998-99 and its importance for peace is illustrated in Tony Jackson's excellent report, *Equal Access to Education—a Peace Imperative for Burundi* (London: International Alert 2000).

trained at all, badly paid and lacking in motivation. A few experiments in pre-school education have shown that this can also be an important way of assisting deprived families.

Hospitals and health centres were destroyed or run down during the crisis and many doctors and nurses were killed or fled. Equipment broke down and medicines were hard to come by. The gap was partly filled by international agencies such as Médecins sans Frontières, International Medical Corps and Memisa. Children die of malnutrition or are seriously underweight and they fall victim to infectious diseases. Poverty and poor health create a vicious circle. The government's aim is to restore the network of health centres so that every family is within reach of one. The abolition of fees for maternity cases and for children under five is part of this strategy, though the change was introduced without enough regard for whether drugs and staff were available. The government has improved the provision of clean water supplies and help for poorer families to construct their homes.

Tradition discriminates against women in Burundi more than the law, but their marriage and inheritance rights are not equal. They are badly under-represented in all the professions. They have a problem obtaining credit. More women than men are illiterate. As a result of the war, many widows have to support their families single-handed. Those with husbands often suffer from violence in the home. Rape became common during the crisis when the army or the rebels descended on a family home, stole the goats and the cattle, and raped women and young girls. The end of the war has not led to a drop in the number of cases of rape, sometimes committed by husbands and fathers. Some still believe that sex with a virgin can cure AIDS. It has been noticed that the number of rape cases goes up during the period of coffee sales when men have more money and are presumably more likely to be drunk. Facing up to all these problems, Burundi has an impressive women's movement, spearheaded by CAFOB (Collective of Burundian Women's Associations and NGOs) and the Association of Women Jurists (AFJ). They may still be a minority, but there are many outstanding educated women playing a full part in public life. Women went as observers to Arusha and the provisions in the Constitution have greatly increased the number of women in government posts (over 30 per cent) and in parliament, where 30 per cent of members of both chambers are women. However, there remains a big gap between the educated élite women and the average woman in the rural *collines* or in the poorer suburbs. Gender is always a consideration in every aid project and in the government's anti-poverty strategy, but the battle for equality is not yet won.

Most of the development plans discussed in this chapter are listed in the Poverty Reduction Strategy Paper 2006, produced by the government in collaboration with the UN agencies. The total budget for three years is US$539 million (£300 million). The bigger items of expenditure include: a fund for agricultural inputs; private sector reconstruction; small irrigation projects; campaigns against major diseases; construction of schools, housing for returning refugees, internally displaced and others people such as orphans; integration of vulnerable people including skills training; provision of anti-retroviral drugs for AIDS sufferers. Burundi's economy is so small that the US$126 million of foreign aid in 2006 was seen by the President as something to boast about.[24] If corruption could be controlled and good management developed, a doubling of international aid would make a huge impact in Burundi and represent a first step towards significantly reducing poverty.

---

24 This consisted of $75m from the World Bank, €10.5m from the European Union, $2m from the African Development Bank, $38m from bilateral donors such as Belgium, France, Germany and the UK. He also announced that customs revenue and tax had increased from $212m in 2005 to $232m in 2006.

20

INTERNATIONAL ORGANISATIONS[1]

In Bujumbura city you will see a large number of 4x4 vehicles painted with the agencies' logo and frequently a young *muzungu* (white) inside. There are large numbers of international non-governmental organisations (INGOs) working in Burundi. Is this the new colonialism? Do INGOs create dependence rather than development? Have they created an internal brain drain by paying better salaries to local staff than the government can afford? To a degree all these questions can be answered in the affirmative. For example, a lot of NGOs moved into Burundi when Rwanda blew up in 1994, some of which were looking for a role rather than responding to a need. Occasionally INGOs are insensitive to local customs and structures. However, I believe the balance still weighs heavily in their favour. They have attracted a lot of extra money to the country—their own funds plus grants from the European Union, 'northern' governments, international companies and foundations. During the crisis years they saved many lives. Basic health services were helped to survive and they enabled a modest amount of development to continue in spite of the embargo and the war.[2] They have propped up the

---

1   See Annex 5 for the web sites of the organisations mentioned in this chapter.

2   Two examples: (1) when Belgian cooperation stopped after the 1996 coup, the agricultural complex at Kimeza (Kirundo province) was abandoned, leaving overgrown fields and orchards and ruined buildings. Christian Aid was able to fund the Anglican church (EEB) who revived this project,

delicate plant that is Burundian civil society. The government quite rightly has power to regulate INGOs, to limit the number and type of organisations in the country and the number of expatriate staff. INGOs cannot easily appoint an expatriate if there are Burundians equally qualified. Expatriates, by the way, are frequently from other African countries. (This is even more the case with the UN agencies. West Africans with their excellent French fill the bill nicely.)

The INGOs mostly fall into three categories. There are the humanitarian relief agencies whose role is to react to desperate situations. They include the various national versions of Médecins sans Frontières and of Caritas; also the French organisations Solidarités and Action contre la Faim. They see their involvement as short term and they therefore tend to show less interest in understanding the cultural context or in training local staff. Given the level of poverty in Burundi, some of them seem prepared to stay on for a longer time, but their main 'mission' is relief, and as soon as conditions in Burundi improve, they will be off to wherever the next disaster has struck. It is sometimes argued that humanitarian aid reduces help for more sustainable development, but that is not a reason to refuse to respond to genuine suffering, even if the action is a just a palliative.

The second category are NGOs that may have started life as relief organisations but now prefer to work for sustainable development, though they still respond to humanitarian needs in the short term. ActionAid, CARE International, Catholic Relief Services (CRS), Christian Aid, International Rescue Committee (IRC), Norwegian Refugee Council, World Vision and Concern Worldwide fall into this category. The third category is a growing number of INGOs concerned with governance, peace, law and human rights issues. Global Rights, RCN and ACAT were described in the previous chapter. Others are Avocats sans Frontières (Lawyers without Bor-

---

laid on irrigation, developed livestock breeding etc. (2) IRAZ (Institut de Recherches Agronomiques et Zootechniques) was a joint research institute at Gitega funded by Burundi, Rwanda and Congo. By the 1990s only Burundi supported it and it could not afford to do any research. World Vision came in and supported research on varieties of potato and Christian Aid on new strains of taro (*colocasia*). Its joint government funding has just been restored.

ders), Search for Common Ground, International Alert and Human Rights Watch.

An awkward question for all international agencies—including the UN—is how to balance the ethnic make-up of their staff. Owing to the history of exclusion from higher education, qualified Hutus have been in short supply (and qualified Batwa like gold dust). Add to that the fact that most the existing staff involved in recruiting and interviewing are also mostly Tutsis, whose enthusiasm for their agency's policy may be less than their interest in placing a friend or relative. Changing from the mainly Tutsi *status quo* has been slow, though a number of INGOs put extra resources into recruiting Hutus and there have been numerous training programmes. Typical of UN agencies was WFP, whose director told me in 1998 that he had been shocked to discover that of 102 staff only two were Hutus.

Quite apart from the security risks of working in a country at war, all the international agencies have faced a problem of death threats—and in Burundi these have to be taken seriously. A driver is sacked and a week or two later the director might receive a letter with a couple of bullets inside it. If an expatriate has an affair with a Burundian girl, he may find her former boyfriend literally on the warpath. Motives are not always clear: former directors of ADRA (the Adventist Development and Relief Agency) and of ActionAid were killed in the 1990s. Reference has been made to the death of Kassy Manlan, head of WHO. Others who faced threats discreetly left the country—or brazened it out.

Although their emphases are different, almost all the INGOs could be said to be working for peace and reconciliation—by creating economic and physical wellbeing, by trying to ensure that staff teams and beneficiaries are ethnically mixed, and through various reconciliation and public education projects. An increasing number of INGOs now try to work through local partner organisations. Christian Aid was a pioneer in this and worked for many years without field offices. Other agencies have developed partnerships with small, local groups which, in many cases, they have helped to create. Choosing the right partners also enables INGOs to direct resources towards people working for peace at a very local level. A few examples of INGOs' peace building activities follow.

The first two INGOs to come into the country with reconciliation as their primary aim were the British-based International Alert (IA)[3] and the American Search for Common Ground (SFCG). The UN Special Envoy, Ahmedou Ould-Abdallah, concerned at the uncoordinated multiplicity of INGOs, planned a conference which International Alert agreed to host in London in 1995, to which all INGOs interested in Burundi were invited. Following this, IA began to work at the level of the political élite to bring the opposing sides into dialogue. At the time it was the only such meeting point. IA has maintained a presence in the country, with different staff members visiting at intervals to collect information, keep in touch with developments and write reports, including a very useful report on education.[4] IA moved on to provide technical assistance, financial resources and sustained accompaniment of civil society groups, particularly women's associations. The strategy is to support local partners working at all socio-political levels in their efforts at reconciliation at community level, promotion of women, action/research and advocacy. On the basis of this contact at local level International Alert is able to make its voice heard at an international level.

Search for Common Ground had a different starting point. As we have seen in chapter 17, its speciality was to work through the broadcast media, through the work of Studio Ijambo and the support of the independent station, Radio Isanganiro. Also from the start, SFCG saw that working with women was likely to be a successful approach to peacemaking. The Women's Peace Centre was opened in 1996, as a contact point for over 200 small women's associations which benefited from training provided by SFCG in conflict resolution, leadership, organisational development and transparency. Regional women's centres were opened all over the country.[5] SFCG has also supported reconciliation activities among youth, including

---

3   The UN Special Envoy, Ahmedou Ould-Abdallah, was critical of many INGOs but worked closely and happily with IA and SFCG. A. Ould-Abdallah, 'Burundi on the Brink' (US Institute of Peace, 2000), pp. 84-7.

4   Tony Jackson, *Equal Access to Education: a Peace Imperative for Burundi* (London: International Alert, 2000).

5   Funding problems have led to the closure of these, but they operated during the vital transition period.

the rehabilitation of child soldiers. It was an important support to JAMAA, especially for the production of the comic books.[6]

Reconciliation can be promoted on a 'bread and butter' level (a more Burundian epithet might be 'cassava and beans'). In the crisis years CRS and Christian Aid were involved in distribution of seeds and tools—bean seeds and hoes. Distribution was organised through local partner organisations, mostly local church people who, with the help of government administrators, would try to draw up lists of the most vulnerable people and to ensure that there was no ethnic bias.[7] This programme could not easily be evaluated in terms of reconciliation. It did, however, enable poor peasants to continue to feed themselves through the crisis years. Hand-outs can create dependency, so it was always made clear that this was a short-term programme. Similar comments could be made about the distribution of 'non-food items' (clothing, pots and pans, roofing sheets[8]) which were distributed at times of special need—and unfortunately sometimes confiscated by the rebels the following day.[9] Vulnerable people such as widows and orphans who were heads of households were targeted when INGOs supported house building programmes, again usually on an ethnically balanced basis, though there have been a number of housing projects specifically for the Twa community.

Some projects are designed to promote development and reconciliation at the same time. An example is the distribution of goats. In Ngozi province CARE International started by identifying the most needy families. Godelieve Ntakarusho, a Hutu, was one who qualified. When her goat had twins, the plan was that one of them was passed on to her former Tutsi neighbour, Evelyn, who had fled to live in a displacement camp. According to plan, the neighbours duly became friends again and Evelyn decided to return to her original home. CARE's programme worker, Rehema Rashid, has helped make many such old and new friendships blossom. It is hard

---

6   Refer to JAMAA in chapter 16.

7   The lists had to be carefully monitored to see that vulnerable people benefited.

8   Often these appeared in anglicised French as *'le non-food'* and *'le sheeting'.*

9   CRS was the coordinating agency for 'non-food items'.

to measure and evaluate the effect on reconciliation of projects like this: the number of baby goats can be counted, and CARE collects anecdotal evidence to see how many Tutsis like Evelyn have returned home, but it is all rather subjective. CARE has also organised training through its local partners, targeting women and young people. Espérance Rudeyideyi is one woman whose determination to do something was sharpened by this training. Instead of killing the thieves who used to come from the neighbouring suburb, she organised her community group to talk with the robbers, and the tactic has worked. She acquired the nickname 'mother of reconciliation'.

ActionAid came to Burundi in 1976, one of the first foreign agencies to arrive. When ActionAid began it was a rather paternalistic British charity mainly concerned with sponsoring children at school. I remember seeing their advertisements in the newspapers with photos of little, thin Burundian schoolchildren. The agency has transformed itself into one of the most progressive, recruiting most of its senior staff from the countries it seeks to help and giving the grass roots maximum influence in the running of its programmes.[10] In Burundi its main work has been in Ruyigi province where it has worked with community groups, helped people return to their homes and supported the revival of agriculture and local health services. After the bloody events of 1993, which even involved killings at ActionAid's office in Ruyigi, reconciliation became the basis of the agency's work. This included seminars and meetings, training of key people such as *bashingantahe* and publishing a successful monthly community newsletter, *Ejo*,[11] which countered false rumours and provided balanced local news. Especially useful was the 'Reflect' project which worked with over 3,000 villagers in 84 centres. Each group had two facilitators, a Hutu and a Tutsi, and ran literacy classes, drama and sports activities. The newly literate villagers wrote many of the articles in *Ejo*. John Abuya, who was ActionAid director during my time in Burundi, told me that before 1998, when there was a rebel attack the Tutsis and Hutus fled in different directions, but as a result of ActionAid's efforts, both groups began to flee together. ActionAid,

---

10 It has set up its international secretariat in South Africa.

11 *Ejo* can mean either 'yesterday' or 'tomorrow' according to the context.

with support from British aid, has also been a main player in the fight against HIV/AIDS.

The African Centre for the Constructive Resolution of Disputes (Accord), based in South Africa, first ran exchange visits between Burundi and South Africa of parliamentarians and youth groups (including youth from the conflict-torn KwaZulu-Natal). When Nelson Mandela took over the role of facilitator, Accord organised consultations with Burundian civil society organisations so that their views could be represented at Arusha. Since it opened an office in 2003, the main activities (supported by DFID) have been training civil society organisations and some government workers in conflict management; contact with rebel groups to help them negotiate; and training of some members of the African peacekeeping mission (AMIB). Burundi was the winner of the Africa Peace Award 2006, hosted by Accord in Durban, for 'outstanding achievements in set-tling years of civil war'. With support from the UN High Commis-sion for Refugees, Accord has also established 'legal clinics', staffed by lawyers and volunteers, which inform returnees about their rights, listen to their problems, provide a mediation service in case of conflict (land being the most obvious cause) and generally promote dialogue and an atmosphere conducive to permanent harmony. The Norwe-gian Refugee Council has also set up legal clinics, especially for land conflicts, in other provinces.

CECI, the Canadian Centre d'Etudes et de Coopération Inter-nationale (Centre for Study and International Cooperation) which is supported by the Canadian government aid agency (CIDA), concentrates on trying to strengthen civil society, organising a series of meetings on the usual priorities: peace and security; democracy and governance; integrated development; humanitarian response. CECI has helped local partners including Action Citoyenne pour la Paix (Citizens' Action for Peace), the Women's Peace Network, the Scouts and Women Heads of Families.

As in most of the poorest countries the presence of United Na-tions agencies is very noticeable. Their 4x4's are also racing round the streets of Bujumbura, but on the roads up country you are less likely to see an expatriate inside than in the INGO vehicles. This is due to the UN system's paranoia about security, which gravely reduces its effectiveness and increases its cost. When, after the incident at Muzye in 1999, almost the whole country was declared to be too dangerous for UN personnel, most of them were sent to vegetate at hotels in Nairobi—and they stayed there for months. INGOs generally continued to work, though they tried to avoid unnecessary risks. Such UN vehicles that did go to the interior went in convoy.

We have noted the conversion of the African peacekeeping force into United Nations Operations in Burundi (ONUB). During its short stay, this force did a lot of useful things. It supervised disarmament and demobilisation of rebels and government forces. It helped train the new police force. It helped with logistics and with the monitoring of the elections of 2005, provided security for some humanitarian operations and support for a few specific development and governance programmes. ONUB left before peace with the FNL was consolidated. In 2006 ONUB was replaced by the UN Integrated Office in Burundi (BINUB), which was an office, not a military force, which reduced its effectiveness. BINUB's priorities were: consolidating peace and democratic governance (mainly helping to build the government's capacity and influence its behaviour); continuing to help with disarmament, demobilisation and reintegration of ex-combatants, including with the FNL; promoting human rights and justice, including helping to set up the proposed 'truth commission' and special tribunal; and coordinating all the UN agencies, along with INGOs and bilateral aid programmes, e.g. USAID, DFID, Belgian and French cooperation.

Burundi, together with Sierra Leone, has been chosen to receive support from the new United Nations Peace Building Commission which provides support and funding for countries recovering from conflict.

In 2011 following a Security Council resolution the UN office in Burundi became BNUB with similar aims: to strengthen the independence, capacities and legal frameworks of key national institutions; to promote dialogue; to fight impunity and protect human rights. BNUB's mandate ended in December 2014 but the UN retains an office in Burundi. The gradually reduced size of the UN presence has been a response to the government's dislike of interference by the UN or any other outside body.

The UN Office for the Coordination of Humanitarian Affairs (OCHA) grew out of the UN Development Programme (UNDP), and traditionally in Burundi the head of the latter is the 'humanitarian coordinator'. The large number of INGOs working in the country need to be coordinated and OCHA, although its remit is only humanitarian, helped coordinate all INGO activities. OCHA tried to build preparedness for human and natural disasters and it collected information on all aspects of humanitarian response. It played a big role in the preparation of the consolidated appeal for funding for all the UN activities in the country. The UNDP has concentrated on reintegration of the population, capacity building and restoring infrastructure. Its 'Consolidation of Peace' programme supported integrated development in seven provinces: health centres, marshland farming, training, youth activities, conflict management. United Nations Volunteers (UNV) are managed by the UNDP and there are usually about 20 of them working in Burundi. Most of them are well qualified Africans who work within the various UN agencies on capacity building within government, environment, gender, community development and documentation.

The Great Lakes Region has seen the movement of huge numbers of refugees since 1959. The UN High Commission for Refugees (UNHCR) continues to have a difficult job. It helped many thousands to return from Tanzania.[12] This involved providing transport and a 'returnee package' (a few months' basic food supply, household goods, seeds, tools). They have also had to cope with Congolese and Rwandan refugees coming into Burundi. The UNHCR appealed for US$23 million in 2007 to continue enabling Burundian refugees to return 'in safety and in dignity' and to find tolerable conditions in their home areas; also to look after Congolese refugees and help them return home. The UNHCR has also encouraged Burundi to pass an asylum law which would enable many vulnerable individuals to have their situation regularised.

---

12 The United States has agreed to receive 13,000 Burundians from the camps in Tanzania. These are people from the 1972 exodus who cannot be integrated in Tanzania, cannot or will not return to Burundi and fit criteria laid down by the Americans.

Food security is a continuing concern in a country which has suffered war, displacement of population, subdivision of land holdings, soil exhaustion, drought, flooding and crop failure due to climate or disease. The World Food Programme (WFP, or PAM in French) supplies food for up to 800,000 people a month, dutifully distributed by INGOs such as CARE and the Tear Fund. The need continues especially when there are periods of drought, which has badly affected Kirundo and Muyinga provinces. The WFP provides the food for returning refugees; for pre-school and primary school children; for vulnerable groups – nursing mothers, malnourished children including orphans, and handicapped people. It understands that handing out food is not the way to self-sufficiency and development, but the UN can often provide surplus food more easily than money and there seems to be some political pressure to keep on doling out food even when there cannot be said to be famine.

An increasing proportion of Burundians are children in spite of a very high infant mortality rate. Most primary schools have no drinking water and many have no latrines. UNICEF tries to intervene wherever children are concerned: helping to provide water supplies to schools, immunising children, helping with the resettlement of former child soldiers. The government's policy of free education has doubled enrolment. UNICEF and its partners have provided materials to over 150,000 newly enrolled children.

Other UN agencies represented in Burundi include the Food and Agriculture Organisation (FAO), the parent of the WFP, which advises on agriculture, livestock, forestry and fisheries and operates (again through INGOs) an early warning system on food security, or the possible lack of it; the World Health Organisation (WHO/ OMS), which oversees and maintains records on immunisation, the incidence of diseases, staffing and provision in the health sector; the UN Population Fund (UNFPA); and UNESCO, which has given support to the secondary schools, to some peace education initiatives and to a proposed definitive history of Burundi.[13] UNESCO has also supported the establishment of a 'Chair of Education for Peace and

---

13 Not to be confused with the government's proposal for a rewritten history, see chapter 21.

Conflict Resolution', in collaboration with the University of Burundi and with financial support from some Belgian agencies. In effect, this is a small independent department aiming to promote research, training, information exchange and documentation on peace education, conflict resolution, human rights, tolerance and democracy; and to link up with universities outside Burundi and with schools. It runs courses for a Diploma (DESS) in Human Rights and Peaceful Conflict Resolution, taught by Burundian and Belgian lecturers, and targeted at magistrates, civil servants and even politicians who spend six months on theory and six months on research in their particular field of work. The department also runs training sessions and workshops for teachers, youth workers and others dealing with young people

This UNESCO project is one of many training schemes that have been started in the wake of the peace process for civil servants, magistrates, army and police personnel. Another was the Burundi Leadership Training Programme, funded by USAID and DFID. Ninety five key individuals, Hutu, Tutsi and Twa, 30 per cent of whom are women, and among whom are ministers, *chefs de cabinet*, media people, police chiefs and army top brass and leaders of political parties, would go on a six-day retreat, followed by training in things like conflict management and decision making. No *per diems* were offered. To many Burundians this is heresy, for a supplement to their meagre salaries is greatly prized. At first many refused to take part because of this, but the reputation of these courses was such that, after a time, candidates were begging for places. Yet another training scheme is provided by Development Alternatives Inc. which developed a curriculum for one week of training for local administrators in every commune in the country.

The World Bank also maintains an office in Bujumbura which helps draw up funding proposals and monitors and evaluates them. It keeps a watchful eye on the government's management of the economy. World Bank funding is an important part of Burundi's development funding and the Bank is able to exert a lot of pressure on the government.[14]

---

14 The scandal over the sale of the presidential plane, described in the next chapter, caused the Bank to threaten to freeze US$70 million promised to Burundi.

THE PRESENT AND THE FUTURE

21

NKURUNZIZA'S FIRST TERM 2005 – 2010

Igiti kigororwa kikiri gito, 'Correct a tree's faults before it is too late.' —proverb

Pierre Nkurunziza came to power in very favourable circumstances. His party had a big majority and he secured almost all the votes in the joint sitting of the National Assembly and the Senate.[1] All the major parties accepted the election result. The prospect of a stable government, an integrated army and an end to the war gave rise to optimism, even among opponents of the new regime. The President's inaugural speech was conciliatory and he took care to be inclusive when forming his government. A Ngozi man himself, he appointed Martin Nduwimana, an Uprona Tutsi from Bururi, and Alice Nzomukunda, a CNDD-FDD Hutu from Bujumbura, as Vice Presidents. While most ministers were from the President's party, three posts were awarded to Frodebu; one each to Uprona and three small 'Tutsi' parties; and the Ministries of Defence and Justice to non-party members. The line-up included technocrats as well as party stalwarts. It was not easy to combine political realism with a complex constitution which laid down ethnic and gender quotas, but, in general, the constitution was respected. Women were rewarded with 30 per cent of government posts including a vice presidency,

---

1 Some say the opposition parties should have named a candidate. It would have been less like the coronation of Peter which helped to create a 'one party' mindset among CNDD-FDD members.

the key ministries of foreign affairs, justice and trade, the presidency of the National Assembly, two deputy presidencies in the Senate and four provincial governorships. Frodebu and Uprona were right to be angry at not being consulted on the appointments as the constitution requires. However, in spite of the criticisms, there were no appeals to the Constitutional Court.

The constitution is vague about the appointment of Governors. In the event, thirteen Hutus and four Tutsis were nominated by the President, including a total of four women. Administrator posts were allocated to Hutus (86) and Tutsis (43) by the electoral commission. The quota for heads of state enterprises is 60/40. The appointments were nearly all from CNDD-FDD and they unfortunately included politicians without management qualifications. Those who lost their jobs were mostly Frodebu people.[2]

Although it followed the rules, it is questionable whether this government is really 'consociative'.[3] The 'Tutsi' parties (G10) had always insisted that the 40 per cent of Tutsis should be from 'Tutsi' parties and they would not be wrong to point out that some of the Tutsis in the majority parties were unprincipled job seekers. The quotas laid down are meant ultimately to provide protection to minority groups. This would be problematic in a case where the minority was determined simply to block the government's actions, as happened in 1993–6. Given the nature of the current Tutsi representation, a more likely scenario would be that the Tutsi members of CNDD-FDD would put their politics above their ethnic group and fail to protect the perceived interests of the 'political' Tutsis. In the Senate the 'eth-

---

2   Information from the Burundi Country Report of the Economist Intelligence Unit (Feb. 2006).

3   The theory of 'consociationalism' was developed by Arendt Lijphart and its relevance in Burundi, Rwanda and the DRC is discussed in René Lemarchand's article in African Affairs (Volume 106 Number 422) op. cit. He characterises it as 'a major restructuring of power relations through a more inclusive participation in policy making, accompanied by corresponding spheres of autonomy for the groups concerned.' See also Stef Vandeginste, 'Théorie Consociative et Partage du Pouvoir au Burundi,' (Institut de Politique et de Gestion du Développement, University of Antwerp). Vandeginste wonders to what extent the new dispensation really integrates both sides and marginalises the extremes.

nic' balance is 50/50 and the size of CNDD-FDD's majority in 2005 was such that the absence of just one opposition senator would have given the government a two-thirds majority and thus carte blanche.

The election defeat threw Frodebu into crisis. Jean Minani, who had a conciliatory approach to the new government, was ousted as leader and replaced by Léonce Ngendakumana, who favoured tougher opposition but also demanded more government posts. In March 2006 Frodebu decided to withdraw from the government coalition, but the three Frodebu ministers put their oath to the President—or their wish to keep their jobs—above their party loyalty. They remained in post but were expelled from their party. In various ways the government seems to have tried to humiliate Frodebu, first by offering only three government posts, without consultation, then by removing nearly all those whom Frodebu had appointed to manage state enterprises and, in August 2006, by arresting ex-president Ndayizeye on clearly trumped-up charges of plotting a coup. Uprona, which did even worse in the elections, was also in crisis and failed to heal the split with the faction led by the hardliner Charles Mukasi.

President Pierre Nkurunziza was born in 1963. His father, one of the many Hutus killed in 1972, had been a member of parliament and Governor of Ngozi and Kayanza provinces.[4] Of Pierre's six siblings, five lost their lives in the crisis and only one sister remains. Pierre graduated top of his class in education and sport at the University of Burundi and he was working there as a lecturer[5] when the campus was attacked by the army, killing many students. 'I was pushed into rebellion by the inter-ethnic massacres that were taking place at the university in 1995.'[6] Attackers shot at his car, but he got out and ran away. He always claims that the war was forced on the Hutus, that they did not start it. His nickname in CNDD-FDD was *umuhuza*, the unifier: he was promoted to the post of Deputy Secretary-General in 1998 and in 2001 he was elected as Chairman,

---

4   Nkurunziza is said to hate wearing a tie as it reminds him of his father's death.

5   He also taught at ISCAM, Burundi's military academy, which was useful preparation for fighting in the bush. He even coached the army football team.

6   Quoted by Charles Bigirimana, BBC Burundi analyst (August 2005).

a post he vacated when he became a presidential candidate. O f t e n anglicised as Peter (or Pita), the president started off well and was popular, especially in the rural areas, playing the role of 'man of the people' convincingly. His arrival in Gitega from exile on a bicycle in 2004 was a brilliant piece of theatre. He is still crazy about sport and regularly plays football with his team, 'Hallelujah 11.'[7] He misses no chance to visit projects and to be seen among the people, and is also a devout born-again Christian, seeming to believe that it is God's will that he should rule Burundi. He explained: 'When I am in church, I pray and devote myself exclusively to God. And when I am in politics, I do the opposite, while at the same time acknowledging that God is everywhere.'[8] It has been said of his style both on the pitch and in politics: 'During much of the match he seems passive, absent. Then, suddenly, he takes control of the ball and shoots at the goal with incredible force.'[9] He spends more time in church and on the football field than in politics[10] and this has not left him much time to run the country: in 2006 critics commented that he did not run the country. He left that to Hussein Radjabu, then president of the party. It was in fact Radjabu who had masterminded Peter's rapid promotion, believing he would be a puppet president he could control. Radjabu was soon to be disappointed.

The government's initial priorities, as indicated in the President's inaugural speech and in several interviews, were national reconciliation; greater transparency and 'an exemplary fight against those embezzling the national riches'; 'fighting poverty and famine in line with the Millennium Development Goals'; and 'the rehabilitation of the truth' by re-writing Burundi's history. CNDD-FDD had not discussed all its policies thoroughly in advance and the impression remained that some decisions were taken 'on the hoof' with a lack of careful planning. However, many of the development proposals

---

7   He has built a football stadium near Ngozi (see chapter 23).

8   Quoted by Charles Bigirimana of the BBC.

9   Maria Malagardis, *Libération*, 31 May 2015.

10 His church is the Eglise du Rocher in the INSS Quarter in Bujumbura.

listed in the Poverty Reduction Strategy Paper[11] were realistic, while others were perhaps too ambitious.

Nkurunziza's desire for reconciliation between Hutus and Tutsis seemed to be sincere, though he ensured that top jobs were held by Hutus. While they were still fighting as rebels, the CNDD-FDD leadership saw things in very 'ethnic' terms but, as they approached the possibility of power, they began to accept that it was the old system that was their enemy, not the Tutsis. Many Tutsis have been welcomed into CNDD-FDD, much of the old military top brass is on board and the extremists on both sides were sidelined. Yet on a political level there was a distinct lack of reconciliation with Frodebu and a very grudging attitude towards reconciliation and negotiation with Palipehutu-FNL which Nkurunziza continued to refer to as a 'terrorist group' and 'now irrelevant'. On transparency, governance and human rights, the slogans have sadly borne no relation to the government's behaviour. Early on the President gained extra popularity by announcing free primary education and free maternity care, and later by stopping prices of electricity and water from being doubled. These decisions have been criticised as acts of faith rather than realism, when teachers, medicines or a sufficient budget were lacking, but they were generally welcomed.[12] The history project is no longer being promoted actively.

The government had limited room for manoeuvre. It needed access to the IMF's Poverty Reduction and Growth Facility. As a Heavily Indebted Poor Country (HIPC) it needed to work towards full debt relief. It needed the World Bank and it needed aid from the European Union and the West. It was therefore susceptible to pressure on its economic policies—it could not, for example, resist privatisation of the coffee industry[13]—and on its governance and human rights

---

11 See chapter 19.

12 Free education and maternity care were policies suggested, I am told, by Alexis Sinduhije before he decided to oppose the government.

13 See chapter 19. Privatisation was pushed by the World Bank and coffee growers 'have been shut out of the reform process, despite coffee producer organisations showing themselves open to reform of the sector' according to experts Olivier De Schutter and Cephas Lumina, who called on the World Bank to consider the human rights implications of privatisation. Peasants

record. The detailed policy proposals for poverty reduction required a lot of donor funding as well as increased tax revenue.

The government began well and there was optimism in the air. However, as all governments do, it started making controversial decisions which offended or disappointed sectors of national and international opinion. In November 2005 a commission began the work of identifying political prisoners. Half of the 7,000 in prison claimed this status. Some were released 'provisionally' even before the commission reported and some of those identified by the commission had been accused of such serious crimes that they should face a proper trial. In this context the government supported the establishment of a Truth and Reconciliation Commission (CVR), as proposed by the UN (this body was finally established in late 2014. The fear among NGOs and churches that the government would influence the appointment of the commissioners and thus protect some of the CNDD-FDD people likely to be accused of crimes committed during the rebellion was justified. It will not help pacify Burundi's demons[14]).

Serious disappointment began early in 2006 at the direction the government was taking. Parliamentary scrutiny of the government had generally been feeble. Frodebu and Uprona were wrapped up in their own problems and the most cogent opposition at that time came from Léonard Nyangoma and his small CNDD party. There may have been an element of sour grapes: Nyangoma had not forgiven those who removed him from the leadership of the main CNDD-FDD. He criticized the sudden decision to provide free primary education and free maternity care as populist and irresponsible. He blamed the President for making wild promises to build dams, airports and universities;[15] and to increase the salaries of the better off civil servants, thus widening the gap with the poor majority.[16]He

---

have lost out and many have destroyed coffee plants and are growing beans instead.

14 See chapter 25.

15 President Nkurunziza promised all these things, including a large new airport at Bugendana to serve Gitega.

16 The civil servants really deserved a raise, though it was not in the budget.

made a number of specific accusations of corruption. He rightly questioned the purchase of a new presidential jet plane. The old one, a perfectly serviceable Falcon 50 jet valued at US$6,848,750 was sold for less than half it was worth.[17] Few were convinced that the president of one of the world's poorest countries, a man who championed the poor, needed a jet plane at all. Nyangoma also claimed that part of the funding for repairing the Bujumbura–Rumonge road was diverted and that the SOSUMO sugar company monopoly had been handed to six CNDD-FDD insiders; he also doubted whether the extravagant acquisition of 200 new cars, one for each member of the National Assembly and Senate went through the proper government tender procedure. Some leading CNDD-FDD members accused Radjabu, who was then president of the party, of profiting from the airplane, sugar and vehicle deals. Nyangoma continued to expose the government's human rights record, its failure to stamp out corruption and its slowness in negotiating with the FLN.

Apologists for the government pointed out that ministers and newly appointed senior civil servants lacked experience and that they had failed to recruit many of the capable people living in exile;[18] also that the government passed an anti-corruption law in April 2006

---

17 It was sold for US$3,150,000 in a sickening story of sleaze. The Ministry of Finance took the decision to sell the Falcon 50 and received a deposit before the cabinet had even considered the matter. It was eventually brought to the cabinet under 'any other business' and ministers were told that the World Bank recommended the sale, which was untrue. The plane was valued by a very questionable company and the sale was only advertised in the government paper, *Le Renouveau*, (not the place you would look if you wanted to buy a plane), with a deadline of several days and with a dossier only in English. Those bidding were given false information that the plane needed expensive repairs and that a payment was owing on the contract. The plane was sold to Delaware Corporation, not the highest bidder. The contract was signed within a week. The plane was resold by Delaware for three times the price it had paid to the Burundi Government—and there is no proof that the money for the sale was in fact paid into the Treasury. (From the preliminary audit report).

18 Eugene Nindorera remarked, 'If you are living in Sweden, England or Canada you will not be tempted to return with your wife and children for a salary of a few hundred dollars.' Those who did return were often frustrated in the face of corruption and either returned abroad or became corrupt themselves.

which created an Anti-Corruption Brigade and a special court and these should be given time to do their job. The Minister of Finance, Dieudonné Ngowembona, who was later dismissed, lacked the political weight to stand up to party leaders, and especially to party president Radjabu.

The UN and the diplomatic community in Bujumbura were becoming aware of cases of torture, arrests, summary executions and corruption even before the end of 2005 but wanted to give the government a little time before bringing pressure to bear. Corruption and internal tensions came out into the open in April 2006 when Matthias Basabose, a member of parliament and a top man in the party hierarchy, accused Hussein Radjabu of corruption and dictatorial tendencies. Journalists crowded into a press conference at his house where they were rounded up and detained by police; some were beaten up. Another journalist, Aloys Kabura, was arrested shortly afterwards for criticising this police action. Terence Nahimana, director of a local peace NGO, was also arrested, merely for complaining about the government's lack of urgency over negotiations with the FNL. In September when he pointed out the irregularities over the sale of the presidential plane, the president of the anti-corruption NGO, OLUCOME,[19] Gabriel Rufyiri, was summarily arrested and held without trial for more than the thirty days permitted by law.

The year's biggest story was the 'coup plot' which the government claimed to have foiled in July 2006. Alain Mugabarabona, leader of FNL-Icanzo,[20] was arrested. He claimed that he was behind the plot and he named former Vice President Alphonse-Marie Kadege and others, who were in turn arrested and tortured. They were joined on 21 August by ex-President Domitien Ndayizeye, whose immunity as a senator had been specially removed. The rumours got wilder, suggesting that ex-President Buyoya and President Museveni of Uganda might have been implicated. Everything pointed to this 'coup' being a fabrication, designed by Radjabu to remove some opponents of

---

19 Observatoire de Lutte contre la Corruption et les Malversations Economiques— Corruption and Misappropriation of Funds Watchdog.

20 FNL-Icanzo is a small former rebel group formed by Mugabarabona when he was expelled from Palipehutu-FNL.

the regime. The Minister of Defence subsequently indicated that he had no military intelligence about any such plot. The likelihood of Ndayizeye and Kadege collaborating was laughable since they had had memorably bad relations when they were in office. Happily the Supreme Court in the end found Ndayizeye, Kadege and most of the others accused not guilty. Signs are that their release was, in fact, a political decision. Pressure and counsel from donor countries and the UN, and from a widening range of public opinion in Burundi, seemed to have worked. Mugabarabona, who had confessed to planning a coup, was sentenced to twenty years.[21]

Coming to the boil simultaneously was the story of the Second Vice President, Alice Nzomukunda,[22] which provided the most glaring revelation of the tensions inside the party. Alice was a loyal and capable party member who had fought in CNDD-FDD's ranks. The first signs of the storm to come were in May when she had undertaken a successful visit to the UN and was due to make an official visit to Belgium. Suddenly, apparently on Radjabu's orders, she was recalled. Shortly after this, during an FNL attack, a rocket was fired at her house.[23] Finally, on 5 September, she resigned, courageously accusing the government of corruption and human rights violations. She openly suggested that the coup plot had been cooked up by Radjabu as an excuse to crack down on his opponents. Radjabu still had enough influence to get his friend, the little known Marina Barampama, named as the new Second Vice President to replace Alice, but even the good news that a ceasefire had been agreed with the FNL that very same day failed to burnish the government's rapidly fading reputation.

Quite apart from these high profile cases, a damning report by Human Rights Watch[24] documented the disappearance of some thirty

---

21 Mugabarabona and his friend, Tharcisse Ndayishimiye, who was also convicted, said their confessions were extracted through torture.

22 Alice Nzomukunda's husband is Herménégilde Niyonzima, the author of *Burundi, terre des héros non-chantés* and a former diplomat.

23 I was told that the rocket in question was of the hand-held variety and therefore could not have been fired from the hills by the FLN.

24 '"We flee when we see them": Abuses with Impunity at the National Intelligence Service' (Report by Human Rights Watch, October 2006).

people in Radjabu's home province of Muyinga, blamed on agents of the National Intelligence Agency (SNR)[25] which had also been responsible for over 200 arbitrary arrests, some involving torture. It reported one case where a detainee was held for over eleven months in the SNR detention centre without trial. In theory the SNR reports directly to the Head of State (here represented by the president of the party) and there is no independent body that monitors it. The number of extra-judicial killings dropped after the ceasefire with the FNL in 2006 but the government did not give clear orders to the police and army to stop abuses. Without this, the ordinary citizen could not feel secure or have confidence that justice would be done.

A lot of reference has been made to the party president, Hussein Radjabu, sometimes nicknamed 'Romeo' or 'le vrai pouvoir'. As he had been behind Nkurunziza's election as head of CNDD-FDD the President was beholden to him. Things had to get really bad before the 'umbilical cord' between them could be broken. At the outset the party played a big part in this government but lacked solid democratic structures. Thus Radjabu was easily able to control the party—and thus the government. A manipulator, he loved power and wielded it for a time with the help of the head of the National Intelligence Agency, Brigadier General Adolphe Nshimirimana. Radjabu was feared and hated, especially by the political 'chattering classes' in Bujumbura.[26] Undoubtedly tensions existed between Radjabu and the President but in mid-2006 nobody expected them to come to breaking point so soon. I was told that the President sheltered behind his religion to avoid having to face the conflict.[27] Radjabu appeared to be

---

25 Service National de Renseignements. On two occasions, bodies were found in a river in Muyinga province. The local military commander was one of those suspected of wrongdoing. He was still on duty early in 2007 and one of the prosecutors in his case was transferred to another post 'for his own safety'.

26 There was an element of anti-Muslim prejudice: he was accused of wanting to Islamise the country—an ambition the born-again President would be the first to resist—but Radjabu had hinted that if the west withdrew aid, the country could turn to Arab countries. He also wanted to clamp down on mini-skirts and adultery—and many Christians would go along with that idea.

27 A newspaper article described a typical party meeting where Radjabu would

the winner in the Basabose case and again when Alice Nzomukunda was driven into exile, but the release, in January 2007, first of the imprisoned journalists and then of Ndayizeye and Kadege, was a sign that his power was slipping. Pressure from outside and inside the country, particularly from some of his CNDD-FDD colleagues, caused the President to realise that Radjabu was leading the government down a dangerous path.

2006 had been a bad year for freedom and good governance. However, early in 2007 the sky brightened. Adolphe Nshimirimana, the Head of the National Intelligence Agency, blamed for the human rights abuses that Radjabu had ordered, turned against the party president, as did the Chief of Police, Brig.-Gen. Alain Bunyoni. The Minister of Defence, Maj.-Gen. Niyoyankana, indicated that he was loyal to Nkurunziza. Finally some leading CNDD-FDD military men met the President and insisted that Radjabu had to go. A special party congress was held in Ngozi on 6 February. This voted by 1,060 votes to 15 to remove Radjabu from the party presidency and replace him with Jérémie Ngendakumana, an intellectual supposedly more open to talking with other parties.[28] Radjabu and nearly all his supporters boycotted the meeting, claiming it contravened the party's rules. Radjabu called an 'official' party conference for 24 February, but he saw that the game was up and cancelled it at the last minute. Radjabu himself sheltered briefly in the South African embassy and many of his supporters were stripped of their posts. In April 2007, he was arrested on charges of plotting an armed rebellion and insulting the president by referring to him as an 'empty bottle'. A year later he was convicted and given a thirteen-year prison sentence (he escaped in March 2015). The fleeting career of Second Vice President Marina Barampama was terminated 'for insubordination'.[29] Only two out of the six ministers who had earlier signed a letter supporting

---

arrive and speak, then the Head of State would say a few words, then Radjabu would resume, one or two others would get a word in and the meeting would end. (From *L'Aube de la Démocratie*, a Frodebu newspaper, so the story may be apocryphal).

28 He was Burundian Ambassador to Kenya.

29 She refused to attend the Ngozi congress.

Radjabu were dismissed. One of them, Karenga Ramadhani,[30] was replaced as Minister of Communication by another Muslim, Mme Hafsa Mossi, a popular choice. Marina Barampama's former *chef de cabinet*, Isaac Bizimana, had been named Governor of the Central Bank, but almost immediately he and Barampama were discovered to have smuggled into the country some containers of Chinese furniture, clothing and building materials worth US$150,000. The continued hounding of other Radjabu supporters did not automatically create better governance. Nonetheless, Radjabu's departure was welcomed with glee in Bujumbura and throughout the country, not least by the international community.

Radjabu's aim had been to create a system of Hutu power and patronage, a mirror image of the Tutsi power that had been overthrown. To control all the levers of power he needed money, which he stole on a large scale, and which would also pay for the militia he had started to create. Radjabu's mistake was being in too great a hurry. He began abusing his power before he had built up his militia or eliminated enough of his rivals.

Where did this small revolution leave Nkurunziza and his government? The military element was greatly strengthened. The Deputy Chief of the General Staff, Godefroid Niyombare;[31] the Chief of Police; the Head of the SNR; and the Minister of the Interior, Evariste Ndayishimiye, began to dominate the government. The immediate effect of Radjabu's elimination was to split CNDD-FDD into two. In spite of harassment by the government Radjabu retained many supporters: his thirty parliamentarians were expelled from parliament.[32] They joined and strengthened an existing opposition party, the Union for Peace and Development (UPD). Unfortunately Nkurunziza failed to seize the moment to reform the structure of the ruling party—and its unity is still further threatened by that old Burundian bugbear, tension between politicians and military from the different regions.

---

30 He was later brought back as Minister of Regional Integration.

31 Who was to lead the unsuccessful coup in May 2015.

32 This was illegal. Deputies are elected as individuals and the government has no right to expel them (but its majority gave it the power to do so!)

The split in the ruling party weakened the government's position in parliament. This encouraged Frodebu and Uprona to demand the full number of government posts which the constitution allows. Frodebu even demanded the impeachment of the president. The work of the National Assembly was completely blocked for months, while deputies turned up only to claim their salaries. The senate frequently had no quorum. A reshuffle of ministers was again attempted but without consultation with the leadership of the parties, so the stand-off with the opposition parties continued. Nkurunziza was finally forced to negotiate seriously with Frodebu and Uprona to enable the government to function properly again, and on 27 September 2007 made it clear that he would work cooperatively with these opposition parties. After this the political ice melted briefly. Alice Nzomukunda, the former Vice President, returned and was appointed First Vice-President of the National Assembly. She was a hate figure for Radjabu's supporters but well-liked by the other parties. Others such as Léonard Nyangoma and Mathias Basabose who had taken refuge abroad also returned. The wholesale sugar market, which had been restricted to only six big CNDD-FDD members, was opened up. The release of most of those accused of the coup plot suggested that the courts were not totally intimidated.[33]

However, the optimism of 2005, which rose again in 2007 after Radjabu's fall from power, was fast evaporating well before the elections of 2010. The people had voted for peace and good government but Burundi's political leaders had put party and personal advantage first and their country second. From the very start, the government pulled every string to ensure that CNDD-FDD would win the 2010 election. As we have seen, the first actions were the populist moves to provide free primary education and maternity care. Its behaviour was otherwise less benevolent, with the government doing its best to block opposition in any form. The recognition of the FNL as a political party even when it had abandoned its 'ethnic' label, Palipehutu, was delayed as long as possible so as to give it less time to organise

---

33 The conviction of Mugabarabona and Ndayishimiye is a sign that the court was still under some pressure from the government. If they had been released they could have revealed a lot more dirt.

before the elections. Alexis Sinduhije founded the Mouvement pour la Solidarité et la Démocratie (Movement for Solidarity and Democracy — MSD) in December 2007. The government, which saw Sinduhije as a real threat, had him arrested on the spurious charge of '*outrage au Chef de l'Etat*'. He was held in Mpimba prison from November 2008 to March 2009 and the recognition of his party was also delayed as long as possible. Frodebu had been alienated over the allocation of posts, as we have seen. The pro-Radjabu UPD was furious at the expulsion of its parliamentarians. In addition, Nkurunziza, following Buyoya's bad example, began engineering splits in the opposition parties. The earlier attempt to get FNL members to expel Rwasa from the leadership is referred to in chapter 10. The government succeeded in cultivating Jean Minani's dissident faction, Frodebu-Nyakuri.[34] Thus relations between the government and all the opposition parties were already very bad-tempered by 2010. Not much progress had been made towards 'correcting the tree's faults.'

---

34 Nyakuri means 'real' but not many voters saw this group as more genuine than the main Frodebu faction.

22

THE 2010 ELECTIONS AND AFTER: A ONE-PARTY STATE?

The unity of the Burundian people will be strengthened when citizens understand that we have to live together, working without respite, in a spirit of mutual understanding and tolerance, imbued with patriotism. We must complement each other, convinced that our differences are in fact a resource... Pierre Nkurunziza before the election

The President was still popular in most of the country in 2010. Free primary education and maternity care still worked in his favour. He lost no opportunity to visit the rural population, share in their sorrows and their worship, drink Fanta and play football with them. The local administration, mainly controlled by the ruling party, kept up pressure on voters—probably giving multiple ID cards to some party supporters and making it known that voting for the opposition would be *mal vu* by the local officials. In the run-up to the elections it is clear that CNDD-FDD spent a lot buying votes, *acheter les consciences*. There is evidence of gifts of cooking pots and other items as well as money and the use of government transport on the party's behalf. This is not to say that some of the other parties did not try similar tricks, but they had fewer resources. The party's radio station, Rema FM, kept up the pressure too.

The plan for the 2010 elections was to have communal elections in May followed by presidential and then parliamentary elections. Ironically it was thought that local issues would be important in the communes and they would not be influenced too much by the President's known popularity. The President, however, (and he was soon imitated by the other parties) put all his energy into winning in May, so that the communal elections became a vote for or against himself, with his portrait even appeared on the party's ballot paper. The official results gave the ruling party over 60 per cent across the whole country, with the FNL leading in Bujumbura Rural and Sinduhije's MSD doing well in much of Bujumbura.[1] International and national observers reported that on the day itself the communal election was generally free and fair. Yet some questions have been raised. The election had been delayed by two days at the very last minute,[2] and according to the electoral commission (CENI) this was due to the late arrival of printed papers from South Africa, but there is evidence that no plane arrived from South Africa during those two days. Polling ended at 4pm but a number of polling stations remained open illegally late (in some cases for acceptable logistical reasons). Counting of votes went on late by candlelight in most places as there was a nationwide electricity blackout at 7pm, which seems highly suspicious. There were questions about the privacy of the polling booths, which meant people feared being watched (and the attitude of local government officials means that many fear this even when there is privacy). Some ballot boxes reportedly spent the night somewhere before reaching Bujumbura. However, the national results when they were eventually announced did reflect those noted by the national and international observers at the polling stations.

The opposition leaders simply did not believe these results. On this basis the presidential election would not go to a second round, denying the opposition the chance to rally round a joint candidate. Some say they were just poor losers, but it is significant that every serious opposition group is of the same opinion about the election, and in spite of their very different party positions and personal antagonisms most of them joined together into a grouping, ADC

---

1   Sinduhije thinks the true result was more like CNDD-FDD 35%, FNL 25%, PSD 15%.

2   So late that it was not mentioned at a meeting between the CENI and the parties the evening before it was announced.

Ikibiri.[3] I was informed that when Alexis Sinduhije and other opposition leaders visited Ngozi province, the President's home area, just after the May poll they received a heroes' welcome, which seems to suggest that the scale of the official majority may have been exaggerated. However, a continent-wide poll in 2011 showed that Pierre Nkurunziza had 81 per cent support and was Africa's most popular president in his own country.

The first decision ADC Ikibiri made was not to take up the places won in the communal vote; the next was for the other candidates to pull out of the presidential election—thus making Nkurunziza's eventual 92 per cent victory a hollow one. More controversially they (with the exception of Uprona) also boycotted the parliamentary election in July in spite of pressure from the international community. Only Uprona and Jean Minani's small Frodebu-Nyakuri faction took part in this election, leaving CNDD-FDD with a huge majority in parliament. The government won an even larger majority in the senate, which is elected by the communal councillors, nearly all of whom were from the ruling party, since those from the main opposition had not taken up their places. Armed with this huge majority the government had the power easily to change the constitution and run the country as a one-party state.

I was an observer of the parliamentary election in Ngozi province. We found the polling stations, the general organisation of the poll and the conduct of the count very good, but the boycott made the election totally meaningless. On a practical level the CENI had done a good job, but if it had shown a little statesmanship the boycott decision might have been avoided. First, CNDD-FDD offered a re-run of the communal election in places where the result was challenged. The CENI refused. There was also a fair chance that the opposition might agree to participate in the parliamentary poll if it could be delayed. Again the CENI refused. Some said this was because it was in the pay of CNDD-FDD, others that it was just arrogance on the part of its members.

---

3   The FNL has since withdrawn from it.

In the end was the opposition wise to opt out of parliament? Those who supported the boycott reckoned that a weak minority in parliament would be useless in the face of an majority imbued with 'military thinking' and that much greater pressure could be brought to bear from outside. Many people, however, believed that an opposition presence in parliament—and it would have been quite a substantial one—could have held the government to account. It is thought that Léonard Nyangoma, leader of the tiny CNDD party, had too much influence on the decision since his party was small and he had little to lose, whereas the FNL, Frodebu and the MSD would have had a reasonable number of seats in parliament and it is thought that they went along with the decision rather more reluctantly.

In retrospect the boycott certainly looks like a mistake. Nyangoma's highly respected deputy, Francois Bizimana, was against it and claims the decision was taken by the leaders of the parties without proper consultation. Former president Sylvestre Ntibantunganya believes so too: not only should they not have boycotted in 2010, he said, but it would have been wise if the opposition had put up a presidential candidate against Nkurunziza back in 2005 as a signal to discourage people from having a one-party mentality. As things turned out ADC Ikibiri's hope that international pressure would bring about a change of heart by the government after 2010 was forlorn. The government seemed impervious to pressure, nor did it have a big problem administering areas where the opposition was strong, such as Bujumbura Rural. In fact in such areas there have been some defections from the opposition by individuals tempted to accept paid jobs.

Fear of a return to violence rose when Agathon Rwasa, the FNL leader, fled into exile but, although there were a number of incidents (dismissed by the government as banditry), it did not develop into war. The high vote for the CNDD-FDD was as much as anything a vote for peace by not disturbing the power in place.

Both Léonard Nyangoma and Alexis Sinduhije also left the country shortly after the election. Visiting Tanzania for talks with other ADC Ikibiri leaders in January 2012, Sinduhije was arrested. He believes his arrival time was leaked in an email and that the Burundi authorities had told the Tanzanian police that a criminal murderer was arriving. When the policeman who arrested him at the airport started abusing him, Alexis explained politely that Tanzania had a good reputation and that the police officer was letting down the memory of Nyerere. The policeman began to realise this was no ordinary criminal and he spoke with his boss on the phone. Burundian agents were standing around to take Sinduhije to Burundi, but to their dismay the Tanzanians took him off and only imprisoned him for a few days. This incident was a clear sign that it would be dangerous for opponents to return home to Burundi.[4]

The President's speech at his 2010 investiture had sounded positive. He committed himself 'to fight against any ideology or practice of genocide and exclusion, to promote and defend individual rights and liberties,' also to 'defend the overall interests of the nation, to ensure national unity and cohesion, peace and social justice.' He promised 'zero tolerance' for corruption and financial irregularities. The rhetoric was not, especially in this last matter, followed by action. However, he still refused to talk to the opposition parties and remained hostile to civil society.

In a 2011 document the ADC Ikibiri parties continued to propose dialogue as the way to behave in a democratic country, while at the same time fiercely criticising the government, accusing it of abandoning the spirit of the Arusha accords, of violating the constitution, of the selective killing of innocent people,[5] of hostility to the media and civil society and of corruption. Such a dialogue would be based on the creation of an open environment where honest and frank talks could take place; on respect for fundamental rights; on the search for truth and reconciliation in the context of transitional justice. There was clearly a fear that the achievements of the peace process would be lost and the country could even return to conflict.

Despite its claims that the sporadic attacks were just banditry, some of the attacks clearly had political motives and Rwasa was blamed for them. The government showed signs of nervousness and

---

4   The Burundi government made another vain attempt to extradite Sinduhije in 2014 at Brussels airport in 2014 for violence against the police by some of his supporters.

5   The UN office counted sixty cases of extra-judicial killings in 2011 alone.

took part in joint exercises with the Congolese forces against supposed FNL groups based in the DRC. There was (and still is) also fear of possible reprisals by al-Shabaab for the Burundi army's role in the African Union mission in Somalia. This threat prompted the erection of barriers across the two major roads that cross outside the President's office and which continue to disrupt traffic four years later (but would be unlikely to deter al-Shabaab!). Jean-Claude Kavumbagu of the Netpress agency was imprisoned for six months for criticising the 'pathetic' inadequacy of Burundi's security.[6] By 2012 the threat of renewed political violence seemed to have diminished, perhaps as a result of infiltration by (perhaps not so pathetic) government agents.

The president's New Year speech in 2012 was less positive. He seemed to rule out any opening to the opposition. He denounced local and international media for supporting armed groups, and he announced plans to change the constitution and to set up the Truth and Reconciliation Commission. The government continued to behave in a very authoritarian way: jobs were linked to party membership; opponents 'disappeared' or arrested; the police highly politicised. The authoritarian tendency may, however, have been moderated slightly by the divisions in the ruling party, by the relative independence of the media and of civil society and by the economic weakness of the country. The government had only limited means to 'buy' support.

At the time of the 2010 election there were serious divisions within the CNDD-FDD. Nkurunziza's position was weak: he had not been the party's first choice as presidential candidate but he was seen to be the most likely to win the popular vote; his lack of interest in the details of policy gave ministers extra power but they were poorly co-ordinated. His relationship with the party president, Jérémie Ngendakumana, who replaced Radjabu back in 2007 and who according to party rules (and according to him) should have been the presidential candidate, was bad from the start. Ngendakumana was also exceptionally corrupt. He was replaced in 2012 by Pascal Nyabenda, who had been leader of the party in parliament and had

---

6   Burundi's role in Somalia pleased the US which rewarded it with some trade benefits.

established the national human rights commission. A civilian and a more moderate man, it was hoped he might be able to heal the continuing divisions inside the party: the dominant military versus frustrated civilians, rigid former fighters versus reformers, members from Gitega versus those from Ngozi.

British direct aid to Burundi before 2012 averaged around US$20 million a year, mostly directed to education, health, governance and economic integration. The British Department for International Development (DFID) stopped this bilateral aid to Burundi in 2012 although it had stated that it had 'a compelling case for aid' to this 'very poor, fragile country' but that the cost of their Bujumbura office was too high in relation to the size of the programme. DFID argued that it would continue funding Burundi through the UN, EU the African Development Bank and Trade Mark East Africa (TMEA). This decision was highly contested in the UK as well as in Burundi. The aid review of 2010 had actually recommended increasing aid and this would have made the local office viable. I was one of a number of individuals and organisations that submitted recommendations to keep the programme going, arguing that Burundi was the poorest of the countries of the East African Community and was now to be the only one with no British aid programme; that Burundi's poverty and the small scale of its economy meant that well directed aid could have a disproportionately positive effect; and that issues of governance and human rights also made Burundi a priority. Some of Britain's aid projects have been picked up by other donors but the end result is a negative one.[7]

2013 started tragically when on 27 January Bujumbura Central Market, the commercial heart of the country, was destroyed by fire. Hundreds of traders lost their stock and their livelihood. Some tried to sell their vegetables and fruit along the streets and the police stopped them. Some of the women organised themselves for an inventive protest, stripping naked and chasing the police away. The loss of the market led to huge price rises and serious shortages of goods.

---

7   One good piece of aid from DFID was the funding of the Burundi Revenue Authority (Office Burundais des Recettes) through TMEA, insisting on an expatriate in charge to avoid corruption.

A commission of enquiry showed that the fire was an accident, but there are rumours and suspicions. A new market was proposed on the site of the old COTEBU textile factory but no immediate action was taken.

In the rural areas conflict over land ownership continued. The rapid population growth and return of refugees ensured that the vast majority of court cases related to land, usually between Hutus occupying the land, and returning refugees whom the land commission tended to favour. In spite of this many of the refugees expelled by Tanzania[8] found themselves homeless. Peasant farmers' plots now average only 0.5 hectares. 80 per cent of the population are engaged in agriculture and yet it only receives 2 per cent of the national budget.

Young people continued to have more problems than most. As children they suffer from beatings, hunger and all the other effects of poverty: ragged clothing, no shoes, poor health. The cost of education, in theory their escape route, is too much for an average family with several children. It helped that primary school fees had been abolished but parents still had to pay for exercise books and school uniforms, often in addition to a contribution for the school building, and they had to pay fees if the child continued to secondary school. Finding a job after leaving school usually involves knowing someone and paying *chai*.[9] Getting married is an even bigger problem for boys as there is a bride price to pay, measured in cows—and the culture, especially in rural areas, requires a couple to marry: illegitimate boys cannot inherit land; the concept of the unmarried mother does not exist in the Kirundi language and abortion is illegal. Social traditions cannot keep up with increasing poverty.[10] Many young people are attracted to join youth wings of political parties, notably the *imbonerakure*,[11] the CNDD-FDD youth, whose activities as 'security men' have increased since 2013 when they began attacking peaceful

8   160 were expelled in August 2013 alone.

9   Kiswahili for tea, the usual term for small bribes.

10   These comments are drawn from a talk at the School of Oriental and African Studies, London, by Marc Sommers.

11   It means 'those who see far'.

citizens at night or taking them as hostages.[12] Complaints about illegal attacks are often ignored by the authorities but many citizens illegally keep guns and sometimes attack and rob innocent people.

The return of Agathon Rwasa to Burundi in August 2013 was a sign that he and the FNL were not planning any further rebellion. It appears that his return was negotiated by foreign diplomats on condition that he stopped contesting the result of the 2010 election. He continued, however, to blame the government for stealing public funds and for extrajudicial killings. The government banned a meeting with his many supporters and considers him a private citizen. Jacques Bigirimana, who has little support, is recognised by the government as the leader of the FNL.

---

12 Their role became more destructive during the crisis of 2015. The MSD also developed a strong youth wing which was to play a major role in the demonstrations of 2015.

23

BURUNDI IN 2014:
THE CALM BEFORE THE STORM

I would say that all of the problems Burundi has faced over the years are related to our system of justice.... A judge should be above the police, but now it is the police that give orders to judges. The result is impunity. —Pierre Claver Mbonimpa

I spent a month in Burundi in 2014 to see what had changed since the first edition of this book was written in 2007 and to look at the prospects for the 2015 elections and the future.

Bujumbura had grown in size and population. More private cars on the road and a huge number of new hotels gave a false impression of increased wealth. In the Kigobe neighbourhood near the parliament building, more recently up the mountainside in Sororezo and along the lake shore stand the large new houses built by those who have grown rich, in many cases from corruption.[1] Investment in building these new hotels was the latest craze—earlier it was petrol stations.[2] Tax exemption on building materials encouraged this but it is a very poor investment: the few foreign visitors who come to Burundi prefer to stay on the lake shore. The new hotels in the city

---

1   They also have large 4x4 vehicles which have been nicknamed 'health centres,' as they cost the same as a village clinic.

2   There are five filling stations within less than a kilometre of eachother on Avenue du 28 Novembre in Bujumbura.

centre or on the hills above the city, many of them very grand, have hardly any clients.[3]

The residential apartheid of the crisis period is no more. Formerly Tutsi suburbs like Nyakabiga and Cibitoke probably now have Hutu majorities. A Tutsi friend had enough confidence that things had changed to build his new house right on the old front line between Kamenge and Cibitoke. In fact, Hutus and Tutsis in emigrant and refugee communities in places like Switzerland and Montreal are more ethnically divided than in Burundi itself: these exiles see Burundi in their memory and cannot always imagine how things may have evolved. At the level of the élite there is, of course, continuing competition for the very limited wealth of the country. Previously this was sewn up in favour of the Tutsis, mainly those from Bururi, but now many Hutus are sharing this meagre *gâteau*. At street or village level poverty and unemployment impel young men (and some women) who feel insecure and lack hope for their future gravitate to the party youth movements—the *imbonerakure* on the government side and those most likely to resist them, FNL supporters of Agathon Rwasa and MSD supporters of Alexis Sinduhije. In March 2014 during a demonstration police entered the MSD headquarters and some of the party youth unwisely took two of them hostage, resulting in sixty-eight arrests and giving their leader more reason to stay in exile to avoid arrest himself.[4]

The ruins of Bujumbura Central Market, yet to be rebuilt, were a truer illustration of economic reality than the glossy new hotels. Over the last few years seven markets in the country have been burned down with no apparent motive. Each time an enquiry is set up but nothing useful is discovered.[5] The opening of the COTEBU site

---

3   Tax on construction materials had been reduced and owning a hotel seemed a smart thing to do. Even the recently deposed Anglican Bishop of Bujumbura built a hotel which stands unfinished as a monument to his folly.

4   Alexis Sinduhije denies that any of the MSD supporters were armed and has asked the government for an independent inquiry which they have refused. The appeal against their conviction was held, abnormally, in secrecy in Mpimba prison, suggesting that the government feared reaction on the streets.

5   The suspicion is that government servants were involved.

promised to the Bujumbura traders has been delayed many times. Nationally, poverty has increased. In other countries the economy expanded after the conflict ended; not in Burundi. Inflation went on rising, affecting the urban salaried classes as well as the rural population. Food production also remained stagnant and it actually dropped between 2010 and 2012. Burundi has been classified as the 'hungriest' nation on earth: 45 per cent of children under five had anaemia and over 800,000 children under five suffered from chronic malnutrition. There are many causes of this: rapid population growth; subdivided farm plots; soil exhaustion and low use of fertiliser,[6] little irrigation despite abundance of water, and lack of cash particularly because of inflation. The climate has become more uncertain and this has affected food crops, especially in drier areas such as Kirundo. The annual feel-good income from the coffee crop was much reduced: production dropped by over 50 per cent as explained above. Attempts to conserve fish stock reduced income from that source.

The government made a commitment to do something about agricultural production but in 2014 withdrew nearly £400,000 from the agricultural budget and transferred it to the election process. Population growth is probably the greatest threat to living standards in Burundi. Burundi had the world's fourth highest fertility rate in 2010. The total fertility rate had even increased in the previous forty years.[7] The use of modern contraceptives has increased but remains low and the government has done little about this.

Up until May 2015 the media retained a certain level of independence. The press law passed in June 2013 was seen by journalists as a threat to their freedom to criticise and advise—and by some as unconstitutional. 12,000 people signed a petition against it. The most widely read printed newspaper is the weekly *Iwacu*. Antoine Kaburahe, the editor, told me that they always try to be balanced but that this was becoming harder as the pre-election atmosphere heated up. In 2014 radio remained by far the strongest media source: 5.5 million Burundians had access and 5 million of them listen in Ki-

---

6   A reform of subsidies may have led to a better supply of fertilisers.

7   From 5.9 children per woman in 1970 to 6.4 in 2010 (Burundi Health Ministry figures 2007).

rundi. African Public Radio (RPA), 'the voice of the voiceless', had easily the largest audience, especially for its midday news broadcast. I met Bob Rugarika, who had just been promoted to Director. He told me that the media climate was tough and they had to step carefully, but insisted that wrongs must be exposed, such as killings, high level corruption and the selling off of national assets, such as the port of Bujumbura, and not putting the proceeds to good use. The national radio station, RTNB, had the second largest audience, well ahead of Radio Isanganiro which had dropped to fourth place behind Radio Bonesha.[8] The audience of Rema FM, the CNDD-FDD propaganda mouthpiece, had dropped to a mere 5 per cent. Television viewing had increased and here RTNB was in the lead[9] over the two private stations, Rema and Télé Renaissance. An increasing number of people got their news via the internet.

Some dramatic landslips caused by heavy rain early in 2014 damaged the RN 1, the vital main road which twists up the escarpment and connects Bujumbura with almost everywhere. For a time all heavy trucks had to be diverted through Gitega and reach Bujumbura from the south, adding an extra 130 kilometres on the route from Kenya, Uganda and Rwanda with a terrible effect on prices. Such emergencies apart, the government can take credit for improving the condition of the roads, using aid from the African Development Bank, the European Union and Japan. The road from Gitega to Karuzi and Muyinga was tarred and a wide new road between Gitega and Ngozi was built. In Bujumbura a couple of new tarmac roads provided some relief to the traffic jams. The programme of paving side roads in most of the city's neighbourhoods continued. I was staying on a road where this work was in progress and I was impressed at the speed at which, after the new concrete gutters had been built, the road was levelled, spread with sand and then with stone sets, women doing much of the work. This project is a model for Africa, for these roads will last for many years without maintenance.

---

8 An independent study reckoned that Bonesha and Isanganiro were more balanced in their coverage than RPA.

9 RTNB was able, with French aid, to broadcast the World Cup on television which boosted its viewing figures.

In his Independence Day speech on 2 July 2014, President Nkurunziza boasted of some other achievements of his government: 1,800 schools and 49 health centres built or rehabilitated in 2013 alone; improvements to water supplies and sports grounds; reforestation and fire prevention measures; 3,000 prisoners released. Rural health centres and schools were a government priority, a way of retaining popular support: 400 health centres were built between 2004 and 2012 and the president controls a special budget line, 'Support for Good Initiatives', which has enabled him to buy support without any bureaucratic supervision.

Burundi's environment continues to be under threat from population growth, deforestation and erosion, but there is increased consciousness of the problem. The slogan in 2014 was: 'Let us raise our voice to protect our lakes and prevent drought'. A new law prevents development within 150 metres of the shore of Lake Tanganyika and 50 metres in the case of the other lakes in the north. The National Institute for the Environment and the Conservation of Nature established a laboratory for testing the degree of water pollution, which should enable measures to be taken to improve water quality. Local NGOs were also working to protect the environment. In the Ruvubu National Park in the east the Association for the Well-being of the People of Burundi is raising awareness among local people; planting trees; re-establishing other endangered plant species and conserving wild animals such as the buffalo, of which this is the only habitat in Burundi. Elsewhere the association promotes methods to improve the quality of the soil and to prevent erosion. Land ownership remains a time bomb: conflicts over land rights make up 80 per cent of court cases and the National Land Commission (CNTB) is not impartial. 350,000 Hutu refugees returned to Burundi between 2002 and 2007. Tanzania has accepted many of the 1972 refugees as citizens, 162,000 in 2010 alone, and many have been assisted to return: 35,000 in 2012 for example. They have continued to trickle back at a rate of about 6,000 each year. Farm plots are too small and pressure on land will continue to increase. This problem is a real threat to social stability in the future and serious thought needs to be given to solving it.

Evangelical churches have continued to proliferate at the expense of the Catholic and older established Protestant churches.[10] A government survey in 2013 found that there were 557 denominations with small groups constantly splitting off, following new pastors and creating new churches. As a result a bill was put before parliament and passed in July 2014 requiring recognised churches to have at least 500 members and a proper building or 1,000 members in the case of 'foreign' churches. The 'mainstream' churches have continued to lose members and even some of them have suffered from splits and breakaways.[11]

Burundi has not been well governed: public mismanagement has increased greatly over the past twenty years. Corruption and nepotism have blossomed. The government's failure to stop this trend, in spite of the president's promises to do something about it, has discouraged foreign investors and damaged relations with donors.[12] In this context, the story came to light in October 2014 that, with no tender procedure, a South African company was given a licence to mine nickel in return for donating a vehicle worth US$800,000 to the foundation run by the first lady. Civil society organisations have, to the irritation of the government, focused attention on corruption and human rights violations and have to some extent made up for the lack of parliamentary opposition. The government has criticized civil society for being Bujumbura-based, predominantly Tutsi-led and funded from abroad but it is clear from the huge support received by Pierre Claver Mbonimpa when he was imprisoned (see below) that is not just an elitist movement. It has also been adept at using the new social media to spread its messages.

On the political front events and opinions in 2014 were already focused on the 2015 elections, especially on what was considered the president's likely candidature for a third term—and the political tension was palpable. Concern had been expressed by the UN Secretary-

---

10 See also Chapter 2.

11 The deposed Anglican Bishop of Bujumbura created a new church. The Quaker EEB has divided into two 'yearly meetings' but remained legally one church.

12 In the Transparency International Corruption Perceptions Index in 2012 Burundi ranked 165 out of 174. In 2013 it had moved up to 157 of 175.

General, the head of the African Union office in Burundi, and the USA and by the European Parliament[13] about human rights abuses, plans to ignore the Arusha agreement and attacks on the opposition. Adama Dieng, the UN Secretary-General's Special Advisor for the Prevention of Genocide, speaking at Arusha on the occasion of the twentieth anniversary of the Rwanda genocide, appealed for dialogue between all political groups to avoid disaster.

Opposition parties were attacked in different ways. Individual party members were kidnapped and tortured or had grenades fired at their homes. Many, especially FNL members, were assassinated. Leaders were harassed. In December 2013 the moderate former Vice President Frederic Bamvuginyumvira was arrested in an irregular manner for adultery; the charge was changed to 'rebellion' and finally to corruption for which he served three months in prison. One of Burundi's least corrupt politicians, in reality he was arrested for strongly opposing the president serving a third term and because he was a credible compromise candidate for the presidency. On 2 October 2014 Léonce Ngendakumana, leader of Frodebu and President of the ADC Ikibiri grouping, was sentenced to a year in prison for 'false accusation and spreading of racial hatred.' His crime was a letter to the UN Secretary-General accusing the government of preparing for the eventuality of losing the elections by building up the *imbonera-kure* youth league and comparing it to Rwanda's *interahamwe* and for comparing Radio Rema to the infamous Radio Mille-Collines in pre-genocide Rwanda. The government's irritation was understandable, but its clear objective was to silence a highly regarded opponent who has had the courage never to go into exile.

The government's other method of destabilising opponents was the bad old habit of engineering divisions in opposition parties causing them to split.[14] Jean Minani had already formed his Frodebu-Nyakuri faction before 2010, and did not join the boycott. Jacques Bigirimana had been elected at a government-backed congress of the FNL in 2013, thus attempting to destroy the legitimacy of the

---

13 The European Parliament passed a strong resolution on 18 September 2014 which also referred to the arming of the party's youth wing.

14 Compare with President Buyoya's 'owl soup' in Chapter 9.

popular leader of the party, Agathon Rwasa. UPD, the party of the supporters of Radjabu, was also caused to split into two factions, an 'official' one led by Zedi Feruzi[15] and an unrecognised one led by Chauvineau Mugwengezo. Uprona was the only major opposition party participating in the government and had been making efforts to overcome its internal divisions. In February 2014 Edouard Nduwimana (Minister of the Interior and 'Doudou' to the cartoonist of Iwacu) stirred up trouble by masterminding the dismissal of Charles Nditije as president of Uprona and, when he protested, causing Nkurunziza to remove Bernard Busokoza (who is also a member of Uprona) from the post of First Vice President. This caused the three Uprona ministers to resign from the government. The outcome was an 'official' Uprona led by Concilie Nibigira, a *muganwa* descended from the royal family, facing a more popular 'illegal' party led by Charles Nditije. To date the only main party which has succeeded in resisting this treatment is Alexis Sinduhije's MSD.[16] In May 2014 Nduwimana called a meeting of the opposition parties, encouraging them to help prepare for the 2015 elections, but of course only the recognised leaders were invited. The others, according to the minister, had no legal status but they were told they could stand as '*acteurs politiques*' rather than party leaders—and it was later made clear that, unless they formed new political parties, they would only be allowed to campaign as individuals in the two weeks of the official election campaign.[17]

In April 2014 a leaked UN document reported that arms were being handed out to the *imbonerakure*[18] and local media confirmed this.

---

15 Feruzi was to be murdered in 2015.

16 The government's tactic appears to be to paint the MSD as a 'Tutsi' party, Sinduhije being a Tutsi. For example, the MSD had nominated two Hutu members to a provincial CENI but the government nominated two Tutsis instead, whereupon the MSD resigned from it.

17 The government made it impossible for these leaders it has deliberately excluded to register their parties. Campaigning in 2015 was virtually impossible anyway, due to fear of death threats and the destruction of the free media.

18 The security chief of the UN in Burundi, Paul Debbie, was expelled as a result. This made the bad relations between the government and the UN office (BINUB) worse. The government has seen the UN office as a

The assumption amongst opponents, as in Léonce Ngendakumana's letter to the UN, is that the youth would be ready to act if the election results were not in the ruling party's favour. The president of APRODH, Pierre Claver Mbonimpa alleged in an RPA broadcast on 6 May that they were being armed, trained and given military uniforms by the government. For this he was summoned and arrested a week later. Pierre Claver has been a policeman and a prisoner himself and is the founder of APRODH,[19] now the country's most respected human rights association. This arrest caused great popular anger and thousands signed a petition. Radio stations encouraged people to wear green on Fridays and for cars to hoot for ten minutes. The government then banned the sale of green cloth so people started draping themselves with green plastic bags, the message being that you can arrest one man but not everybody. Mbonimpa was conditionally liberated on 29 September. The government denied that this was the result of outside pressure.

The structure of Nkurunziza's regime was complex. Power lay in theory with the majority party, the CNDD-FDD, in the National Assembly of which the president was leader. The reality was different: a president surrounded—and to some extent controlled—by several powerful military men. All important decisions were taken by this group, and their approval by the party and parliament was just a formality. Ministers, civil servants or party members could only access the president only through these 'strong men,' all Hutus. The two strongest were Adolphe Nshimirimana, head of security, and Alain Guillaume Bunyoni, *chef de cabinet civil*. In the event they were both moved from their posts in November 2014 but remained close to the president and very influential.[20] Evariste Ndayishimiye, military *chef de cabinet*; and Guillaume Nabindika, the police chief, were also moved. These men had been above the law and, although co-ordinated by the president, were the power brokers. They would override parliament, the judiciary and even the executive (Radjabu had a

---

constraint on its independence.

19 See also Chapter 18.

20 Interestingly, Adolphe was replaced by Godefroid Niyombare, the leader of the 2015 coup (see next chapter).

similar role in 2005 but he operated as a civilian). The president went on playing football and allowed ministers to take the blame if things went wrong. According to Manassé Nzobonimpa, (a former advisor to the party turned critic) the party president, Pascal Nyabenda, was chosen as someone who could improve the party's public relations, but in reality neither he nor ordinary members of the party had any voice. The Tutsis in the government and in the party have been described as mere 'window dressing.'On 3 December the long-awaited Truth and Reconciliation Commission (CVR) was constituted with the respected head of the Catholic Justice and Peace Commission, Mgr Jean-Louis Nahimana, as president and the Anglican Archbishop, Bernard Ntahoturi as his deputy. The eleven commissioners appointed, four of whom were women, included six Hutus, four Tutsis and Libérate Niyacenzi representing the Batwa. The pro-Tutsi parties declared that it was just a creature of the CNDD-FDD and that reconciliation required justice to be done. The line-up, however, included a number of widely respected personalities. The CVR was given four years to find the truth behind the killings committed between 1962 and 2008, assess personal and collective responsibility for them, identify and map mass burial sites, propose a reparation programme and promote forgiveness and reconciliation.

Despite the many ominous signs, the country remained calm and generally peaceful at the end of 2014 while people awaited the president's decision to stand—or not—for a third term.

24

THE STORM

Tout va bien. —President Nkurunziza

Merci Dieu, merci de nous avoir protégé ...puisqu'au sein de notre partie Dieu occupe la première place. 'Thank you, God for having protected us.... since in our party God ranks most highly.' —CNDD-FDD communiqué, 13 August 2015

The government started 2015 by jailing the popular director of African Public Radio (RPA), Bob Rugurika, on 20 January for complicity in the killing of three Italian nuns in 2014. In fact RPA had done some good investigative reporting on this incident, which infuriated the government, suggesting that the influential Adolphe Nshimirimana was somehow linked to the killings. When he was freed on bail a month later the huge crowd that cheered his release amazed him, a modest man, and shocked the government. Big street demonstrations had been rare in Burundi and this one set the pattern for what was to follow.

Excitement mounted when, on 2 March, Hussein Radjabu, the president's right hand man back in 2005 and the man who pushed him into the leadership of the party, escaped from Mpimba prison where he had languished since 2007. The ease of his escape suggested complicity at quite a high level. Radjabu went into hiding, making clear that he was against the president serving a third term. Soon after this, many in the president's own party, the '*frondeurs*', took the risk of opposing a third term. Seventeen leading members circulated a petition to this effect, including the president's own spokesman, Leonidas Hatungimana. (They all lost their jobs and many have since fled the country.)

The government had tried in March 2014 to amend the constitution so that the president could stand for a third term with no legalistic questions asked. For this an 80 per cent majority was needed: 85 votes. The National Assembly voted[1] and at the last minute the Uprona MP, Bonaventure Niyoyankana, withdrew his support and the proposal failed by one vote (Niyoyankana became something of a hero to the opposition). Despite this setback there is no doubt that Nkurunziza wanted to stand in 2015.[2] There was some argument as to whether this would be against the constitution or not: Stef Vandeginste, an expert in Burundian constitutional affairs,[3] explains that the constitution states clearly that the president cannot serve more than two terms. However, it also states that the president must be elected by a direct vote (whereas he was elected by parliament in 2005) and that exceptional arrangements may be made at the time of the constitution coming into force. Looking back at the Arusha Accord it seems clear that the intention was to limit any president to two terms—but although Arusha was the basis for the new constitution it is not enshrined in it. Thus it could be argued that the president had the right to stand again, though almost all informed opinion suggests that this would be a breach of the constitution. Vandeginste remarked that the fact that the argument was taking place in the context of the constitution and not as simple power-play

---

1   This indicates some courage on the part of the small opposition parties in parliament and especially the members of the ruling party who voted no.

2   In 2014 I met one CNDD-FDD senator who hoped the president would not stand as it was likely to divide the country, especially because the constitution would have been violated. He was very pessimistic about the future of the country, and how right he was.

3   Stef Vandeginste, *L'éligibilité de l'actuel Président de la République du Burundi aux élections présidentielles de 2015: une analyse juridique* (Institute of Development Policy and Management, University of Antwerp, 2012). Stef has also set up a website *Droit, pouvoir et paix au Burundi*: www.uantwerpen. be/burundi

was an encouraging sign that Burundi's institutions were taking root. The President, interviewed by BBC World Service Radio in June 2014, insisted that the decision was a matter not for him alone but for the constitutional court. Yet the law does not insist that the court has to confirm a candidate's right to stand. Nor does the electoral commission (CENI) have the authority to put matters to the constitutional court. One improvement was that in April 2014 parliament unanimously adopted a new electoral code. The CENI would have increased power; there would be a single ballot paper; and the rule that presidential candidates must be graduates was dropped.[4]

In April opponents of the third term began to organise. The ruling party organised two big demonstrations supporting a third term, the first by former CNDD-FDD combatants, the second by youth. These were more than counterbalanced in March by the decision of the Catholic Church to oppose the idea, by the creation of the 'Stop the Third Term' movement by fifteen organisations and by pressure from abroad, notably from the UN Secretary-General and the American Secretary of State. The removal of President Blaise Compaoré in Burkina Faso was a kind of inspiration for many opponents, who said they wanted to 'compaoriser' Nkurunziza!

The president must have been aware that on 25 April, when he announced his fateful decision to stand for re-election he was taking a big risk, but nothing would deter him. He hinted in his speech that the CNDD-FDD was divided and then went on immediately to expel from the *Conseil des Sages* of the party all those who were opposed, including the former party chairman Jérémie Ngendakumana, Second Vice President Gervais Rufyikiri and the president of the National Assembly, Pie Ntavyohanyuma. On 30 April the Constitutional Court gave Nkurunziza the decision he wanted, despite having earlier endorsed the Arusha accord's clear indication that presidents should serve for only two terms. The vice president of the court, Sylvère Nimpagaritse, fled the country saying that the six other members faced 'enormous pressure and even death threats.' His brave remarks effectively destroyed the president's chances of

---

4   This restriction had been a way of preventing Agathon Rwasa from being a candidate.

having the election result being seen as acceptable by his critics inside the country and abroad.

The following morning demonstrators took to the streets. Mostly young men, Tutsi and Hutu, they set up road blocks and effectively stopped normal life in the capital. The police reacted ferociously and were supported by members of the party youth league, the *imbonerakure*. Interestingly, the Minister of Defence made a statement suggesting that the army was neutral between the demonstrators and the police, implying that it was in fact divided.[5] On 3 May, the government marked World Press Freedom Day by banning RPA from broadcasting and stopping other free radio stations from broadcasting outside the capital. They also closed the *Maison de la Presse*, so the journalists had to meet instead at the premises of Iwacu whose courageous editor, Antoine Kaburahe, said in his speech: 'The independent media opened their columns and their radios to the CNDD-FDD when it said it was fighting for freedom. Today they are the ones who are closing our radios and stopping us from working.'[6]

Then on 13 May came the day of reckoning. *Iwacu* reported that a column of armoured cars and pick-ups carrying machine guns drove into town, followed by an immense crowd of jubilant demonstrators. RPA began broadcasting again. Crowds surrounded police headquarters to liberate their colleagues. The attempted coup was led by Major General Godefroid Niyombare,[7] whom the president had dismissed as head of security three months earlier. He announced that Nkurunziza had been deposed to 'save the Arusha accord' and the government dissolved by the *'forces vives de la nation'* for illegally standing for re-election and for many other wrongs committed. But the army was not united. Forces loyal to the president—and these included the chief of staff, General Prime Niyongabo—prevented Niyombare from taking the state broadcaster, RTNB, which meant

---

5   He got the sack for this.

6   '3 mai, journée mondiale de la liberté de la presse — Au Burundi, des journalistes tristes mais fiers,' Iwacu, 3 May 2015. http://www.iwacuburundi.org/3-mai-journee-mondiale-de-la-liberte-de-la-presse-auburundi-des-journalistes-tristes-mais-fiers/

7   Niyombare had been Chief of Staff in 2009 and was made Head of Security (CNR) in 2014.

that the news of the coup did not reach the provinces. The airport was only closed briefly. By the evening the coup had failed. Hopes that had been raised high were quickly dashed.

That night the independent radio stations were physically attacked. RPA's premises and equipment were set on fire, Radio Bonesha and Télé Renaissance were also smashed up and Radio Isanganiro closed down. The president, who had been away at a meeting of the East African Community in Dar es Salaam, returned more determined than ever to crush his opponents. He sacked ministers whose loyalty seemed less than 100 per cent: the Minister of Defence, Pontien Gaciyubwenge, who had affirmed the neutrality of the army (see also below); the Minister of Foreign Affairs, Laurent Kavakure, for failing to convince the international community that the president was justified; and the Minister of Trade, Virginie Ciza, for the shortage of petrol. He announced that 99 per cent of the country was at peace and suggested that al-Shabaab was the greatest threat he faced. The president's apparent confidence that he was still in control (and his spokesman's remark that the coup was a joke) added to many people's suspicions that this coup was a put up job aiming to flush out those who were against the president. I do not believe that the regime would have taken such a risk, for the coup might indeed have succeeded. Clearly Niyombare himself was highly motivated to stop the president, but the failure to capture the national radio station or to control the airport for more than a few hours were crucial. General Léonard Ngendakumana, another military opponent of the president, said that 12 army and police commanders were involved but that the plot failed due to 'misunderstandings.' It seems that what happened was that General Niyongabo, the chief of staff, played a double game, giving Niyombare and his friends a green light, telling him that he could announce the coup on the private radio and that he would take care of RTNB. The Minister of Defence, thinking that the coup was approved, told Pierre Claver Mbonimpa that it was going ahead smoothly. Niyombare attacked, only to discover that the chief of staff had remained loyal.

On 23 May Zedi Feruzi, leader of the pro-government wing of the party supporting Radjabu, UPD-Zigamibanga, was assassinated, causing other key opposition figures who were still in the country to go into hiding. (The government expressed regret and denied responsibility.) Burundi's four former presidents supported a letter to regional heads of state asking for intervention by a *force d'interposition*. The journal *Iwacu*, which had stopped publication, was able to resume. Demonstrations continued, mainly in the suburban quarters such as Musaga, Nyakabiga, Cibitoke and Buterere, but also in some provincial centres, despite heavy police presence.

As I write the number who have fled the country has exceeded 200,000. Some are Tutsi and Twa fearful that the conflict might turn ethnic. Many are people active in politics and public life who feel threatened, including Maggy Barankitse (see chapter 16) and Pacifique Nininahazwe, President of the Forum for Conscience and Development. Those in the ruling party who had the temerity to oppose Nkurunziza's third term fled, notably Gervais Rufyikiri, the Second Vice President;[8] and Pie Ntavyohanyuma, president of the National Assembly, both, like the coup leader, long standing Hutu members of the ruling party. 200 students tried to get refuge in the US embassy. All the staff of the free media were to be found in Kigali, Rwanda. The World Bank and the IMF threatened to leave the country. Belgium withdrew its funding of the elections and threatened to stop all bilateral aid and collaboration with the police. The European Union withdrew its electoral observer mission and the US suspended co-operation with the CENI. France suspended security co-operation. The Catholic Church announced that it would not co-operate with the electoral process. Calls for elections to be postponed until normality returned came from the East African Community, the African Union, the US and the UN, but the government was determined to go ahead and simply added to the budget deficit to pay for them, even appealing for donations on Facebook.

The final dates chosen were 26 June for the communal and parliamentary elections and 15 July for the presidential. Even before this new crisis had blown up there had been a total determination on the part of the ruling party to win these elections and continue rul-

---

8   Rufyikiri wrote to the president: 'I ask you to ask yourself what the economic future of Burundi will be deprived of foreign aid for an economy of which, in normal times, 52 per cent depends on technical and financial support.'

ing. Ten years of almost uncontrolled corruption had allowed the big military men to grow rich.[9] They knew they could be prosecuted and stripped of their wealth if the CNDD-FDD were to lose. Registration of voters had been in progress in 2014. As many had no identity cards, a million and a half of these had been distributed, in some areas only to party supporters, and often to people too young to vote. The government later accepted that there had been irregularities, but the damage had already been done. The party had also carried out a secret census of its members in some rural areas to help recruit more of them, but also with the aim of intimidating (or eventually eliminating) non-members. The government counted on the fact that there was no appetite on the part of the people to return to violence and therefore that the mere threat of force from their side was enough to discourage voters from taking risks. The controversial arming of the youth wing[10] was thus a kind of insurance policy and a reminder that it could be dangerous to vote against the regime. Visits and meetings of opposition parties up country had long been restricted or sabotaged. By the time of the election the heavy police presence in the 'hot' parts of town, coupled with the desperate economic situation, meant that the demonstrations were diminishing.

The government need not have worried about the result. The conditions for a fair election on 26 June were absent and the ruling party won a large majority. The boycott was not very effective outside Bujumbura, due mainly to fear of not being seen to have voted. In Bujumbura some of those who did vote were seen trying to remove the evidence by washing the ink off their hands. Although they had called for a boycott, the alliance of Agathon Rwasa and Charles Nditije (Amizero y'Abarundi) managed to win 21 seats. Rwasa described the results as 'prefabricated.' The CNDD-FDD won 74 and the 'official' Uprona 2. The figures have to be adjusted for ethnic and gender balance and to include six Batwa. The results of the presidential election on 15 June were also no surprise, with Nku-

---

9   Gabriel Rufyiri of OLUCOME has compiled a list of people who have enriched themselves illegally.

10 Denied by the government.

runziza winning 69.41 per cent on a 73 per cent turnout.[11] Despite the impossibility of campaigning Rwasa obtained 18.99 per cent, winning a majority in Bujumbura Rural and Rumonge. This may have encouraged him to take his seat in parliament despite having called for a boycott and refusing to recognise the election results. He said he wanted to 'play the game' to help resolve the crisis,[12] and was elected second vice president of the assembly to the dismay of his coalition partner, Charles Nditije of Uprona, and to the disappointment of the other opposition leaders. The election to the senate (by the councillors elected at the communal elections) on the same day gave the CNDD-FDD 33 out of 36 seats. To the UN, the African Union, the European Union, the USA and other Western countries these elections were not fair or credible. President Putin congratulated Nkurunziza, while China, and African members of the Security Council considered that it was an internal affair for Burundi.

President Nkurunziza has never taken kindly to interference or even advice from outside. As he has grown in confidence his relationship with the UN has become more and more prickly. The new UN mediator who arrived on 23 June, Abdoulaye Bathily, only stayed for a few weeks. It was similar with the African Union representative, Boubacar Diarra, who had represented the AU since 2012, and was driven out in April 2015 for speaking 'too frankly.' The President had also snubbed his hosts at recent summits at Johannesburg and Dar es Salaam. In July the EAC nominated President Museveni of Uganda to mediate, and he may also come to feel unwelcome. In any case this president, who is seen in Burundi as a Hima (Tutsi), was not the man to question Peter's desire to serve for more than ten years.[13] The president is unlikely also to welcome the EAC's proposals that

---

11 The 'official' Uprona won 2.14 per cent, Jean Minani (Frodebu-Nyakuri) 1.36 per cent, Jacques Bigirimana ('official' FNL) 1.01 per cent, ex-presidents Domitien Ndayizeye 0.71 per cent and Sylvestre Ntibantunganya 0.14 per cent.

12 Rwasa also said: 'Should we now abandon to their fate all those who voted for us...?'

13 Frederic Bamvuginyumvira commented: 'It is hard to understand how someone who has been in power since 1986 can find arguments in favour of a limitation of terms.'

militias in Burundi should be disarmed under AU supervision and that there should be an investigation as to whether the Rwandan FDLR rebels had any presence in Burundi.

Considering his increasingly beleaguered position, Nkurunziza would be wiser to make friends rather than alienating them. If the other EAC members show some irritation this is especially true of Rwanda. Earlier Peter had been an admirer of Kagame's regime and in some ways he has tried to imitate it. But the relationship between the 'twins' is a sensitive one. Tutsi dominance disguised by 'ethnic amnesia'[14] in Rwanda contrasts with Burundi's ethnic rules laid down in the Arusha Agreement. Burundi stopped co-operating with Rwanda against the FDLR *génocidaires* in 2014 but denies helping them. Rwandans also see the *imbonerakure* as something very similar to the genocidal *interahamwe* of 1994. Burundi thinks that Rwanda may have had a hand in the failed coup and blames Rwanda for harbouring many of the Burundians who have fled the country, including the coup leaders. Kagame can hardly blame Peter for wanting a third term as he is planning one himself, but he blames him for failing his people, a comment that went down very badly with the president's supporters in Bujumbura.

A fateful month began on 1 August when the president's increasing number of opponents met in Addis Ababa. A strong group of opposition leaders created the National Council for the Respect of the Arusha Agreement and the restoration of the Rule of Law (CNARED) headed by Léonard Nyangoma, the founder of the original CNDD. At the same time the National Resistance Council chose the exiled Second Vice President, Gervais Rufyikiri, as its leader. The charismatic coup leader, Godefroid Niyombare, was also present. Then, early the next morning six men in military uniform blocked the road in a pick-up truck at the Gare du Nord, where they stopped and killed the president's right hand man, Adolphe Nshimirimana. Nshimirimana had served Peter for ten years as security chief and was regarded as the power behind the president, responsible for building up and arming the *imbonerakure* youth movement and for much of the government's violent response to

---

14 Filip Reyntjens' description.

the protests.[15] Perhaps as revenge, the following day the much-loved fighter for human rights, Pierre Claver Mbonimpa, was shot and wounded.[16] Lawlessness continues daily and there have been reports of killings all over the country, including the murder on 15 August of Colonel Jean Bikomagu, suspected of being behind the 1993 coup against President Ndadaye. For those who regarded the elections as illegal, the president became illegitimate on 26 August. On 11 September the army commander, Prime Niyongabo, another leader of the harsh reaction to the demonstrations, was attacked by uniformed men in an army vehicle but survived.

As this book goes to press tension and fear in the country continues to increase. The President's ultimatum on 2 November, directed at the opposition strongholds in Bujumbura, threatening to attack and confiscate arms has led to a number of deaths and to many families fleeing their homes. Rwandan President Kagame's bitter criticisms of Nkurunziza have added to the explosive atmosphere. The economy continues to deteriorate and it is not only the poor who are getting poorer. International news coverage of the situation is increasing and perhaps the world will start to take Burundi's latest crisis seriously.

---

15 Bob Rugurika of Radio Publique Africaine, who traced the death of the Italian nuns to Adolphe, remarked that he always saw the hand of Adolphe behind the president's worst crimes.

16 Pierre-Claver's son was taken by the police and killed on 2 November 2015 and another relative of his was killed in October.

25

THE FUTURE: PEACE OR WAR, DICTATORSHIP OR DEMOCRACY?

Ahari amahoro, umuhoro uramwa, If there is peace you can shave with a machete
—proverb

A surprising and immediate effect of the 2005 elections was the sudden side lining of Hutu-Tutsi tension. This did not mean it totally disappeared but, as Alexis Sinduhije remarked at the time, it was having a siesta. Most people remembered the fear and tension during 'the crisis' and were prepared to be tolerant if not provoked. Burundi may be a tiny country with a feeble economy but the political struggle was and is about power, and the 2005 elections turned out to be a contest between two 'Hutu' parties, the CNDD-FDD and Frodebu, with the Tutsis out of the equation. The so-called 'Tutsi' parties, including Uprona, failed to attract the votes of many of their targeted supporters.[1] Different opinions are expressed as to how many Tutsis voted for the CNDD-FDD but certainly quite a number did, perhaps bowing to the inevitable. The number of Tutsi members of parliament and in other government posts is not always, of course, an indication of political conviction but more likely a sordid scramble for jobs. I was surprised to learn that a former pro-Tutsi hardliner of my acquaintance entered parliament in 2005 for the CNDD-FDD. He was not the only 'chameleon.'

---

1   Their representation in all organs of the government is less than 12 per cent.

The ethnic factor was even less evident in the 2010 election and, although the president has tried to re-awaken it, there is little evidence of it in 2015. In an excellent article Benjamin Chemouni considers that Burundi had moved 'beyond the question of ethnicity in its politics. Despite promising to free the country from Tutsi domination, the CNDD-FDD has appalling results in terms of development and governance. This situation does however have a silver lining: it deconstructs the ethnic stereotype of the exploitative Tutsi. ...Hutu can exploit Hutu as well.'[2] The FLN and Frodebu have collaborated with a very Tutsi party, Parena. Agathon Rwasa, leader of what had been the violently Hutu FNL, went into alliance with the traditionally Tutsi Uprona, which in turn had as its leader Charles Nditije, a Hutu. Edouard Nduwimana, until 2015 Minister of Home Affairs and scourge of the opposition, is in fact a Tutsi. The government's apparent fear of the MSD is not because it has a Tutsi leader but because it appears to transcend ethnicity.

The army also demonstrates the fading away of the ethnic factor. As we saw in chapter 11, integration went well and until May's events the army remained 'republican', ethnically well integrated and fairly efficient. It had been praised for its contribution to peacekeeping in Somalia. Tutsis and Hutus from the old army as well as former rebel fighters had been promoted. However, the junior ranks have complained about low pay and lack of equipment and there is resentment at the glaring corruption of many senior officers. It was Nkurunziza's decision rather than ethnicity that divided the army during the coup of 14 May and this political schism in the army remains. The police on the other hand are neither well integrated nor well trained, and its members have been involved in a number of human rights violations. According to Transparency International, the East African Community and Burundian civil society, the police force is the most corrupt institution in the country. The government's lack of confidence in both army and police in the event of a political crisis probably accounts for the strengthening of the party youth wing, the *imbonerakure*.

---

2   African Arguments, 19 May 2014.

Among the population in general there has been a genuine degree of reconciliation and a change in attitudes. The contrast with 1994 is very striking. The many peace projects I have described had a cumulative effect, as did sheer war-weariness and the daily struggle to feed the family. Yet violent crime continued to occur every week somewhere in the country and it is increasing horribly as result of the new crisis of 2015. Is it fair to ask whether violence is endemic in Burundi? Can we generalise and ask whether Burundians (and Rwandans) kill more easily than, say, Congolese or Zambians? Is it a cultural thing? In the history of both countries there have been merciless killings even of women and children; men have even killed their wives. One explanation is impunity: few killers are ever brought to justice. A cultural factor is that Burundians (and Rwandans) are highly disciplined and obey their leaders: a call for revenge can be answered by fearless, perhaps excessive, obedience as was seen in Burundi in 1972 and 1993—and in Rwanda in 1994. Deaths are accepted with incredible stoicism. Emotions are buttoned up. Many suffer from trauma, as we have seen, but to talk openly about it is very difficult for a Burundian. Discipline, obedience and stoicism can work both ways and there is no reason why this quality cannot create a just and well-ordered society. There are cultural parallels with the Japanese, who in their history have also been capable of great cruelty. Their country is now one of the best ordered and most law-abiding in the world.

In Burundi even very moderate intellectuals see history differently depending on their 'ethnic' upbringing. Was Micombero's government provoked into massacring Hutus in 1972? Was the reaction to Ndadaye's death an instant response to shock or a pre-planned genocide? There is still a tendency to recall—and rewrite—history as a way of accusing the other party. It was a brave idea for the government to propose a new national history project but this seems to have been sidelined. This could be a good thing, as a 'Hutu version' would do no more for national reconciliation than the 'Tutsi' monument at Kibimba. Perhaps the only way that history can become common property is for mutual forgiveness to be coupled with justice.

Genocide should be admitted and not forgotten. Up to now, where individuals have been charged, it has usually been the small fish not the *grandes légumes*,[3] that have been tried and executed—and it has often been the wrong small fish at that.[4] Justice involves facing the past and seeing two sides to it. Tutsi groups like AC Génocide and PA Amasekanya are now weak. They saw genocide only on one side, and there were Hutus who, equally, downplayed the savagery of 1993. The Truth and Reconciliation Commission now exists but in the confusion of 2015 it is having difficulty starting its work, and even when it does it could awaken memories and arguments which might in fact damage the chances of reconciliation. Will Burundians speak openly and frankly to the commission at all, and, if they do, should this then exonerate them from being charged by a tribunal? Burundi is not South Africa and there is no-one of the stature of Mandela or Desmond Tutu to validate the process and calm things down. Louis-Marie Nindorera, Director of Global Rights, told me he thought a commission could make things worse: 'I am convinced we should search for the truth but this is not the way to do it....It should not be organised by the government or the UN but ...civil society people, well organised, well prepared ... can research on it gradually—or you risk having the same cycle of violence.'

There is never a good moment to publish a book which tries to bring a story up to the present. By the time this edition is published, much more 'stuff' will have happened in Burundi. The first edition covered the record up to mid-2007; this edition takes it to mid-2015. Pierre Nkurunziza's obstinate decision to stand for re-election has released Burundi's demons. They are not the same demons as in 1993, but they pose huge risks for this lovely and fragile land. I hope readers will forgive me if none of the possible scenarios I suggest turn out to be correct.

At the time of writing President Nkurunziza is increasingly isolated and weakened. He had already lost many prominent members of his party and has now lost Adolphe Nshimirimana. He has offended and lost most of his friends abroad. There may be many in the

---

3 Big vegetables, the Congolese name for 'big fish'.
4 Refer to the case of Samson Gahungu in chapter 6.

army and police who may jump if he starts to look like he is fighting a losing battle—and there have already been desertions. He does still have two strong man behind him, Alain Guillaume Bunyoni and the army commander Prime Niyongabo who narrowly escaped assassination, and he still has support in the villages, *les collines*, but it is not clear how much of this is genuine affection for him or a mixture of fear of and obedience to authority. And although they have lost their leader, Adolphe, the *imbonerakure* are still strong, armed and violent. Nkurunziza has also succeeded in neutralising (or buying?) that old and popular rebel, Agathon Rwasa, five of whose supporters have been given quite important government ministries.[5]

One scenario is that the president will remain in control, refusing compromise or negotiation and the police, the army and youth league will continue using strong arm tactics against the population and manage to resist any possible violent attacks by opposition forces. Burundians who can will continue to leave, creating huge gaps in crucial manpower. In such a scenario there would be no free media, civil society would be sidelined and the country would become even more of a repressive backwater. The East African Community can try to isolate the virus but Burundi is not strategic enough for the international community to play as big a role as it could. There may be just enough stability to satisfy those investing in nickel production but in the short term the economy would remain broken, and this might in the end force the president to negotiate.

Peace in Burundi came through the Arusha settlement rather than through the kind of military victory that brought Kagame and Museveni to power in Rwanda and Uganda. The shattering of the fragile settlement means that, tragically, the second scenario of a new civil war seems very possible—and there are a lot of weapons left over from the last conflict. Whether the forces of opposition are capable of more than guerrilla tactics is not certain, and the decision of Rwasa to work within the system must gravely weaken the opposition's chances. But again the constant destabilisation that guerrilla

---

5   Rwasa's supporters are ministers of Youth, Sport and Culture; Labour; Community Development; Trade, Industry and Tourism; and Good Governance and the Plan. The new government contains twelve Hutus and eight Tutsis.

attacks and assassinations would cause might in the end bring the president to the negotiating table. If he were to try to harness the support of the Rwandan FDLR he would risk bringing Rwanda into the conflict against him.

The best scenario would be for pressure from inside and outside the country to lead to real negotiations. Colette Braeckman, a Belgian commentator, suggests that some form of transition could be achieved where Nkurunziza, having 'won' his election, would remain in power, rather as Buyoya was, for a limited time before being retired honourably. Any agreement would have to include the reinstatement of the free media,[6] disarmament of the *imbonerakure*, the return of refugees and exiles, dropping of charges against opposition leaders, promises of free elections with a reformed electoral commission, and agreement with investors in nickel production. Every effort would have to be made to treat all Burundians with respect and to build trust. It is not obvious who could be the most plausible leader to replace Peter if he should depart or be removed. Key figures, all Hutu, are Agathon Rwasa and Léonard Nyangoma but many would suggest Godefroid Niyombare who was active in the rebellion and in the CNDD-FDD until he broke with the president. He has charisma and could be acceptable across the political and ethnic spectrum.

Whatever form of government prevails it will face enormous challenges.[7] The 2015 crisis has cut economic activity by more than half; government revenue is estimated to be down by 35 per cent; international aid was responsible for 52 per cent of the budget and this is likely to be drastically reduced. Even without these extra blows the reality is that the country is small and the population is already more than three times greater than at independence in 1962. This population growth must be slowed—and by more humane methods than civil war, AIDS and malaria. Even with im-

6   RPA is likely to be able to get funding to restore its equipment. The other media should also be able to get help.

7   Burundi-watchers like to predict who could be future leaders—Nyangoma (clear ideas but maybe a bit old?), Sinduhije (inspired but rather unpredictable?), Niyombare (another umuhuza who could unite people?), Rwasa (something of a 'lone wolf'?).

proved agriculture and irrigation it is not going to be easy to feed the people and still grow crops for export. People are moving to the capital, which will lead to a big growth in urban poverty, and rural poverty will also worsen. The country needs major investment. The known nickel deposits are said to be worth US$330 billion and mining would be a long-term programme; doubtless the government is already trying to borrow money on the strength of this. But in the short term a 'Marshall Plan', which—given the small scale of Burundi's economy—amounts only to a few minutes' worth of the US defence budget would enable Burundi to take advantage of the agricultural potential of the Imbo plain, of its membership of the East African Community and of its links south by the lake to develop industry and trade. The Democratic Republic of Congo is in an equally sensitive post-conflict phase and events here can also, as in the past, have a good or bad effect on what happens in Burundi. A peaceful and developing Congo can only enhance Bujumbura's economic importance.

Such dreams of development will get nowhere if Burundi's meagre resources are dissipated through corruption and mismanagement and if key cadres remain in exile. Before 1993 corruption was rare in Burundi. Now low level corruption—payment of *chai* to civil servants and the police is commonplace and higher up it is worse. If the government cannot act, donors will have more difficulty in finding the aid money that Burundi desperately needs. Without this, many more long-suffering Burundians, most of whom live on less than $1 a day, will turn to crime and banditry: 'We can't eat the constitution.'[8] International donors will find many reasons to forget Burundi. $400 million was pledged in Paris in 2000 with Mandela twisting their arms, but donors still dragged their feet, muttering about insecurity.[9] Corruption and abuse of human rights will be a reason, or an excuse, to put their money elsewhere.

---

8   This is the title of a paper by M.B. Jooma (Pretoria, 2005). The gap between the incomes of villagers and those in employment is wide. Between lowly civil servants and high officials it is wider. There is bound to be jealousy and resentment.

9   I represented the international NGOs working in Burundi at this meeting. Many delegates were hesitant to make pledges but it was hard to refuse

Throughout this story it has been hard to forget Rwanda, Burundi's non-identical twin. When one twin sneezes, the other catches a cold. Thus the 'revolution,' which brought a Hutu regime to power in Rwanda in 1959 and the consequent ill-treatment of Tutsis, caused the flight of refugees to Burundi. This poisoned the inter-ethnic climate in Burundi and reinforced the anti-democratic instincts of Presidents Micombero and Bagaza. The killing of Ndadaye hardened the attitude of the Hutu extremists in Rwanda. The genocide in Rwanda reinforced the determination of the Burundi army leadership and Tutsi politicians to resist reform. As mentioned above, Rwanda has been watching the events of 2015 nervously and is not likely to tolerate any apparent risk to its own security. Whatever happens, the two twin states cannot escape from each other. Today Burundi is infectious but if convulsions ever occur again in Rwanda then Burundi will not escape the fall-out.

Whatever the future holds for Pierre Nkurunziza, his life throws light on some very real problems and realities about politics in Africa. I do not believe he was an evil man when he first came to power. He was known as *umuhuza*, a person who brings people together. He plays football and worships with villagers because he likes them. (He never felt the same about town kids as he spent all his youth in the rural areas.) Yet once he was in the presidential chair he began to grow in confidence, self-assurance and eventually arrogance. The first evidence of this was his removal of Radjabu. After ten years in the job, convinced he was still loved by most of the population and that God was behind him, he could not see that his decision to run for a third term would be disastrous for his country and for his reputation. The obstinacy of this one man has thrown the country back into chaos and darkness—and many people warned him of this. He could have gone down in history not only as the first freely elected president to serve not only one but two terms, but even as some kind of 'father of the nation.' Law and tradition in Burundi, as in other African countries, have a split personality: traditionally, although there were some restraints, chiefs and kings laid down the law and ruled until they died; 'modern' law and political practice (though

Mandela.

often perverted by dictatorships) meant constitutions, individual freedoms, civil society, media and the need to conform to international rules. Nkurunziza felt much more at home in the traditional mould, arriving like a king every time he visited a *colline*, and he ended up as a 'big man' prepared to use any method, however brutal, to stay in power. He had no programme for his third term, nor even for his second, but power, even in such a small country, has its attraction and dreams of income from nickel made the future look brighter, whereas loss of power could mean retribution, especially for all those close to him who had grown rich on the spoils of office. This highlights another common African problem, what to do with former rulers. There is no continental 'House of Lords' where they could keep their dignity and be quietly forgotten.

My original sub-title for this book was 'An African success story.' I quickly realised that this was too optimistic an assessment and that the post-2005 government was making too many mistakes. I am more pessimistic in 2015 than I was in 2007, but I still believe Burundi has the potential for success. The successful integration of the army may have faced a setback in 2015, but its divisions are no longer ethnic and could be resolved. The old army had been the core of Burundi's problem since 1966: senior military saw their role as defenders of Tutsi hegemony. Rebel forces were equally determined to destroy Tutsi power, symbolised by the army. Both eventually saw that war could not be won, but I believe they were also influenced by the change in public attitudes resulting from the many reforms described in the preceding chapters. Most of the refugees of 1972 and 1993 have returned home, some who had been in exile for more than thirty years. Hopefully those who fled in 2015 will be reintegrated quickly. Education has expanded. There is more chance for women, and not just in government. The countryside is still green and fertile. If negotiations result in peace and the rule of law there could be a real chance of economic development, and hopefully the media and civil society could regain their vigour. People have a sense of humour and still make fun of politicians over a beer. The remarkable peacemakers and other outstanding personalities I have described in this book are backed up by millions of honest Burundians hoeing their fields, bringing charcoal to the market, sitting at their sewing machines, driving minibuses, nursing, teaching, fishing, preaching. They are Burundi's greatest resource and for their sake there must be liberty, a representative government, economic development and peace.

ANNEX 1

BIBLIOGRAPHY

Acquier, Jean-Louis *Le Burundi* (Collection Architectures traditionnelles) (Marseilles: Editions Parenthèses 1986).

Ben Hammouda, Hakim *Burundi. Histoire Economique et Politique d'un Conflit* (Paris: L'Harmattan 1995).

Bentley, Kristina and Roger Southall *An African Peace Process* (Cape Town: HSRC 2005).

Berwouts, Kris *Burundi* (Amsterdam: Landenreeks, Koninklijk Instituut voor de Tropen, 2007) (in Dutch).

Bihute, Donatien *Parcours publique et privé d'un Burundais* (Paris: L'Harmattan 1999).

Chrétien, Jean-Pierre *Burundi, l'histoire retrouvée* (Paris: Karthala 1993).

——*Le défi de l'ethnisme—Rwanda et Burundi 1990-96* (Paris: Karthala 1997).

——and Melchior Mukuri *Burundi, la fracture identitaire* (Paris: Karthala 2002).

Chrétien, Jean-Pierre (tr. Scott Straus) *The Great Lakes of Africa, Two Thousand Years of History* (New York: Zone Books 2003).

Chrétien, Jean-Pierre and Jean-François Dupaquier *Burundi 1972: au bord des génocides* (Paris: Karthala 2007).

Cochet, Hubert *Crises et révolutions agricoles au Burundi* (Paris: Karthala 2001).

Daley, Patricia *Militarism, Gender and Genocide: The Search for Spaces of Peace in Central Africa* (Oxford: James Currey, 2007).

De Lespinay, Charles and Emile Mworoha (eds) *Construire l'Etat de Droit* (Paris: L'Harmattan 2000).

Eggers, Ellen K. *Historical Dictionary of Burundi* (Lanham, MD: Scarecrow Press 2006).

Frey, Claude *Le Français au Burundi* (Vanves: Edicef 1996).

Furley, Oliver and Roy May (eds) *Ending Africa's Wars: Progressing to Peace* (Aldershot: Ashgate 2006).

Gahama, Joseph *Le Burundi sous administration belge* (Paris: Karthala 2001).

Greenland, Jeremy *Tangled Pattern* (Winchester: Apologia Publications 2004).

Guichaoua, André (ed.) *Les crises politiques au Burundi et au Rwanda 1993-94* (University of Lille/Paris: Karthala 1995).

Guillebaud, Meg *After the Locusts* (Monarch Books 2005).

Guillet, Claude and Pascal Ndayishingije (eds) *Légendes historiques du Burundi*

Harroy, J.-P. *Burundi 1955-62* (Brussels: Editions Hayez 1987).

Hatungimana, Alexandre *Le café du Burundi au XX siècle* (Paris: Karthala 2005).

Hatungimana, Jacques and Nahimana Salvator *Inaburundi, épouse Mutwe* (Paris: L'Harmattan 2002).

—— (eds) *Melchior Ndadaye pour le Burundi nouveau—campagne 1992-93* (Paris: L'Harmattan 2004).

Kabarahe, Antoine *La mémoire blessée* (Brussels/Paris: La Longue Vue 2002).

Kabuta, Daniel *L'autre face du clandestin* (Paris: Editions du Panthéon 2004).

Kamatari, Esther *Princesse des rugo* (Paris: Bayard 2001).

Kayoya, Michel (Tr. Aylward Shorter and Marie-Agnes Baldwin) *My Father's Footprints* (East African Publishing House 1973). The original was *Les traces de mon père* (Bujumbura: Presses Lavigerie 1971). He also wrote *Entre deux mondes* (Bujumbura: Presses Lavigerie 1971).

Kimonyo, Jean-Paul and Damase Ntiranyibagira *Reform of the Coffee Sector in Burundi: Prospects for Participation, Prosperity and Peace* (London: International Alert 2007).

Kounzilat, Alain and Evode Twagirayezu *Le Burundi—Perspectives et Réalités* (Corbeil-Essonnes: ICES 2004).

Krueger, Robert and Kathleen *From Bloodshed to Hope in Burundi: Our Embassy Years during Genocide* (Austin: University of Texas 2007).

Le Coz, Martine *La reine écarlate* (Paris: Albin Michel 2007).

Lemarchand, René *Burundi: Ethnic Conflict and Genocide* (Cambridge University Press 1996).

Malkki, Liisa *Purity and Exile: Violence, Memory and National Cosmology among Hutu Refugees in Tanzania* (University of Chicago Press 1995).

Manirakiza, Marc *La Déviance d'un Pouvoir Solitaire: le régime Bagaza 1976-1987* (Brussels/Paris: La Longue Vue 1997).

Mariro, Augustin *Burundi 1965, la première crise ethnique* (Paris: L'Harmattan 2005).

Martin, Christel *La Haine n'aura pas le dernier mot* (Hate won't have the last word—about Maggy Barankitse) (Paris: Albin Michel 2005).

Melady, Thomas Patrick *Burundi: the Tragic Years* (New York: Orbis Books 1974).

Meyer, Hans *Les Barundi (*Société Française d'Histoire d'Outre-Mer 1984).

Mvuyejure, Augustin *Le Catholicisme au Burundi 1922-62* (Paris: Karthala 2003).

Ndayirukiye, Sylvestre (ed.) *Bujumbura Centenaire 1897-1997 Croissance et Défis* (Paris: L'Harmattan 2002).

Ndarubagiye, Léonce *The Origins of the Hutu-Tutsi Conflict* (English edition self-published, available in SOAS Library, London).

Ndegaya, Vénérand *Répression au Burundi: journal d'un prisonnier vainqueur* (Paris: L'Harmattan 1993).

Ndeta, Patrice *Ikiza (le fléau) 1972* (Paris: L'Harmattan 2007).

Ndoricimpa, L. and C. Guillet (ed.) *L'arbre-mémoire. Traditions orales au Burundi* (Paris: Karthala 1984).

Niemegeers, Marcel *Les Trois Défis du Burundi* (Paris: L'Harmattan 1995).

Nimubona, Julien *Analyse des Représentations au Pouvoir—le cas du Burundi* (ANRC).

Niyonzima, David and Lon Fendall *Unlocking Horns* (Newburg, Oregon: Barclay Press, 2001).

Niyonzima, Hermenegilde *Burundi, terre des héros non chantés* (Switzerland: Editions Remesha 2004).

Nsanze, Augustin *Le Burundi Ancien—l'économie du pouvoir 1875-1920* Paris: (L'Harmattan 2001)

——*Le Burundi Contemporain—l'Etat national en question 1956-2002* (Paris: L'Harmattan 2003).

Nshimirimana, Perpétue *Lettre à Isidore* (Vevey: Editions de l'Aire 2004).

Ntabona, Adrien (ed.) *Au Coeur de l'Afrique*, a bi-annual review (Bujumbura: CRID).

Ntahombaye, Philippe *Des noms et des hommes: Aspects psychologiques et sociologiques du nom au Burundi* (Paris: Karthala 1983).

Ntamwana, Simon *Laissez partir mon people*

Ntibantunganya, Sylvestre *Une démocratie pour tous les Burundais* (2 volumes, Paris: L'Harmattan 1999).

Ntibanzonika, Raphael *Biographie du Président Melchior Ndadaye.*

——*Au royaume des seigneurs de la lance.*

Nyamitwa, Alain Aine *J'ai échappé au massacre de l'Université du Burundi le 11/6/95* (Paris: L'Harmattan 2006).

Nyberg Oskarsson, Gunilla *Le Mouvement Pentecôtiste* (Uppsala: Swedish Institute for Missionary Research 2004).

Ould-Abdallah, Ahmedou *Burundi on the Brink 1993-95* (US Institute of Peace 2000).

Petit Futé *Burundi Country Guide* (Nouvelles Editions de l'Université 2007)—an excellent detailed guide book with a lot of accurate background information (in French).

Pézard, Stéphanie and Nicolas Florquin *Small Arms in Burundi: Disarming the Civilian Population in Peacetime*, published jointly with Ligue Iteka (Small Arms Survey, Geneva 2007).

Potier, Emilie *Au pays de Lottie: journal d'une mission humanitaire* (Paris: Les Quatre Chemins 2005).

Reychler, Luc, Tatien Musabyimana and Stéfane Calmeyn *Le Défi de la Paix au Burundi. Théorie et Pratique* (Paris: L'Harmattan 1999).

Reyntjens, Filip *Burundi, Prospects for Peace* (Mimority Rights Group 2000).

—— 'Burundi: A peaceful transition after a decade of war?' (*African Affairs* vol. 105, no. 418, January 2006).

Rwabahungu, Marc *Au cours des crises nationales au Rwanda et au Burundi* (Paris: L'Harmattan 2004).

Sebudandi, G. and Pierre-Olivier Richard *Le drame burundais* (Paris: Karthala 1996).

Sindayigaya, Jean-Marie *La saga d'Arusha* (Charleroi: Editions ARIB 2002).

Sommers, Marc *Fear in Bongoland* (Oxford: Bergbahn Books 2001).

Thibon Christian *Histoire Démographique du Burundi* (Paris: Karthala 2004).

Tuhabonye, Gilbert *The Running Man* (John Blake, London 2007), published in the US as *This Voice in My Heart* (Harper Collins 2006).

Wilson, Richard *Titanic Express* (London: Continuum 2006).

ANNEX 2

WHO'S WHO

BAGAZA Jean Baptiste—President of Burundi 1976-87

BAMBONEYEHO Venant—leader of AC Génocide

BAYAGANAKANDI Epitace—army commander, Tutsi politician

BIKOMAGU Col. Jean—army commander at the time of Ndadaye's death

BUDUDIRA Mgr Bernard—Bishop of Bururi in 1993

BUYOYA Pierre—President of Burundi 1987-93 and 1996-2003

COURTNEY Mgr Michael—Papal Nuncio to Burundi, killed in 2003

GAHUTU Rémy—founder of Palipehutu killed in 1990

HARROY Jean-Paul—Belgian Governor of Ruanda-Urundi

KABURA Cossan—leader of Palipehutu-FNL 1991-97

KARAGEORGIS—assassin of Prince Louis Rwagasore

KARATASI Etienne—leader of Palipehutu 1990-

KARUMBA Joseph—leader of Frolina

KAVUMBAGU Jean-Marie Vianney—President of Ligue Iteka 2005-

MANDELA Nelson—ex-President of South Africa, mediator at Arusha

MAUS Albert—leader of white settlers in Ruanda-Urundi prior to Independence

MELADY Thomas Patrick—American Ambassador in 1972

MICOMBERO Michel—President of Burundi 1966-76

MINANI Jean—Frodebu leader

MIREREKANO Paul—co-founder of Uprona, Hutu politician

MPAWENAYO Prosper—Palipehutu politician, later Minister of Education

MUKASI Charles—leader of hardline faction of Uprona

249

MWAMBUTSA—King of Burundi 1915-65 d.1977
MWEZI Gisabo—King of Burundi 1850-1908
NDADAYE Melchior—President of Burundi briefly in 1993
NDAYIKENGURUKIYE Jean-Bosco—CNDD-FDD leader 1998-2001
NGABISHA, Eustache—father of President Pierre Nkurunziza
NGENDABANKA Gérard—State Prosecutor 1998-2001
NGENDADUMWE Pierre—Prime Minister 1963-64 and 1965 d.1965
NINDORERA Eugène—first President of Ligue Iteka, Minister under Buyoya II
NINDORERA Louis-Marie—former General Secretary of Ligue Iteka, Director of Global Rights
NTAKARUTIMANA Pie—President of Ligue Iteka to 2006
NTARE Ndizeye—the last King of Burundi 1966, d.1972
NTARE Rugamba—King of Burundi 1796-1850
NTARE Rushatsi—the first King of Burundi c.1680-1709
NTARYAMIRA Cyprien—President of Burundi briefly in 1994
NTIBANTUNGANYA Sylvestre—President of Burundi 1994-96
NTAHOTURI Bernard—Anglican Archbishop of Burundi 2005-
NTAMWANA Mgr Simon—Archbishop of Gitega, previously Bishop of Bujumbura
NYANGOMA Léonard—Frodebu minister 1993-94, leader of CNDD
NZOJIBWAMI Augustin—former Secretary General of Frodebu
NYERERE Julius—former President of Tanzania, mediator at Arusha
RADJABU Hussein—President of CNDD-FDD party until 2007
RUKINDIKIZA Captain Gratien—Ndadaye's security man in 1993
RUHUNA Mgr Joachim—Archbishop of Gitega, killed in 1997
RWAGASORE Prince Louis—Prime Minister 1961 d.1961
RWASA Agathon—leader of PALIPEHUTU-FNL 2001-
RYCKMANS Pierre—pre-Independence Belgian Resident in Urundi
SEBUDANDI Christophe—Ligue Iteka, LDGL, President of OAG 1999-2005
SENDEGAYA Pierre-Claver—Royalist candidate in 1993 election
SIBOMANA Adrian—Prime Minister 1988-93
SINDAYIGAYA Jean-Bosco—leader of a faction of Palipehutu-FNL

ANNEX 3

GLOSSARY OF FRENCH,
KIRUNDI AND KISWAHILI WORDS

(Words beginning with *mu-* or *umu-* have plural *ba-* or *aba-*)
amahoro—peace
Banyamulenge—Congolese ethnic group of Rwanda Tutsi origin
banyaruguru—people of the interior (usually referring to Muramvya)
brochette—shish kebab
colline—hill, a scattering of homesteads, the usual settlement pattern in
         Burundi
dot—betrothal ceremony
école normale—teacher training college
ethnie (ubwoko) —ethnic group
génocidaires—perpetrators of genocide
Imana   —God
Kiranga—high priest
levée de deuil—ceremony to mark the end of mourning
muganwa—member of the extended royal family
mushingantahe—notable, wise man, counsellor
muzungu, umuzungu—white person (Swahili, Kirundi)
Mungu—God (Swahili)
mwalimu—teacher (popular name of President Nyerere)
mwami—king
quartier—neighbourhood in town
rugo (pl. *ingo*)—homestead
ruguru—up country (*banyaruguru*—people from up country)
soukous—type of Congolese (Zairean) music
ville morte—'dead city' —demonstrations blocking the city
ubugererwa, ubugabire—leasing of land/cows

ubumwe—unity (Charter of Unity)
umuryango—clan, also family
Urupfu—death, Devil

ANNEX 4

ACRONYMS

ACAT	Action by Christians for the Abolition of Torture
ACCORD	African Centre for the Constructive Resolution of Disputes
AMIB	African Union Mission in Burundi
A.PRO.DH	Association pour la Protection des Droits Humains et des Détenus
AU	African Union
Bancobu	Banque Commerciale du Burundi
BCB	Banque de Crédit de Bujumbura
BINUB	Bureau Intègre des Nations Unies au Burundi (Integrated UN Office in Burundi)
CAFOB	Collective of Women's Associations and NGOs of Burundi
CECI	Centre d'Etudes et de Coopération Internationale
CIDA	Canadian International Development Agency
CNDD	Conseil National pour le Défense de la Démocratie
CNEB	National Council of Churches of Burundi
COMESA	Common Market of Eastern and Southern Africa
Cotebu	Complexe Textile du Burundi
CRID	Centre de Recherches pour l'Inculturation et le Développement
CRS	Catholic Relief Services
DDR	Demobilisation, Disarmament and Rehabilitation
DFID	Department for International Development (British aid)
EEA	Eglise Evangélique des Amis (Quaker)
EEB	Eglise Episcopale du Burundi (Anglican)
EU	European Union

FAB	Forces Armées du Burundi (army pre-2005)
FAO	Food and Agriculture Organisation (UN)
FBU/BIF	Burundian Franc (currency)
FDD	Forces pour la Défense de la Démocratie
FIDH	Federation International des Droits de l'Homme (International Human Rights Federation)
FNL	Forces Nationales pour la Libération
Frodebu	Front pour la Démocratie au Burundi
Frolina	Front pour la Libération Nationale
GDP	Gross Domestic Product
HIPC	Heavily Indebted Poor Countries
HRW	Human Rights Watch
IA	International Alert
ICRC	International Committee of the Red Cross
INGO	international non-governmental organisation
IRAZ	Institut de Recherches Agronomiques et Zootechniques
IRC	International Rescue Committee
JPH	Jeunesse Patriotique Hutu
LDGL	Ligue des Droits de la Personne dans la Région des Grands Lacs
Meproba	Mouvement des Etudiants Progressistes Barundi
MFPH	Mouvement des Femmes Patriotiques Hutu
NGO	non-governmental organisation
OAG	Observatoire de l'Action Gouvernementale
OAU	Organisation of African Unity
OCHA	United Nations Office for the Coordination of Humanitarian Affairs
Olucome	Observatoire de la Lutte contre les Malversations Economiques
OMS	Organisation Mondiale de la Santé
Onatel	Organisation Nationale de Télécommunications
ONUB	United Nations Operations in Burundi
Palipehutu	Parti pour la Libération du Peuple Hutu
PAM	Programme Alimentaire Mondial (WFP)
PDC	Parti Démocrate Chrétien
RCN	Réseau Citoyens Network
Regideso	State Water Company
RPA	Radio Publique Africaine (African Republic Radio)
RTNB	Radio Télévision Nationale du Burundi
Sosumo	Société Sucrière du Moso

THARS	Trauma Healing and Reconciliation Services
UCEDD	Union Chrétienne pour l'Education et le Développement des Déshérités
UNDP	United Nations Development Programme
UNESCO	United Nations Educational, Scientific and Cultural Organisation
UNHCR	United Nations High Commission for Refugees
UNICEF	United Nations Children's Emergency Fund
Uniproba	Unissons-nous pour la promotion des Batwa
Uprona	Union pour le Progrès National
USAID	US Agency for International Development
WFP	World Food Programme
WHO	World Health Organisation

INDEX